# ❧ SEXUALITY AND FORM

# SEXUALITY and FORM

## Caravaggio, Marlowe, and Bacon

### GRAHAM L. HAMMILL

THE UNIVERSITY OF CHICAGO PRESS
*Chicago & London*

GRAHAM L. HAMMILL is assistant professor of English at the
University of Notre Dame.

The University of Chicago Press, Chicago 60637
The University of Chicago Press, Ltd., London
©2000 by The University of Chicago
All rights reserved. Published 2000
Printed in the United States of America

10   09   08   07   06   05   04   03   02   01   00      5   4   3   2   1

ISBN (cloth) : 0-226-31518-5

Library of Congress Cataloging-in-Publication Data

Hammill, Graham L.
    Sexuality and form : Caravaggio, Marlowe, and Bacon / Graham
L. Hammill.
        p.   cm.
    Includes bibliographical references and index.
        ISBN 0-226-31518-5 (hc : acid-free)
    1. Homosexuality and art.   2. Caravaggio, Michelangelo Merisi
da, 1573–1610—Psychology.   3. Marlowe, Christopher,
1564–1593—Psychology.   4. Bacon, Francis, 1561–1626—
Psychology.   5. Europe—Intellectual life—History.   I. Title.
NX180.H6 H36   2000
305.3′09′031—dc21

                                                                00-008740

⊗The paper used in this publication meets the minimum requirements
of the American National Standard for Information Sciences—
Permanence of Paper for Printed Library Materials, ANSI Z39.48-1992.

# CONTENTS

# ILLUSTRATIONS

## Figures

## Plates (following page 84)

# ACKNOWLEDGMENTS

Many more people than I could ever name helped me as I wrote this book. Even so, I would like to make a few acknowledgments. The English Department at the University of Notre Dame has provided a warm and lively intellectual environment in which to work, which I deeply appreciate. For helping to make it so, I want to single out Gerald Bruns, Stephen Fallon, Cyraina Johnson-Roullier, Theresa Krier, Maura Nolan, Katherine O'Brien O'Keeffe, Kathy Psomiades, Ewa Ziarek, and Krzyzstof Ziarek. For many provocative conversations that have deeply influenced my thinking, though not always in the ways these interlocutors have wanted, I also thank Kathleen Biddick, Charles Daniel Blanton, Harry Berger, Jr., and Judith Feher Gurewich. For their advice, criticism, and friendship, I am deeply grateful to Leigh DeNeef and Barbara Baines. My thanks to Clarissa Lawrence and Priscilla Harrison should go without saying. Daniel Boyarin and Julia Reinhard Lupton gave my manuscript careful readings; I am indebted to both for their support. Dan Gates was a valuable research assistant. (All mistakes, of course, are mine). Carlisle Rex-Waller copyedited my manuscript, and it is much improved because of that. Doug Mitchell is simply a marvelous editor.

The second chapter of this book developed from some work I did during a summer seminar at the Folger Library sponsored by the National Endowment for the Humanities. I am very grateful to Lena Orlin, then the director of the Folger Library, for organizing the seminar and to Harry Berger, Jr., for directing it. A fellowship for junior faculty awarded by Notre Dame's Institute for Scholarship in the Liberal Arts as well as a generous leave of absence granted by Notre Dame's English department gave me the necessary resources and time to do my work. Notre Dame's Institute for Scholarship in the Liberal Arts also provided funds for research assistance and a subvention to pay for the color reproductions in this book. I happily thank Don Costello, Julia Douthwaite, Christopher Fox, and Chris Vanden Bossche for their assistance and support.

An earlier version of chapter 4 appeared in *English Literary History* 63 (1996): 309–36. Johns Hopkins University Press has generously granted permission to reprint it here.

Finally, I want to thank Audrey Threefoot, Henry Threefoot, and Ashley Hammill, who are supportive even though they have to be, and to acknowledge the memory of Harry Hammill.

History is the subject of a structure whose site is not homogenous empty time, but time filled by the presence of the now.
Thus, to Robespierre ancient Rome was a past charged with
the time of the now which he blasted out of the continuum of
history. The French Revolution viewed itself as Rome reincar-
nate. It evoked ancient Rome the way fashion evokes cos-
tumes of the past. Fashion has a flair for the topical, no matter where it stirs in the thickets of long ago; it is a tiger's leap
into the past. This jump, however, takes place in an arena
where the ruling class gives the commands. The same leap in
the air of open history is the dialectical one, which is how
Marx understood the revolution.
Walter Benjamin, *Theses on the Philosophy of History,* thesis 14

If it is true that as soon as philosophy declares itself to be
reflection or coincidence it prejudges what it will find, then
once again it must recommence everything, reject the instruments reflection and intuition had provided themselves, and
install itself in a locus where they have not yet been distin-
guished, in experiences that have not yet been 'worked over,'
that offer us all at once, pell-mell, both 'subject' and 'object,'
both existence and essence, and hence give philosophical
resources to redefine them. Seeing, speaking, even thinking
(with certain reservations, for as soon as we distinguish
thought from speaking absolutely we are already in the order
of reflection), are experiences of this kind, both irrecusable
and enigmatic. They have a name in all languages, but a name
which in all of them also conveys significations in tufts, thickets of proper meanings and figurative meanings, so that,
unlike those of science, not one of these names clarifies by
attributing to what is named a circumscribed signification.
Rather, they are the repeated index, the insistent reminder of
a mystery as familiar as it is unexplained, of a light which, illu-
minating the rest, remains at its source a mystery.
Maurice Merleau-Ponty, *The Visible and the Invisible*

ONE

# Introduction:
# History and the Time of Sexuality

*Sexuality and Form* argues that sex is a limit of the civilizing process. It examines some of the epistemological and aesthetic spaces created by Renaissance painting, drama, and science—by Michelangelo Caravaggio, Christopher Marlowe, and Francis Bacon, to be more specific—that permit attempts to think sex at the limits of civilized, social judgment. It is my contention that Caravaggio, Marlowe, and Bacon share the attempt to construct experimental lines of sexed thinking—minor literatures, as Gilles Deleuze and Félix Guattari might put it—that rework, overturn, modify, and drain the normative force of civilized judgment from within.[1] Specifically, I will argue that each of these thinkers is able to produce a temporal pose that is irreducible to social thought. What makes these experimental lines of thinking sexed is not simply the content of their thought but the various disjunctions between forms and substances upon which these lines of thinking insist, disjunctions whose locus in all three figures—Caravaggio, Marlowe, and Bacon—is the epistemological space of the body being judged.

The works that I will consider conceive of sex not simply as one aspect among many to be read, discussed, and historicized but rather as a horizon of interpretation and a threshold of thinking. In other words, these works urge a much more extreme argument than the now fashionable claim that a responsible, historically sensitive, cultural poetics needs to include attention to sexualities outside the domain of the seemingly all-encompassing modernist division of sex into homosexual and heterosexual. Current cultural studies encourages investigations into the construction of sexed personages and communities, the terms for understanding experience as sexual, the relations of particular individuals to deviancy from historically constructed erotic norms, and the expressions of same-sex or nonnormative erotic relations both in aesthetic works and by way of cultural production—all unarguably indispensable to much of what this book will assert. But, I shall argue, the reduction of sex to historical information does not constitute interpretation as such. The horizon of sex demands more than the introduction of new material for cultural analysis. With the works of Caravaggio, Marlowe, and Bacon, it demands a shift from modes of critical analysis that conceive of the aesthetic as a reflection of the social toward modes that reconceive the social and its relation to history through the aesthetic.

One of the greatest challenges confronting my argument is just how to locate sexuality historically. The problem is only in part that, as Eve Sedgwick explains, sexualities "are being discovered to possess a diachronic history—a history of significant change—and to be entangled in particularly indicative ways with aspects of epistemology and of literary [or, more generally, aesthetic] creation and reception."[2] More pointedly, the aesthetic—broadly conceived—gives form to a history of sexuality in such a way that some changes are rendered significant while others go simply unrecognized. The question of sexuality, that is, urges the problem of historiography. In particular, while a social history of sex may help by giving rough sketches of general trends in relation to socially sanctioned patterns of relatedness or to historical patterns of geographic and economic movement, social history tends to be incapacitated when confronted with queer sexualities. For all its importance, social history tends to be fairly reductive when faced with the aesthetic. Nor can historically situated taxonomies that "recover the [erotic and sexual] terms in which the experience of individuals belonging to past societies were constituted," for which David Halperin argues, entirely solve the problem.[3] Sexualities emerge *in their particularities* precisely in the interstices of the social—neither outside nor prior to the social, but in and between social thought. And, because of the spacing of this emergence, these sexualities tend to be recalcitrant to easy social reassimilation.[4]

The problem of sexuality as an object of study therefore strongly concerns cultural memory. How do we recall and commemorate a sexed thinking recalcitrant to the operations of the social, including cultural memory? And how do we do this while neither reifying nor debasing either this recalcitrance or the thinking of sex? Or, as Louise Fradenburg and Carla Freccerro ask, "what does it mean to practice a discipline [e.g., history] whose designs on life and death, pleasure and suffering of the body have, however often effaced or repressed, nonetheless been a central part of its work?"[5] To state the problem in a more philosophical register, how might we recall this sexed thinking in its historicality?[6]

The crucial difficulty in locating sexuality historically lies in the relation of sexuality to time. Sexualities of the past, especially queer sexualities, demand modes of cultural memory in our present and their future (the two are not the same) that attend to temporality. This is why when Valerie Traub argues for a temporal consistency of female homoeroticism as enacted on the Renaissance London stage—"[figured] not only in terms of the always already lost, but the always already about to be betrayed"—she also begins her well-known essay "The (In)Significance of Lesbian Desire" with a tease: "The 'lesbian desire' of my title is a come-on. If this is the last you hear of it, it is because, enticing as it may sound, it doesn't exit."[7] This is also why in his analyses of sodomy in relation to Renaissance English literature Jonathan Goldberg will suggest that "a deconstructive method of reading" with its attentiveness to the retroactive reconstruction of meaning is the "only way" to approach questions concerning "the sites of sexual possibilities, the syntax of desires not readily named," even at "the risk of dehistoricizing."[8] While I do not agree with Goldberg's methodological assessment, I would propose that both Traub and Goldberg begin a mode of ethical criticism that commemorates what is not spoken by introducing a difference between what is not spoken in the past and the naming of it in the present *in the very act of naming*. But, I will argue, these relations between sexuality and time are not just problems for the present. Sexualities that think emerge "in their moment" with a temporal form distinct from official history and expressed primarily in the refusal to collapse form with substance. For this reason, the time of sexuality calls for modes of critical analysis that maintain external relations with the historical.

Most boldly put, any attempt to historicize sexuality that does not afford some difference between temporal and social forms risks repeating the conscription of time upon which social force is predicated.

Time's local irreversibility almost always serves as the grounds upon which the social constructs stable, sanctioned identities. By translating that irreversibility into repeated corporeal habits and practices, the social uses bodily movement to construct social being. As Pierre Bourdieu demonstrates, the social organizes movements of the body in and over time by granting certain poses and gestures social significance. By rooting "the most fundamental structures of the group in the primary experiences of the body," society reproduces the body moving in time as the posed, gestural body aglow with social significance.[9] In the repetition and ossification of movement, the social creates what Cornelius Castoriadis calls "identitary time," the social institution of time and of the self in that time.[10]

What sanctifies these habits and practices and what secures the continuation of this identitary time is not the social as a material field but the consolidation and abstraction of juridical authority that as a mode of evaluation occurs in the establishment of identitary time. While Freud proposes that narcissism grants the ego "the self-respect" in a way that is similar to the anthropological concept of "prestigious imitation," he adds that social movement relies on the portability of social judgment.[11] In order to move with civility in civilized spaces, the ego must learn to anticipate and, ultimately, to incorporate social demands such that imitative reciprocity—produced by parenting, pedagogy, and so forth—is preempted by the abstraction and introjection of social judgment in the form of the superego, the function of which is to regulate an individual's actions and motives before these can be regulated by some external authority.[12]

The force of the social is to produce an isomorphic relation between an increasingly sedimented body and an increasingly abstracted judgment, the result of which is a regularized expression of social form as psychic space. As Judith Butler proposes in her readings of Freud and Nietzsche, "the social implicates the psychic in its very formation—or, to be more precise, *as* its very formation and formativity."[13] Psychic space, posited in the act of bringing social judgment to bear upon oneself, gives regularized form to social force insofar as that force attempts the ossification and regularization of bodily movement in the creation of identitary time.

Thus, it is easy to understand how a social historian's focus on poses and gestures can "offer a key to some of the fundamental values and assumptions underlying any particular society," as Keith Thomas puts it.[14] But it is also easy to understand how these "underlying" values, assumptions, and generic protocols explicitly rely on relinquishing the particularities of thinking to a conscriptive and regularizing social thought that amounts to repetition of the same. For those of us who wish to think about sexualities of the past, therefore, the usefulness of social history and its cousin cultural studies must be matched by a strong suspicion of both when either one refuses the social and the force of its institutions any limitation, refuses to grant thinking any particularity, and refuses to distinguish between history and temporality in assuming that the time of history is, as Benjamin puts it, homogenous.[15]

My main assertion in this book is that certain sexualities recalcitrant to the consolidation of judgment in the formation of identitary time take the spaces in between the repetition of social thought. I came to this assertion through analyses of Caravaggio, Marlowe, and Bacon. For previous generations, one critical issue that pertained to each of these figures was homosexuality. Certainly the last fifteen years of gay studies has taught that such an imputation seriously ignores the historical specificity of homosexuality by universalizing it. Even so, it seemed to me when I began my analyses that the historically wrenching misnomer "homosexuality" got at something significant in each of these figures, something that has a great deal to do with the sexed body and its relation to history and to interpretation, if not a great deal with object choice per se. I came to the conclusion that each of these thinkers situates his work at a certain threshold of civility that frustrates and extends social norms and the protocols of reading and spectatorship, the historical modes of evaluation that support them. In so doing, Caravaggio, Marlowe, and Bacon each posit different relations between the body and aggression, between practice and thinking, between posing and judgment, and between form and substance. What each develops is sexed thinking as *poiesis* of the body that extends and modifies social thought.

## A *Poiesis* of the Body

To some extent, my analyses of this *poiesis* rely on a psychoanalytic understanding of the body and sexuality—not on the developmental account of the ego to be sure, but on the psychoanalytic insistence that both the body and sexuality necessitate an account of thinking and its relation to aggression. Psychoanalysis is of interest not because it attempts to tell a universal truth of the body or of sexuality, but because it serves to explain in a general way the violence of the social reproduction of the body from the vantage point of particular, individuated symptom formation. Its critical value, then, lies in its capacity to explain sexuality as a relation to the social, at best in a way that neither collapses into dominant ideology nor forgets the complexities of corporeality.

As the work of Freud, Lacan, Kristeva, and others would suggest, the body is constituted in relation to an aggression that society constitutively wishes to avoid, such that the body of the socially created individual—and for Freud, the ego "is first and foremost a bodily ego, . . . the projection of a surface"[16]—is a strategy for negotiating social dissolution. Psychoanalysis doesn't assume a binary relation between society and the body; it asserts a three-part relation between society, the body, and aggression. In his essay "On Narcissism," Freud proposes a primary narcissism grounded in autoerotic libido and a secondary narcissism "superimposed" upon the first.[17] In primary narcissism, the subject discovers what Lacan calls a "profound lack of co-ordination of its own motility." It "is invested with all the original distress resulting from the child's intra-organic and relational discordance during the first six months."[18] Neither corporeality nor its spacing is "civilized." Secondary narcissism defends against the aggressivity of this initial formation of space by alienating the subject from it. "The human individual fixes upon himself an image that alienates him from himself," Lacan writes, an image formed through the critical judgments of others.[19] This image, the ego-ideal as projected image of the mirror stage, allows the subject to display itself being loved by the critical judgments of some group—nation, family, church, ethnic group, and so forth—by conforming to the image that these critical judgments offer in the consolidation of identitary time. From this perspective, of course, one can recall the gratification of primary narcissism through identification with the ideal-ego, whose task is to remember with nostalgia a gratification once enjoyed. But in effect this nostalgia, too, defends against primary narcissism by screening the subject from it. Thus, in secondary narcissism, the very splitting of the ego defends against the space of primary narcissism either through a memory that screens or by initiation into a social identity that refuses particularity.[20]

Perhaps most fundamental for my analysis is that this relation of subjectivity to aggression grounds the capacity for a sexed thinking irreducible to social thought. For Freud, thinking defers the satisfaction of social signification by positivizing what civilized subjectivity wishes to avoid as *jouissance*.[21] On an initial level, Freud argues, thinking begins when the psychical apparatus makes a link, or what Freud calls a "perceptual identity," between satisfaction and a mnemic image.[22] This link effectively cathects that image with satisfaction. However, this link affords no basis for a distinction between thought and reality, no basis for a distinction between conscious and unconscious thought. There is, simply, a network of associated memories of satisfaction. On this level, "all thinking is no more than a circuitous path from the memory of a satisfaction (a memory which has been adopted as a purposive idea) to an identical cathexis of the same memory which it is hoped to attain once more." Here, what counts is movement: thinking "must concern itself with the connecting paths between ideas, without being led astray by the *intensity* of those ideas."[23] On another level, Freud argues, thinking must stop simply remembering and start making distinctions, first and foremost distinctions between remembered satisfaction and present reality. And it is the avoidance of satisfaction that allows it to do so. Rather than just remembering moments of satisfaction, thinking separates from a network of memory and creates a path of "deviation" precisely by orienting itself toward what perceptual identities reject—"painful excitation."[24] In so doing, thinking positivizes as an aggressively insistent and unthinkable index what memory avoids. As Freud explains in his *Project for a Scientific Psychology*, the rejection of painful excitation allows for a reference point external to thinking, what Lacan calls "the Thing," that can serve as its "criterion for distinguishing between perception and memory."[25]

It is through an enjoyment in aggression qua painful excitation that a sexed *poiesis* can recuperate this index and disengage from satisfying social truth. By aggression, I do not at all mean the brute stupidity of a violence whose objective is to overcome or to destroy others. Nor do I mean passive submission to that violence. By enjoyment in aggression I mean to designate the force of a creation that gives thinking the capacity to extend beyond itself and beyond social thought. This force of creation cannot be divorced from corporeality: in this enjoyment the body has the capacity to think what the social does not want to say. Following Monique David-Ménard, I propose that this thinking is expressed in certain aesthetic formations that, as "elaboration[s] of the body in a modeling of movement" irreducible to social movement, have no other aim than the goal of "struggling with the shaping of a jouissance," formations that disarticulate an isomorphic alignment between abstract social judgment and the sedimentation of the body in identitary time.[26] The effect of this *poiesis* is not to consolidate the judgment of the superego but to do exactly the opposite: to make space for different modes of evaluation with different relations to the body, aggression, and identity. Morever, this *poiesis* cannot be fully elucidated by a historicism of sexualities, no matter how detailed, because historicism is a mode of judgment and criticism that to date remains unable to separate history from temporality. Instead, what this *poiesis* calls for is a kind of historically minded phenomenology of sexualities that, as such, refuses to compress the relationalities that various sexualities posit into social truth—that refuses to interrogate with the goal in mind of a singular, historical solution.

The potential problem in beginning with psychoanalysis is that it risks positioning the social at the vanishing point from the get-go, avoiding the social in a symptomatically ahistorical forgetting rather than working through the social and its conscriptive force. For this reason, and in order to focus more clearly on what emerges in the spaces in between the repetition of social thought, Freud's psychic apparatus needs to be continually rethought within historically specific versions of the social that recognize and thematize both the force of the social and its limits. For a study of the Renaissance, as I will argue much more extensively in chapter 2, this means beginning with Norbert Elias's civilizing process and especially the civilizing process's double articulation of power: on the one hand, the formation of pacified, psychic spaces; and on the other, the insistence on the immanent force of exteriority that, for civility, war comes to represent. The relation between psychic space and exteriority that Elias proposes isn't simply one of inside/outside; it is, as well, a relation of competing strategies for dealing with aggression. In part, the civilizing process organizes aggression by positing the anticipation of aggressive judgment through the regulation of the body as its identitary time: in anticipation of the possible judgment that one is uncivilized, illmannered, the civilized subject takes on the strictures of civility as corporeal practices, introjecting the force of judgment by bringing that judgment to bear against itself as a preventative measure against violence. This identitary time actively rejects as violent a version of immanent force characterized by war, but since civility's interiorization of power consistently implies a rejected exteriorization of force, war inevitably returns with increasingly well-developed technologies demonstrating what civility has organized as its most dangerous threat.[27]

I do not mean to suggest that the relation between these two articulations of power are, on the level of the subject, causal. The civilized subject's introjection of judgment is not a direct response to the threat of war. It is, rather, as I shall develop in chapter 2, a duplication of the distinction between interiority and exteriority by which the subject attempts to affirm a limited sense of freedom, primarily economic, in relation to communal mores that the civilized subject sees itself as having superseded. As Elias argues, civility received its "specific stamp and function" in the first quarter of the sixteenth century, when generic shifts in structures of observation in books of manners consolidated a form by which one strategically submits to a system of courtesy neither out of an inherited obligation to that system nor out of some magical respect for that system, but as an act of upwardly mobile self-assertion. Especially with Erasmus's *De Civilitate Morum Puerilium* and Della Casa's *Galateo,* Elias argues, manner books were no longer written as if they were spoken by the voice of authority; the very same rules are authorized with the voice of observation and experience.[28] This genre shift recasts manners not as obligatory strictures that one must follow but as socially produced rules that one brings to bear upon oneself in order to stylize a mode of participation in civic life: "[T]his situation gave, among others, the representatives of a small, secular-bourgeois intellectual class, the humanists, . . . not only an opportunity to rise in social situations, to gain renown and authority, but also a possibility of candour and detachment that was not present to the same degree either before or after. This chance of distancing themselves . . . permitted individual representatives of the intellectual class to identify totally and unconditionally with none of the social groups of their world."[29] Elias argues that the emergence of an intellectual humanist stratum at courts and other bases of civic power is predicated upon the notion that those who "naturally" belong there—members of the nobility and aristocracy—are duped because they unproblematically believe in a system that the intellectual humanist can see "for what it is." The intellectual humanist proposes a perspective from which one believes in the system and is duped by it in order to legitimate an alienated self not duped by that system even in the process of submission to it. By folding the force of strictures, by bringing the force of judgment to bear upon oneself, this intellectual humanist is able to eke out a space for social mobility and political maneuvering. Moreover, the humanist perspective also posits a fairly rigidly consolidated virtual reader in extremely homosocial psychic space who regulates the possibilities of candor and detachment that Elias here describes.

For Caravaggio, Marlowe, and Bacon, the limit of the civilizing process is to be found neither in its strategies of subjection nor in its double articulation of power, but in its relation to the flesh. Whereas the body is the *product* of the civilizing process, the flesh is its *asserted precondition*. I do not wish to argue that the flesh precedes the production of the civilized body; rather, I propose that the civilizing process's syncopated organization of the body and the flesh readdresses the Christian problematic of the history. As the well-mannered body becomes the iconic referent for a civility that offers upward mobility to the merchant classes, it also reoccupies the function of the Christic body of Paul's epistles, especially insofar as the function of both Christianity and civility is to incarnate a community that paradoxically attempts to transcend the body through spiritualized corporeal practices. In order to secure the historical centrality of Christ's death and resurrection, Paul elaborates an ethics of corporeal transcendence by which he defines Christian community. Against circumcision, which he reads as an insistence upon the flesh by which the Jews build a genealogical community bound by law, Paul opposes baptism, which binds members of a Christian spiritual community into "one body in Christ" (Rom. 12:5).[30] In effect, rather than cutting the body in an attempt to fulfill the strictures of God's law, as the Hebrew Bible demands (Gen. 17:10–14), Paul proposes a historical, epochal cut from

Judaism as Christians enact a transcendence of the flesh in order to come together in the spiritual body of Christ.

> You cannot have forgotten that all of us, when we were baptised into Christ Jesus, were baptised into his death. So by our baptism into his death we were buried with him, so that as Christ was raised from the dead by the Father's glorious power, we too should begin living a new life. If we have been joined to him by dying a death like his, so we shall be by a resurrection like his; realising that our former self was crucified with him, so that the self which belonged to sin should be destroyed and we should be freed from the slavery of sin. Someone who has died, of course, no longer has to answer for sin.
>
> But we believe that, if we died with Christ, then we shall live with him too. We know that Christ has been raised from the dead and will never die again. Death has no power over him any more. For by dying, he is dead to sin once and for all, and now the life that he lives is life with God. In the same way, you must see yourselves as being dead to sin but alive for God in Christ Jesus.
>
> That is why you must not allow sin to reign over your mortal bodies, and make you obey their desires; or give any parts of your bodies over to sin to be used as instruments of evil. (Rom. 6:3–12)

To secure Christ's death and resurrection as the central historical event for members of the Christian community, Paul establishes a practice, an ethics of the self, whose historiographic work is to cut Christianity from its Hebrew past.[31] It will be up to Origen, Augustine, and other of the church fathers to recuperate that past by positing a full-fledged hermeneutics, based on Paul, whose function is to convert that past and its fleshiness through allegorical interpretation.

In asserting a political and social organization based on a self-effacing performance that attempts to supersede an organization based on kinship and genealogy, the civilizing process repeats the gesture of Pauline Christianity in a different register. The complex self-assertiveness that Elias describes amounts to an existential program that repeats Christianity's efforts to secure a historical break while translating Christian eschatology into political utopianism. As Hans Blumenberg has demonstrated, the modern age recuperates the Christian attempt to preserve eschatology through transcendence and the allegorization of history by reasserting Christian otherworldliness into a general "responsibility for the condition of the world as a challenge relating to the future."[32] That is, while the modern age explicitly turns from a theological version of history, nevertheless it also recuperates Christianity's eschatological thinking in the form of political utopianism.[33] And, to a certain extent, this recuperation solves the tension between Christian spirit and Jewish flesh. In civility, the function that the spirit serves for Paul is *already* rooted in the body. By grounding itself in the performing and self-effacing "constructed" body, this new civility comes up with a relation to embodiment that always just allows identity to transcend the flesh in a kind of corporeal instantiation of the radical Renaissance formula for subjectivity, "I am not I." But this new civility isn't so much a secular synthesis of Christianity and Judaism as it is a rearticulation of that tension in the two dominant modes of embodiment of the civilizing process: the civilized, aestheticized body and the carnal, sexed flesh.

To make space for thinking in this extremely cunning social and aesthetic formation means effecting a consistent undoing of the civilized subject's relatively organized psychic space and of the relatively consolidated virtual readers that regulate through the flesh. This undoing serves as the grounds for building, giving shape, and forming a minor, sexed mode of thinking such that what will come to thinking is radically exterior and unanticipated. This, I shall argue, is the work that in various ways and to various degrees Caravaggio, Marlowe, and Bacon all attempt, each asserting temporal forms through sexed modes of thinking at odds with that of the civilizing process in both its psychic and historiographic forms of identitary time. To this extent, the sexed *poiesis* of Caravaggio, Marlowe, and Bacon radicalizes a developing baroque metaphysics that insists on understanding the universe as a restricted, plural determination mediating between absolute necessity and absolute possibility. Effectively controverting Augustinian allegory, Nicholas of Cusa argues that the universe, as God's creation, must be understood as "possibility actually determined," which expresses and explicates God as Absolute Necessity.[34] Perhaps most significant for my analyses, this understanding shifts away from the life of Christ as Christianity's focal event and centers instead on plurality and possibility as modes of explication. Building off the Cusan's arguments, Giordano Bruno posits matter as both substratum and a potency whose mode is neither activity nor passivity but instead merges both active and passive in a kind of "capacity-to-be." This capacity-to-be coincides with a "being-in-act" that is dispersed and multiplied in the plurality of the universe, a capacity to be affected, which Spinoza most forcefully links to the body as a mode of expression.[35] Instead of using the self-regulation of the body to problematize the flesh, I shall argue, Caravaggio, Marlowe, and Bacon each mobilize this capacity to be affected in varying degrees precisely in order to reformulate relations between history, possibility, judgment, and the flesh.

## History, Theory, and Sexuality

Even though my analyses rely on psychoanalysis, I don't want simply to assert psychoanalysis as the untroubled theoretical center of this work. I do think that the problems I am raising cannot at present be thought outside a psychoanalytic register, but by the same token no raising of these problems should serve only to consolidate that register. In other words, I am not interested in psychoanalytic polemics; nor am I interested in allegorical readings, however ingenious, that "prove" the so-called truths of psychoanalysis: the Oedipus complex, its figurations of maternity, the phallus, and so forth. If there can be such a thing as psychoanalytic thinking, it must maintain at its "center" a notion of psychoanalysis always differing from itself. Nowadays, it seems to me that especially for a study of sexuality this will mean an engagement between the works of Lacan and Foucault. Since in Renaissance studies Lacan is, with a few notable exceptions, simply dismissed and Foucault is, though usually praised, generally underread, I want to spend a few pages discussing what might be for my arguments the relevant ground as well as the possible horizon of such an engagement.

In *Le séminaire livre XX: Encore,* Lacan raises the following problem: How can psychoanalysis rethink sexuality and contemporary versions of sexual difference (e.g., early 1970s) such that the history of sexed being can open up onto something else? In Lacan's diagnosis, contemporary sexuality has been a way to sustain the subject as subject to the desire of the Other. It is, he argues, our current metaphysics. For Lacan, desire is generally subjectifying insofar as it is a result of turning the fact of the unspoken, the fact that "saying it all is literally impossible," into a sign of meaning.[36] Sexuality, of any kind, is a particular way to support this desire by positing in specific and specifiable, unconscious fantasy a substantialized enjoyment that is not necessarily satisfying to the subject but is satisfying to the supposed desire of the Other. And to maintain these unconscious fantasies, the subject will make all sorts of sacrifices and endure all kinds of hardships. For example, Lacan's main critique in *Séminaire XX* is of a courtly love tradition (of which, Lacan argues, Freud is a part) in which desire for One Truth, a truth of sexual difference, substantiates enjoyment in a fantasmic phallic *jouissance*. For Lacan, the primary problem is that the subject of desire forgets itself as what he calls the subject of the statement. As he puts it, in desire "the fact that one says remains forgotten behind what is said in what is heard."[37] The speaking subject as subject of the statement lags behind its subjectivization by the desire of the Other. In order to counter this problem and in order to develop a different relation to a courtly love formation of sexual difference, Lacan argues, first, for the admittedly brutal, analytic transformation of the One of the phallus into a one of pure difference. Second, he posits a resituation of the subject of the statement in relation to an untimely *jouissance* that does not congeal into a fantasy that supports the subject in the desire of the Other.[38]

The problem Lacan raises is quite similar to the one Foucault confronts between his writing of volumes 1 and 2 of *The History of Sexuality*, although for Foucault the problem more obviously concerns temporality and history than temporality and language. In what over the last ten years has become perhaps the most oft-quoted and infamous passage from *The History of Sexuality*, volume 1, Foucault distinguishes the epoch of modernity from "the premodern" in the difference between the sodomite and the homosexual:

> As defined by the ancient civil or canonical codes, sodomy was a category of forbidden acts; their perpetrator was nothing more than the juridical subject of them. The nineteenth century homosexual became a personage, a past, a case history, and a childhood, in addition to being a type of life, a life form, and a morphology, with an indiscreet anatomy and possibly a mysterious physiology. Nothing that went into his total composition was unaffected by his sexuality, it was everywhere present in him: at the root of all

his actions because it was their insidious and indefinitely active principle; written immodestly on his face and body because it was the secret that always gave itself away. It was consubstantial with him, less as a habitual sin than as a singular nature. . . . Homosexuality appeared as one of the forms of sexuality when it was transposed from the practice of sodomy onto a kind of interior androgyny, a hermaphrodism of the soul. The sodomite had been a temporary aberration; the homosexual was now a species.[39]

Foucault's opposition is most forceful about the conditions that allow for the specific debasement of being that characterizes modernity, a debasement that the invention of the homosexual both figures and instantiates. As David Halperin writes from a slightly different perspective, this "schematic opposition between sodomy and homosexuality is first and foremost a discursive analysis, not a social history, let alone an exhaustive one. *It is not an empirical claim about the historical existence or nonexistence of sexually deviant individuals.* It is a claim about the internal logic and systematic functioning of two different discursive styles of sexual disqualification—and, ultimately it is a heuristic device for foregrounding what is distinctive about modern techniques of social and sexual regulation."[40] Thus, as both Traub and Goldberg have argued, Foucault's distinction cannot be used to prevent or deny questions of sexuality before modernity. Nor, as both also argue, can its seeming status as paradigm shift be used to foreclose questions concerning relations between "premodern" and modern sexualities.[41] However, in light of the introductory chapters to *The Use of Pleasure*, Foucault's second volume of *The History of Sexuality*, I would go a few steps further. The distinction Foucault makes between the sodomite and the homosexual marks an epochal division in which history threatens to triumph over temporality by turning the difference between the sodomite and the homosexual into broadly conceived periods that would then divide the history of sexuality into "the period of the sodomite" and "the period of the homosexual." But in *The Use of Pleasure*, Foucault's approach to the question of practice modifies this potential drive toward epoch making. Rather than allowing the difference between the sodomite and the homosexual to expand into broadly conceived periods of time, Foucault radically repositions temporality and exteriority in relation to the writing of a history of sexuality, underlining the critical necessity of accounting for what Nietzsche calls the unhistorical and the untimely as the basis for resisting cultural and ethical stagnation.[42]

This repositioning is most productively read, I think, against Foucault's discussion of what he calls the Greeks' aesthetics of existence. In *The Use of Pleasure,* Foucault argues that the moral reflection of the Greeks allowed for the practice of an aesthetics of existence in which the individual could stylize a certain freedom. Neither reducible to the laws of the city-state, which asserted freedom for a certain collectivity, nor separable from these laws, this aesthetics of existence allowed the individual to exercise freedom as a kind of active mastery of oneself in relation both to pleasure and to others—women, boys, and slaves—over whom one had the rights of domination. "This freedom was more than a nonenslavement," Foucault writes. "In its full, positive form, it was a power that one brought to bear on oneself in the power that one exercised over others. . . . In order not to be excessive, not to do violence, in order to avoid the trap of tyrannical authority (over others) coupled with the soul tyrannized by desires, the exercise of political power required, as its own internal principle of regulation, power over oneself." By folding the force of law in bringing it to bear on the self, the Greeks reformulated force from a series of codified rules into "a stylization of attitudes" more open to future possibility than simple submission to the law.[43]

Most radical about this practice of folding force was that it established a relation to exteriority, only the relation that it established was also deeply conservative. Recall Foucault's definition in *The Archaeology of Knowledge* of the statement as ground zero for discourse analysis. The statement is an "event" that "defines the possibilities of appearance and delimitation of that which gives meaning." To this extent, the statement asserts an exteriority that has "no adverse form of interiority."[44] In other words, the statement does not contain some secret or hidden meaning—no nomenon behind the phenomenon— but instead has a relation with something else, something foreign and outside of thought that is specifiable not by reference to the meaning of the statement, but by reference to its formal, enunciative modality, deduced from its quasi-systematic repetition. And it is here at the statement and its "space of exteriority" that Foucault locates not the "speaking, showing, thinking subject," but "a totality in which the dis-

persion of the subject and his discontinuity with himself may be determined," not the subject of desire, but the subject of the statement.[45]
The aesthetics of existence of the Greeks established a relation with
this exteriority not by acceding to it, but by commemorating it in the
substantialization of *jouissance* that Foucault calls the problematicization of pleasure. As Deleuze explains, "[T]he folding or doubling is
itself a Memory: the 'absolute memory' or memory of the outside. . . .
Memory is the real name of the relation to oneself."[46] This commemo-
ration is not archival memory. It is formal. Nor therefore is it opposed
to forgetting. Rather, in the very form of their practices, the Greeks
commemorated the possibility of exteriority while in almost the same
gesture refusing this possibility by translating the folding of force into
a problem concerning pleasure, virility, and being. That is, the transposition of the possibilities of exteriority into practices of *jouissance*
allowed this *jouissance* to locate the possibility of exteriority while also
serving as a stop-gap to it. As they developed, these practices repeatedly translated the subject of the statement into a subject of desire
who recognized "in desire the truth of being."

   The main effect of this translation was to congeal exteriority qua
possibility into an inertia of the untranslated that these practices
tended to manifest, or "presentify" as Lacan puts it, as the flesh.[47] Foucault's diagnosis of desire and sexuality is not all that different from
Lacan's. The flesh as utter contingency becomes a necessary component of these practices as they translate the possibility of exteriority
into a hermeneutics of desire. Thus, as Lacan consistently argues
throughout his works, the cunning of this misguided attempt to find
in desire the truth of being is that it refuses to understand the flesh as
the effect of moral practices, instead understanding it metaleptically
as these practices' substantiated cause—as the problem that necessitates them.[48]

   Of course, *The Use of Pleasure* is no celebration of these practices.
Foucault's analysis of "the *problematicizations* through which being
offers itself to be, necessarily, thought" implies an "etho-poetic" that
cannot be reduced to "the *practices* on the basis of which these problematicizations are formed."[49] And here, I think, is where *The Use of
Pleasure* is most instructive. Instead of claiming the supposed homosexuality of the Greeks as the historical predecessor by which homosexual being can find the truth of its desire, Foucault approaches the

Greeks' problematicization of pleasure with a problematicization of history that potentially permits thinking to open history up in such a way that one can "learn to what extent the effort to think one's own history can free thought from what it silently thinks, and so enable it to think differently." Against the aesthetics of existence, Foucault proposes as his own the rather intoxicating philosophical activity of *askesis,* "an exercise of oneself in the activity of thought":

> There is always something ludicrous in philosophical discourse when it tries, from the outside, to dictate to others, to tell them where their truth is and how to find it, or when it works up a case against them in the language of naive positivity. But it is entitled to explore what might be changed, in its own thought, *through the practice of a knowledge that is foreign to it.* The "essay"—which should be understood as the assay or test by which, in the game of truth, one undergoes changes, and not as the simplistic appropriation of others for the purpose of communication—is the living substance of philosophy, at least if we assume that philosophical activity is still what it was in times past, i.e., an "ascesis," *askesis.*[50]

As opposed to "the determination of an ethical substance" through "modes of subjection" in which "the individual establishes his relation to the rule and recognizes himself as obliged to put it into practice," this activity of thought approaches the practice of knowledge obliquely, in a quasi-regularized movement that oddly substantiates thought in its approach to knowledge from the outside.[51] In short, rather than continue the potential project of epoch making at work in the first volume of *The History of Sexuality,* in *The Use of Pleasure,* Foucault returns epoch to its Greek meaning—*epoche,* a pause in movement or turn in direction—through the activity of his own thought in that thought's irreducibility to the practices of the Greeks. Here, Foucault presents neither an antiquarian nor a monumentalizing display of the terms by which the sexual experiences of individuals have been constituted. He presents the possibility for a phenomenology of "intercorporeity," as Merleau-Ponty puts it, in which one allows oneself to be seduced into a different relation with exteriority than the one established by Cartesianism and its prop, the civilizing process.[52]

The condition for this phenomenology is what Lacan calls a "passion for ignorance"—*not* a desire not to know but, more like Nicholas

of Cusa's learned ignorance, a passion for producing as such the unthought (or the unhistorical).[53] One of Lacan's main theses is that because the desire to know allows one to maintain a distance from the
limits of thought, "there's no such thing as a desire to know."[54] Every
desire to know is also a desire not to know. Hence, Lacan's question
concerning knowledge is how the flesh—as what he calls the *objet a*—
gets mobilized by the subject to support the imputed omnipotency of
the Other who claims all *jouissance,* all rights to enjoyment and to
transgression. How, that is, does the subject substantiate the enjoyment of the woman or the homosexual (though the latter is not a
figure that Lacan will seriously question) in relation to this imputedly
omnipotent Other in order to sustain itself as subject of desire—that
is, in order to forget itself as subject of the statement? How does the
subject suppose some knowledge of the *jouissance* of the Other on the
part of these figures—a knowledge supposedly felt in the flesh—such
that the subject can maintain its own relation to that Other?

It is not just the case that the practices of the Greeks determined
an ethical substance through modes of subjection; it is also the case
that the substantialization of the homosexual as a categorical figure
sustains the subject of modernity in relation to the supposed omnipotence of history.[55] To this situation, one must bring a passion for ignorance that refuses to allow the flesh to become history's support.
When one is confronted with the possibility of *jouissance* that would
satisfy being in history, Lacan argues that one must continually reply,
"That's not it," continually fracturing relations between the phenomenon and the supposed nomenon, between insufficiency and expectation, in order to situate oneself in the time of what he calls "para-
being," *par-être.*[56]

Neither Foucault nor Lacan fully develops a phenomenology of intercorporeity and exteriority. It stands as a horizon of engagement
between the two, although Foucault does explicitly and forcefully
underline its relation to contemporary homosexuality. Insofar as this
activity of thought is granted its mode by the relation between the
invention of the homosexual and the "homosexual lifestyle," which
Foucault discusses most fully in his interviews, it takes up the difference between sodomitical activity and the invention of the homosexual in order to write what Foucault elsewhere calls "a history of the
present."[57] The invention of the homosexual is so interesting and so

important, then, because the supposed transposition from sodomitical activity into homosexual being substantiates instead a form of being that, contrary to the aesthetics of existence, actively turns against
its own substantiation in the specific lines of thinking it permits.[58] As
Foucault proposes, part of what defines homosexuality is the problematicization of history: Two men, Foucault argues, "face each other
without terms or convenient words, with nothing to assure them
about the meaning of the movement that carries them towards each
other. They have to invent, from A to Z, a relationship that is still
formless."[59] For this reason, Foucault speculates, what makes homosexuality so disturbing is "much more than the sexual act itself"—
"the homosexual mode of life"—a mode without a final cause. Foucault's point is neither to claim nor to invent a final cause, nor in fact
to claim a material cause, but "to advance a homosexual *askesis* that
would make us work on ourselves and invent, I do not say discover, a
manner of being that is still improbable," a homosexual ascesis between historiographic discourses.[60] If it is to respect and mobilize this
between-ness, the application of historiography to homosexuality
must avoid the historicist fall into substantiated cause. "We must
make the intelligible appear against a background of emptiness, and
deny its necessity."[61] The opposition that Foucault draws between an
aesthetics of existence and the problematicization of history implicitly
specifies what Foucault elsewhere calls the intellectual's reason for being, to do "the work of modifying one's own thought and that of others," as more precisely the "work of becoming homosexual" by mobilizing sexuality to arrive at "a multiplicity of relationships," including
relationships between oneself and history, oneself and thinking, oneself and truth.[62]

Leo Bersani rightly cautions against desexualizing Foucault's emphasis on a homosexual mode of life. "The intolerable promise of 'un-
foreseen kinds of relationships' which many people see in gay lifestyles
cannot be dissociated from an authentically new organization of the
body's pleasures," Bersani writes. Moreover, he continues, "such a program may necessarily involve some radical, perhaps even dangerous,
experimentation with modes of what used to be called making love."[63]
Rather than reducing homosexuality to an aesthetic and practical program of courtly love, homosexual thought must involve aesthetic and
practical forms of relationality invented through, with, and against the

body's pleasures, in relation to a pain that coexists with human beings' willingness "to give up control over their environment," to experience the "self-shattering" of *jouissance* in order to imagine "a nonsuicidal disappearance of the subject."[64] Bersani's main polemic is not so much against Foucault, I think, as it is against a banal and conservative version of queer theory that naively claims to have superseded gay identity in its insistence on the performativity of all identity. In rendering all identity formally the same, this claim concerning performativity amounts to avoiding history, often quite piously in history's name. Foucault's move is entirely friendly to Bersani's point, although it is a bit more complex. Foucault aims at this nonsuicidal disappearance of the subject through a rethinking of being and history in order to move from a *jouissance* of being that substantiates "the homosexual" as a support for modernist history to a *jouissance* of thinking through and with the body that problematicizes history and its relations to corporeality. This nonsuicidal disappearance does not occur in corporeal practices per se; it occurs in the body as the means of translation back from the subject of desire to the subject of the statement, from being to thinking, not as something one can be but as something thinking can do. The *jouissance* of thinking that Foucault locates *is* homosexual thought, although it most likely will not always be so. Since this nonsuicidal disappearance of the subject is a temporal stance in relation to *jouissance,* a sexed *poiesis* that risks futurity, what it calls for is an understanding of the various forms of this *poiesis* neither through a narrative of supercession nor as a mode of identification, but as a proliferation whose collection must, in its very activity, allow homosexual thought to remain open to becoming something else.

What forms of sexed thinking might posed bodies permit? What thinking emerges around the pose of the courtier that Della Casa's quite ridiculous narrator urges in the *Galateo* (chapter 2), the posed male body in Caravaggio's paintings (chapter 3), the sodomitical pose of Doctor Faustus at the end of Marlowe's play (chapter 4), or the pose of Bacon's experimenter, subject to epistemological violence (chapter 5)? In raising these questions, I do not only mean to ask what cultural or social truth these bodies tell. I also wish to ask how these posed bodies might offer lines of thinking at society's threshold that cannot be reduced to culturally and socially produced truths. How might poses and gestures attempt to disengage knowledge from social truths and dominant values? And in what ways do these attempts involve rethinking relations between being, violence, and the body?

In chapter 2 I investigate the normative relations between masculine posing, judgment, and equivocation of Renaissance aesthetic culture as expressed in Albertian perspective and in the forms of reading established by Della Casa's *Galateo.* I will demonstrate how civilized aesthetic space locates sexuality and violence at its psychic and geographic limits. Chapter 3 offers an exploration of queer formalism and its relation to history in Caravaggio's boy-paintings and religious paintings. I argue that Caravaggio attempts to traverse the social identificatory mechanisms of Renaissance aesthetics by forcing as the basis of spectatorship an erotic, specifically queer identification with a rather violent historical openness. Chapter 4 considers Marlowe's constructions of corporeality, spectatorship, and readership in *Doctor Faustus.* In this chapter, I argue that Marlowe's play uses forms of literary reception to translate a political jurisprudence of sodomy into a sexual hermeneutics that can read the sodomitical outside the disciplinary strictures of the law. Specifically, I argue that in *Doctor Faustus* sexuality congeals in the relations between, on the one hand, a division of corporeality into the performative body and the textualized flesh and, on the other hand, the splitting of an audience that suspends disbelief from an audience that sustains disbelief. Chapter 5 proposes that Bacon's experimental science emerges out of his attempt to form a counterjurisprudence to the consolidation of judicial authority by jurists such as Plowden and Coke. The result, I argue, is not simply the establishment of inductive reasoning but also an eroticization of experience of time instantiated in the capacity of the body to be affected. In this eroticization, the sexed body embodies not history monumentally, but history in the process of change. Chapter 6 concludes with a discussion of the significance of Irigaray's analyses of sexual difference, history, and ethics for contemporary gay studies and queer theory. In this conclusion, I come full circle back to the problems I have been discussing here.

Finally, a brief word about theory. From a historicist perspective, theoretical readings—and especially theoretical readings influenced by psychoanalysis, as are the ones that follow—are nothing but dubious attempts to tell the ahistorical "truth" of art, attempts that historicism tends to forbid in its dreams of a history that keeps intact firmly established boundaries between past and present, then and now. I hope it is clear from this introduction that I do not imagine this simplistic fantasy of truth telling to be theory's job. Nor do I intend to support a universal truth of sexuality. Rather, throughout this book I engage in theoretical readings performatively—aiming not at some version of *moi* criticism, but at a theoretical practice that accounts for theory's Greek root, *theoria*—as the basis for thinking history, aesthetics, and sexuality. Throughout the writing of this book, I never intended to grant this engagement the status of a method; I meant it quite simply as an approach, a mode, a technique of shaping, if you will, whose primary effort was not to determine the outcome of its movements.

# Reading Bodies: Recognition and the Violence of Form

Consider, as an opening gambit, the juxtaposition of the following two images, both Italian, both dating from the first part of the sixteenth century: on the one hand, the Baltimore Panel, an "ideal city" genre painting (fig. 1); on the other hand, Leonardo da Vinci's sketch of an imaginary military weapon, a horse-drawn scythed cart (fig. 2). One only need look at the sliced body parts strewn around Leonardo's cart to understand that this sketch has an interest in movement and its capacity to produce violence against the body. Exactly the opposite seems true for the Baltimore Panel, with its extremely pacified, regulated, architectural space. In the Baltimore Panel, there is no violently wild motion. Nevertheless, isn't something similar to Leonardo's interest at work in its quite monumental assertion of emptiness? To the extent that the movements of the body are not frozen into the highly allegorical statues standing atop the four columns in the city's piazza, motion in this painting is burdened by vacancy. Notice, for example, the various lone figures and couples that haunt the empty space so forcefully asserted by the painting's architecture. Especially when measured against the solidity of the statues in the piazza, these figures and couples have a certain placelessness. They are, after all, transparent. Moreover, various of these figures are literally cut through by the lines that give the painting its pronounced perspectival feel. Isn't the Baltimore Panel attentive to how the assertion of supposedly ideal civic space affects corporeal violence, albeit in a fashion less immediately obvious than Leonardo's drawing of military weaponry?

When it comes to the question of violence, what distinguishes the Baltimore Panel from Leonardo's drawing is that the violence of the

Fig. 1. The Baltimore Panel. Walters Art Gallery, Baltimore.

Fig. 2. Leonardo da Vinci, sketch of a scythed cart, MS B, 10ʳ.
Bibliotèque Nationale, Paris.

Baltimore Panel is primarily a violence of form, not a violence of content. As such, this violence occurs most forcefully in the field of spectatorship. The Baltimore Panel implies that civic space should be orderly, regulated, and pacified. Moreover, the Baltimore Panel urges one to make its civic space one's own. To take this painting as an ideal is also to bring its judgment to bear upon oneself in hopes of making one's own space equally regulated and pacified. Leonardo's drawing prompts no strong impulse to see oneself in it. If anything, it is a space to be avoided.

The violence of the Baltimore Panel is a violence that Norbert Elias describes as integral to the civilizing process—the violence, that is, by which civility establishes its monopoly of force. It is, in other words, the violence of the civilizing process. In Elias's account, the civilizing process begins with the passage from a masculine warrior society to a world in which institutional monopolies of force form pacified social spaces. As "the battlefield is, in a sense, moved within," Elias writes, the tensions and passions "that were earlier directly released in the struggle of man and man, must now be worked out within the human being." The result is that "the passionate affects, that can no longer directly manifest themselves in the relations *between* people, often struggle no less violently *within* the individual against [the] supervising part of himself."[1] Contrary to Elias, I wish to propose that this passage is not one that happens between epochs. There is not an epoch of the battlefield and an epoch of its internalization. Rather, I shall argue, war bears an "extimate" relation to civility that is constitutive of civilized psychic space: war appears to be intimate to the civilized subject because it is what the state wants most to exteriorize in its monopolization of violence.[2] The civilizing process masks itself as a form of violence by positing a pacified subject who sustains a slight distance from raw force through increasingly focused practices of self-regulation and the concurrent instantiation of abstract forms of judgment, but this masking also posits as exterior an aestheticized version of immanent force for which war comes to stand. The apparatus by which civility commemorates a founding distinction between itself and war, I shall argue, is civilized psychic space, an apparatus of constitutive forgetting by which the state sustains its monopolies of violence. To this extent, and only to this extent, war permits the development of aesthetic forms that recontextualize the civilizing process and its concurrent forms of judgment.

The form upon which the civilizing urges of the Baltimore Panel depend is, most simply, perspective. There appears to be no violence in the Baltimore Panel, but its lines conspire to produce an illusion of depth that fixes its spectators and attempts to capture them within the emptiness it pretends to represent. Quite the opposite is the case with Leonardo's drawing. There, the line translates imaginary military technology into an aesthetics of motion that resists capture by civility. These lines attempt to portray the force of absolute exteriorization, even to the extent that the advancement of military technology is not the object of this sketch. Its object is to gesture toward the production of a diagrammatics of force that exceeds the cunning of civilization's monopoly on violence sustained through modes of judgment and forms of recognition. This gesture involves a two-part risk: the sketch fails to the extent that one sees what it portrays as simply horrifying, a fall of *poiesis* into referentiality, and it also fails to the extent that someone actually builds and uses the machine, a fall of *poiesis* into technology.

To assert, as I did in chapter 1, that sex is a limit of the civilizing process is to place sex at the threshold of a certain mode of judgment. In this chapter, I shall discuss how this mode of judgment develops through and in relation to aesthetic form. I shall argue that the civilizing process sustains a mode of judgment that situates the flesh at its limits, between its insistence on self-regulation and the version of force for which war comes to stand, as the stop-gap that locates the possibilities the civilizing process refuses.

## Posing and Judgment

Perspective, especially as elaborated by Alberti, responds to the political crises of the late Florentine republic by abstracting Florentine apprehensions concerning the sexed body into formal, aestheticized space. As Florence faced financial and political instabilities in the opening decades of the fifteenth century, worries over civic and sexual morality, especially sodomy, became extremely pronounced.[3] In 1403, as a response to a law that called "for the elimination and extirpation of this vice and sodomitical crime, and for its purging and its punishment" by whatever means necessary, the Signoria established the Ufficiali dell' Onestà, whose main function was to import and regulate foreign female prostitutes in order to turn young Florentine men away from sex with other men. Dissatisfied with this solution, in 1404 the council of the Popolo called for the Onestà to "make a law on the vice of sodomy" in order to "suppress it."[4] In the 1410s, sodomy was increasingly located by the clergy and by civic authorities as *the* moral problem of Florentine civic life. Although they were not put into practice, in 1418 and 1419 two provisions were passed demanding that

magistrates root out Florentine sodomy and calling for candidates for
public office to be screened for evidence of sodomitical activities and
for sodomites to be prevented from holding guild or public offices.[5]
And in 1432, the Florentine *reggimento* created the Ufficiali di Notte,
whose specific task was to track down and punish sodomites. To enable the Ufficiali di Notte to fulfill its task, the *reggimento* gave the
council's six elected members (each of whom had to be married) summary justice and the right to disregard legal principles and statutory
customs in their proceedings.[6]

The troubling of the citizen's body through sodomy enforced a social strategy of disidentification through purging perhaps best expressed by Bernardino of Siena in the Lenten sermons he delivered in
Florence in 1424:

> Whenever you hear sodomy mentioned, each and every one of
> you spit on the ground and clean your mouth out well. If they
> don't want to change their ways by any other means, maybe they
> will change if they're made fools of. Spit hard! Maybe the water of
> your spit will extinguish their fire. Like this, everyone spit hard!
>
> [*Quando udite ricordare parole di sodomia, ogni e catuno isputi in
> terra e spurghisi bene. Poi non si vogliono ammendare in altra forma,
> almeno s'ammenderanno che sarà fatto beffa do loro. Sputate forte!
> L'acqua del votro sputo, forse, ispegnerà el loro fuoco. E così ognuno
> isputi fortemente!*][7]

The ritual logic could hardly be any clearer. Even the word *sodomia*
enacts a bodily intrusion, if not an invasion, and threatens at least
figuratively to identify those who hear it with the passive *fanciullo,*
whom Bernardino especially excoriates throughout his sermons. To
disidentify with this possibility, the hearer spits, the act of spitting
ritually cleansing his body and revising his sexual history such that
the only contact with sodomy is and was through the ear. At the same
time, the act of spitting conjures the shamed, fantasmic figure of the
sodomite in opposition to the righteous hawkers. Both the cleansed
and the sodomitical body are abstractions produced through ritual,
social magic. As Peter Stallybrass and Allon White argue in a different
though related context, "the *exclusion* necessary to the formation of
social identity at [the level of official identity] is simultaneously a *pro-*

*duction* at the level of the Imaginary, and a production, what is more, of a complex hybrid fantasy emerging out of the very attempt to demarcate boundaries, to unify and purify the social collectivity."[8] Bernardino's attempts to establish ritual spitting produced Christian Florentine citizenship in opposition to the fantasmic sodomite. According to the scribe who recorded the sermon, the spit that hit the pavement after Bernardino's exhortation "seemed like thunder" [*che parve un tuono*]. Bernardino's 1424 Lenten sermons culminated in a repetition of this cathartic, symbolic violence. Several days later, after delivering a sermon on lust, which concluded with the "vice of sodomy," Bernardino cried out, "To the fire! They are all sodomites! You are in mortal sin if you try to help them!" [*Al fuoco! Tutti sono sodomiti! e se' in peccato mortale se per lui prieghi!*]—upon which the listeners in Santa Croce thronged to the piazza outside the church to watch Bernardino set fire to a massive pile of wigs, cosmetics, and clothing previously collected for the purpose.[9]

The substantialization of the sodomite through a ritual logic of purging amounts to a translation of the political problem of the subject split between civic duty and familial interests into a moral problem of the flesh. The Florentine constitution, which more or less held from 1282 to the fall of the republic and its takeover by the Medici in 1433, attempted to prevent citizens' private interests from influencing governmental decisions through two main features. First, the constitution called for short-term citizen participation in which officeholders were most often chosen by lot and not by election. The eight magistrates that made up the Signoria, which along with the Gonfaloniere di Giustizia comprised Florence's most powerful and certainly most visible executive council, held office for only two months. By making office holding brief and unpredictable, the constitution attempted to prevent government offices from becoming the bases for individual citizens or families to further their own interests. Second, the constitution demanded that citizens act according to conscience, foreclosing the possibility of representational government by forbidding both voter solicitation as well as prior negotiations among citizens, which might lead to block voting. To ensure a rigid separation of the civic personage from his familial, commercial, and other selves, members of the Signoria were immured in the Palazzo Vecchio during their tenures of office, quite literally separating familial and commercial activities from civic duty.[10] The Florentine Gino di Neri Capponi expressed with precision the opposition upon which this system of government and its notions of integrity relied when, in 1420, he wrote: "[T]he Commune of Florence will keep its authority only if it does not let any particular citizen or family or group of conspirators within it to be more powerful than the Signoria" [*Tanto terrà il Commune di Firenze suo stato, quanto terrà la spada in mano contro alli strani ed intra sé non lascerà niuno particulare cittadino o famiglia o congiura essere piú potente che la Signoria*].[11] However, in its attempts to prevent the incursion of particular interests into civic decisions, the Florentine constitution only solidified an opposition between civic duty, on the one hand, and the will of the "particular citizen" or the "family" as possible "conspirators," on the other. The Florentine constitution thus produced a constitutive fracturing of the citizen as political subject.[12]

The effect of this fracturing was that the integrity of public officials became a crucial if also extremely troublesome location for developing and consolidating forms of civic judgment. By the beginning of the fifteenth century, Florence's governmental structure had made the distrust of public officials a primary means, a "vortex," as Andrea Zorzi terms it, for competition between various factions vying for their own political and commercial interests.[13] The confused flow of this vortex became more and more regularized as it increasingly allowed Florence to consolidate its sovereignty against the rule of the Holy Roman Empire. While de facto the relation between the two was more complex, up until the mid-fourteenth century, de jure Florence was subject to the empire. Questions and problems concerning the integrity of Florentine officeholders were referred to a group of foreign, itinerant judges—the syndics—who worked for the empire and whose job was to examine and evaluate all financial, executive, and judicial activities of public officials.[14] But as Florence began to assert its sovereignty both de facto and de jure, the city replaced these syndics with its own political authorities. The Otto di Guardia was established in 1378, after the Ciompi revolt, to track down and prosecute political conspiracies, and the Conservatori delle Leggi in 1429, after various crises of the 1420s, to enforce the integrity of public officials.[15] These councils did not simply replace the Office of the Syndics but substantially expanded both the syndics' jurisdiction and procedures for obtaining conviction. For example, the Otto di Guardia widened its juridical territory to include villages and districts outside the city walls, which made up approximately three-fourths of its cases. It also began to consider vendettas under the categories of homicide and assault rather than under the category of honor, in effect redefining what counted as violence against the state.[16] And the Conservatori delle Leggi relied on anonymous denunciations, since the public denunciations required by prior councils often resulted in criminal retaliation by the families of those charged with wrongdoing, thus exacerbating the problems the trials and punishments were meant to resolve.

Because the Florentine constitution in essence created the crisis over the integrity of public officeholders, the increasingly urgent attempts during the last fifty years of the republic to express public distrust in terms of sexual behavior represented the translation of political ordering into a problematicization of the flesh. This process, because it relied on a difference integral to translation, inevitably failed to resolve the issues it imagined itself to be addressing. Instead, relations between subject and judgment were reiterated in ever more abstract and aestheticized forms—merchant ethics, *perspectiva artificialis,* and ultimately the civilizing process—while the flesh became consolidated into a highly equivocal, troublesome, and mobile excess. What emerges here is a practical logic that grants the civilizing process the force of a magical thinking by which civility can obtain a certain semiotic mobility through reiterated, formal homologies that exceed any simple relation to material cause.

In Alberti's *I Libri Della Famiglia,* Florentine merchant culture attempts to stylize a solution to this historical crisis by insisting on absolute visibility as both the expression and guarantee of honesty and integrity. Only this stylized solution doesn't replace the division between particular interestedness and civic duty. It repeats that division within the merchant family and in the merchant's relation to his body. As the merchant Giannozzo explains in book 3 of *Della Famiglia,* commerce—an occupation he claims is both "as honorable as possible and one useful to as many people as possible" [*quanto potessi onestissimo, e quanto più potessi a molti utilissimo*][17]—works properly when a merchant manages through observation. And not to manage through observation or to delegate the duty of management entirely to someone else is tantamount to being immoral. "Laziness, negligence, and not watching carefully [*non spesso rivedere*] over one's business, these are the things that injure our condition, my children, and bring us down. A man who cannot report on his affairs except by the mouth of another is a fool. He is blind who sees only with another's eyes [*occhi altrui*]. You must be solicitous, alert, and diligent and examine our affairs daily [*rivedere spesso ogni nostra cosa*]" (198/206). The managers one hires, Giannozzo asserts, must themselves be managed through observation and examination. "I would employ managers and workers with whom I should not interfere in any way," he explains, "except to oversee and regulate everyone's performance of his task [*a provedere e ordinare che ciascuno facesse il debito suo, e a tutti così comanderei*]. . . . I should, first, exercise extreme care in choosing the best possible manager and, second, I should often examine and verify everything in order not to let him become careless [*rivedere spesso e riconoscendo ogni mia cosa*]" (196, 198/204, 206).

This stylization also necessitates that the merchant submit himself to observation. As Giannozzo explains, a merchant must always be clear and careful in keeping records (197), always ready to be examined concerning his honesty. "Messer Benedetto Alberti used to say. . . that it was a good sign if a merchant had ink-stained fingers [*avere le mani tinte d'inchiostro*]. . . . He considered it is the duty of the merchant and anyone who has to deal with many people always to write everything down—contracts, sales, and purchases—and check everything so often that it seems he is always with pen in hand" (197/205). Not only must the successful merchant assert his authority through claims to absolute visibility, but also he must reproduce his deeds and even his body within that field in such a way that his past appears open for all to see. Responding to the various needs to prove one's honesty when paying taxes, when dealing with customers, and when encountering charges concerning one's ability to hold public office, the graphic practices that emerged around merchants' memory books translate into an aestheticization of the body—a demonstration through the body that one is a record keeper—as the expression of general integrity.[18]

In *I Libri Della Famiglia,* absolute visibility formally attempts to secure what Bourdieu would call irresistible analogies between merchant honesty, patriarchal authority, and good citizenship. The trea-

tise opens by raising the problem of continuity. Alberti's father, Lorenzo, on his deathbed, asks his brother, Alberti's uncle Ricciardo, to
assume his paternal function in the raising of the young Alberti and
his other son, Carlo. What will give patriarchal power its continuity
over and against the death of any particular father is not this substitution, though, but submission to absolute visibility. Reciting the dic-
tums of his own father, Benedetto, Lorenzo explains, "The head of a
family must be vigilant and observant above all [*vegghiare e riguardare
per tutto*]. He must know all the family's acquaintances, examine [*es-
saminare*] all customs both within and without the house, and correct
and mend the evil ways of any member of the family with words of
reason rather than anger" (17/36–37). By the same token, Lorenzo
continues, it is the duty of the young to make themselves transparent
to their fathers and elders, "to refer every wish, thought, and plan of
their own to their fathers and elders" (41). He explains:

> [L]et the elders be always watchful and ready to act for the well-
> being and honor of the entire family, by counseling, correcting,
> and guiding all its members. [*Però siano e' maggiori al bene e onore
> di tutta la famiglia sempre desti e operosi, consigliando, emendando
> e quasi sostenendo la briglia di tutta la famiglia.*] . . . Let the elders
> remember that it is their first duty to look after all members of
> the household, just as those good, ancient Lacedonians who con-
> sidered themselves the fathers and tutors of every young person,
> corrected the ways of any of their young citizens, and held them-
> selves indebted if their closest relations were shown better ways by
> anyone at all. Fathers consider it a privilege to thank anyone who
> took pains to make the young more reasonable and responsible.
> And with this good and most useful supervision of customs they
> made their city glorious and honored it with well-deserved and
> everlasting fame. (18–20/38–39)

Absolute visibility, figured by the watchful elders and the transparent
youths, and not the particularities of any individual father, magically
guarantees and organizes a set of seamless homologies between merchant ethics, family, education, citizenship, and civic history through
the promises of mastery and the demands of submission.

The result of this submission is the positing of a virile masculine
integrity opposed to that of the chivalric tradition, determined by the
active management of one's capacity to be excessive, and figured as an

earnest though belated acknowledgment of the edicts and "wisdom" of the previous generation. Book 3 of *I Libri Della Famiglia* begins with Giannozzo reminiscing about the jousting festivals of his youthful days and the conflicts that these festivals caused between himself and his elders: "I remember when I was young, in those days when our country was in a prosperous state, there were many jousts and other similar tourneys. They caused the strongest and only disagreements between my elders and me, for I always wanted to go forth with the others to show what I could do" (157/159). The elders tried to prevent Giannozzo from participating in these contests of male prowess because, they warned, "jousting is a dangerous game, useless, very expensive, and more likely to give rise to envy than friendship, to criticism more than praise. They would say that too many mishaps occurred in them, and then they would add that they caused quarrels. And then they would add that they loved [him] more than [he] could imagine or, perhaps, deserved" (157/159–60). Eventually, Giannozzo learns the elders' lesson as an economic lesson about management:

> They did seem hateful to me when they opposed me and stood firm against my too obstinate, though manly will. I was angrier still whenever I thought they acted as they did from motives of economy, for they were, as you know, they were careful and thrifty managers, as I, myself, have since learned to become. [*E molto più mi dispiacevano quando io stimava lo facessino per masserizia, come egli erano, sai, pur buoni massaiotti, quale io testé sono diventato.*] But in those days I was young and open-handed and spent my money. (158/160)

But it is not just in this imaginary prehistory that we can find what motivates Giannozzo to accept a merchant ethos of *masserizia* (thrift). Giannozzo's nephew Lionardo asks how his uncle is different in his old age, to which Giannozzo responds:

> Now, my dear Lionardo, I have become wise. I know that it is madness to throw away what you possess. The man who has never experienced the sorrow and frustration of going to others for help in his need has no idea of the usefulness of money. [*Chi non ha provato quanto sia duolo e fallace a' bisogni andare pelle mercé altrui, non sa quanto sia utile il danaio.*] (158/160)

Giannozzo accepts the ethic of *masserizia* to avoid experiencing the pain and uncertainty of asking others for help. To prevent the tyrannizing effects of being dependent upon others, Giannozzo submits to self-management as a principal of internal regulation. And it is in order to instill in the young men of his family the values of the previous generation that Giannozzo elaborates upon this merchant-ethic of *masserizia:* management of spirit, management of time, management of one's body, and management of one's wife.

Albertian perspective translates this ethics into a more rigorous logical, formal, and aesthetic field of absolute reason. According to Alberti, in *perspectiva artificialis* the painter creates the illusion of depth and architectural, spatial relations by harnessing the capacity of the line to produce illusions of surface and quantity. The relation of the shapes on the canvas—all organized around what Alberti calls "the centric ray"—anticipates the position from which the viewer can experience the canvas not as a surface but as "an open window."[19] Alberti proposes that "surfaces are measured by certain rays, ministers of vision as it were. . . . These rays, stretching between the eye and the surface seen, move rapidly with great power and remarkable subtlety, penetrating the air and transparent bodies until they encounter something dense or opaque where their points strike and they instantly stick" (40). The painter should anticipate the "visual pyramid" that these lines imply in order to posit a point in space from which the relations of lines on the surface of the canvas will give the illusion of depth. Hence, to be positioned at the "original" point of the centric ray that the painting anticipates for the viewer is to be positioned as a kind of master of form, to be positioned in such a way that the images on the canvas produce the correct and meaningful illusion of depth. But to pose as the master of form is also to be constrained by the perspectival organization of space: one must be situated at precisely the point anticipated and posited by the particular painting.

This positioning amounts to an active submission to reason. In describing Brunelleschi's early-fifteenth-century experiments, Manetti writes that he

> produced and himself practiced what painters today call perspective since it forms part of that science [*quella scienza*] which, in effect, consists of setting down properly and rationally [*che è in effetto porre bene e con ragione*] the reductions and enlargements of near and distant objects as perceived by the eye of man: buildings, plains, mountains, places of every sort and location, with figures and objects in correct proportion in which they are shown

[*di quella distanzia che le si monstrano di lungi*]; and it is he who
originated the rule [*la regola*] that is so important for everything
of the sort done between that time and this.[20]

Perspective begins as a curious set of experiments that Brunelleschi
demonstrated, that Alberti, della Francesca, Dürer, and others formalized with mathematics, and that some (though not a lot of) quattrocento painters produced with systematic coherence. But perspective is
able to pass from these particular manifestations to a symbolic form
that holds sway over Western subjectivity and epistemology precisely
because it is a form of what Leonardo da Vinci calls "rational demonstration" [*ragione dimostratiua*]—what Damisch terms "demonstrable
reason" and Joan Kelly a kind of "rational seeing"—that gives coherence to the apprehension of space, the prerequisite for much modern
physics and philosophy.[21] In that it translates the viewer into a subject
situated at a point that is thought by a reason not the viewer's own, a
reason implied by the shapes composed on the canvas, perspective is
a form that demonstrates the capture of a subject by the rationaliza-
tion and mathematicization of space. As Damisch quite succinctly
puts it, "perspective posits a point 'encompassing' space within a space
that encompasses the point and that, insofar as it appeals to vision,
is always already *thought*."[22] Or, as Panofsky argues in *Perspective as
Symbolic Form*, Renaissance perspective projects space as mathematical, reasoned relations between bodies and intervals of empty space.
The result, Panofsky concludes, is "the objectification of the subjective."[23] The sense of subjectivity that perspective assumes is not particularized because that subject is grounded in ineffable emotions and
feelings; what renders the subject subjective is its capture by a system
of reasoning that objectifies and formalizes social thought. It is not
subjective thinking per se but its relation to this formalized social
thought that is particular to the subject.

Merchant culture's insistence on absolute visibility responds to the
problems of office holding in Florence with an ethics of active submission and self-management. Renaissance perspective reiterates this ethics as its form of expression and, in so doing, attempts the objectification of subjective space in such a way that renders its formal reasoning
absolute—specifically, by promising the mastery of the visual field by
positioning the subject at a point that the system has already, objec-

tively thought. The main effect of this process of abstraction is the consolidation of a new form of power. Since Renaissance perspective collapses mastery and constraint into one subjective position, the position of "absolute master" is emptied out. That is, within the space created by perspective, there is no place for a master who isn't already subject to the system. In its stead is the space of perspective consolidated around an abstraction of judgment. In a certain sense, of course, this evacuation of the absolute master, or at least the absolute patriarch, is already at work in *I Libri Della Famiglia,* which is poignantly haunted throughout by the dying father. The interlocutors in *I Libri Della Famiglia* attempt to sustain the father's authorized place even as the treatise portrays his graphic decay. Renaissance perspective simply finishes him off—place and all.

In its validation of the doubting humanist who knows the constructedness of the social field, the civilizing process simply accepts this evacuation. But if the absolute master formally disappears from these aesthetic and social fields, this master returns through a temporality of anticipation that binds the observer to the social field. According to Elias, this binding occurs through narcissism. But note, narcissism here takes on a very specific meaning. In a well-known example, Elias writes:

> The increased tendency of people to observe themselves and others is one sign of how the whole question of behaviour is taking on a different character: people mold themselves and others more deliberately than in the Middle Ages.
>
> Then they were told, do this and not that; but by and large a great deal was let pass. For centuries roughly the same rules, elementary by our standards, were repeated, obviously without producing firmly established habits. This now changes. The coercion exerted by people on one another increases, the demand for "good behaviour" is raised more emphatically.[24]

Instead of transmitting manners simply through commandments— for example, "[T]hose who like mustard and salt should take care to avoid the filthy habit of putting their fingers into them"[25]—manners are transmitted and sustained through a set of expectations deduced in the process of reading social practices by which, one imagines, one will be judged. This narcissism does not depend on simple mimesis as the imitation of an image given by juridical strictures. Instead, it depends on the lack of discretely articulated juridical strictures. Owing to this lack, one is forced to deduce possible judgments from observing and interpreting the behaviors of others. And, in the process, one imputes these deduced strictures to some abstracted master in order to anticipate and prevent this master's judgment by enacting the supposedly correct behavior of others.

What gives this anticipatory logic an aesthetic enjoyment is Renaissance perspective. In his very fine and formative study *Painting and Experience in Fifteenth Century Italy,* Michael Baxandall has argued that perspective formalizes a cognitive style based primarily on the interpretive practices of gauging and discerning proportion so crucial to the Italian merchant classes. What merchants are trained to do in everyday life, paintings executed more or less in accordance with the rules of perspective have them do when they look at art. To support this argument, Baxandall proposes a general social theory of taste that explains the experience of looking at paintings:

> Much of what we call "taste" lies in this, the conformity between discriminations demanded by a painting and skills of discrimination possessed by the beholder. We enjoy our own exercise of skill, and we particularly enjoy the playful exercise of skills which we use in normal life very earnestly. If a painting gives us opportunity for exercising a valued skill and rewards our virtuosity with a sense of worthwhile insights about the painting's organization, we tend to enjoy it: it is to our taste.[26]

I want to take Baxandall's social theory one step further. It is not *our* enjoyment in exercising the skills of everyday life that underwrites taste; it is the enjoyment of some abstracted juridical authority for whom we pose in front of the canvas and for whom we exercise these skills. Baxandall writes that "Renaissance people were, as has been said, on their mettle before a picture, because of an expectation that cultivated people should be able to make discriminations about the interests of pictures."[27] The effect of shifting the skills of everyday life to the realm of aesthetics is the consolidation of this abstracted authority who judges us. It is not just a playfulness that "Renaissance people" enjoy when they look at a painting; they pose for the enjoyment of the Other, in order to be recognized as one among the cultivated. The motivations of taste are based on narcissism, but this is not a narcissism that follows the logic of the mirror. It is, rather, a narcissism of reading and self-presentation whose coercive moment of social judgment is implied in the act of imagining oneself being read in the ways in which one reads others.

Purportedly, according to the aesthetic imaginary that accompanies this consolidation of judgment, perspective organizes the body represented on the canvas in such a way that it charms the viewer captured by the regulated, mathematicized, virtual space projected by the canvas. In *Della Pittura* (which Alberti wrote at the same time that he was drafting books 1 through 3 of *I Libri Della Famiglia*), it is not just the case that by taking the correct position the viewer comprehends as meaningful the shapes, lines, and images on the canvas. Owing to its abilities to charm, the painting itself freezes and masters its spectator for the particular economic and professional benefit of the painter. Alberti expresses this capture through an aesthetic discourse that negates economic motives:

> The function of the painter is to draw with lines and paint in colours on a surface any given bodies in such a way that, at a fixed distance and with a certain, determined position of the centric ray, what you see represented appears to be in relief and just like those bodies. The aim of the painter is to obtain praise, favour and good-will [*grazia e benevolenza e lode*] for his work much more than riches. The painter will achieve this if his painting holds and charms the eyes and minds of the spectators. [*E seguiranno questo I pittori ove la loro pittura terrà gli occhi e l'animo di chi la miri.*] (*DP*, 87/90)

If it works, perspective inverts the patron/painter relation so that the patron as spectator, held and charmed by the illusion of mastery promoted by the painting, accords the painter a symbolic capital that rhetorically exceeds, but practically leads to, economic compensation.

In Alberti's treatise the locus of this charisma is the compositional and aesthetic theory of *istoria*. In part, *istoria* is a version of painterly composition that takes as its fundamental unit the represented body. "The great work of the painter is the *istoria;* parts of the *istoria* are the bodies, part of the body is the member, and part of the member is a surface" [*parte della istoria sono i corpi: parte de' corpi sono i membri:*

*parte de' membri sono le superficie*] (67–68/58). Here, the main goal of *istoria* is to have the painter manage the actions, movements, and poses of the represented body, so that "in every painting the principle should be observed that all the members should fulfill their function according to the action performed [*che ciascuno membro segna, a quello che ivi sa fa, al suo officio*], in such a way that not even the smallest limb fails to play its appropriate part, that the members of the dead appear dead down to the smallest detail, and those of the living completely alive" (73/64). In contrast with a medieval theological aesthetics based on a combination of luminosity and allegory, both of which conspire to transcend the represented body, *istoria* refuses to move from the body but instead renders the body entirely functional and well-managed.[28]

Formally, the problem with Albertian perspective is that, while it works mathematically with extraordinary precision, practically perspective must fail because it assumes monocular vision. The body that it requires is that of a Cyclops. "If you want to put it into operation in any work," writes Leonardo da Vinci, "you must ensure that this perspective is only viewed through a single aperture." And even then, since "every part of the pupil possess the visual power, and this power is not reduced to a point as the perspectivists require," there will of necessity be some difference between the body required by the logic of perspective and the body practically positioned within its geometric space.[29] This difference, an instantiation of the impossibility of embodying the space organized and prescribed by Albertian perspective, informs the subject of that perspective, embodying it in a flesh always different from the functional and well-managed bodies continually proposed by perspective's visual forms and textual discourses.

## Logistics and the Fold

Louis Hjelmslev's linguistic analysis of form and substance, and especially its revision by Deleuze and Guattari, is quite useful in characterizing the alignment of forms I have been discussing. In attempting to break with the form-content duality, Hjelmslev proposes splitting both form and substance into expression and content. Thus, he argues for four terms, not two. There is, he argues, a form of expression and a form of content as well as a substance of expression and a substance of content.[30] These four terms—form, substance, content, and expression—are no doubt interdependent and obtain relative invariance only within particular historical instantiations. Even so, over any repeated series, Deleuze and Guattari argue, there is an initial differentiation between content and expression. "There is not an articulation of content *and* an articulation of expression—the articulation of content is double in its own right and constitutes a relative expression within content; the articulation of expression is also double and constitutes a relative content within expression."[31] There is not, for example, an articulation of manners as a form of content and a separate articulation of civility as a form of expression. The civilizing process can become a dominant form of power insofar as various forms of content (manners, medicine, merchant ethics, pedagogy, bureaucracies, etc.) line up as a prop for civility as a form of expression.

In this alignment various substances are submitted to increasing sedimentation. When the civilizing process conscripts the body within civic modes of discipline, it also leans on the fact of the body in order to substantiate a sedimentary residue as the "problematicized" equivocation that the civilizing process in its normative drive toward pure form attempts to control. But also, substance is the site for a more radical differentiation from these forms of power. At least, this would be the a priori assumption for a history of sexuality as historical materialism, as opposed to, say, cultural materialism. Substance is not an unmoved essence, no matter how much the ideological urges of an alignment of forms might attempt to make it that. Substance is "chosen" matter. It is not simply an effect of sedimentation, an effect of the alignment of forms, but comprises the nonce-ordered traces that matter as movement leaves as its wake. Matter, I wish to propose, is simply the ground for historical potentiality—the troublesome matter that in his *Metaphysics* Aristotle asserts "is capable if being otherwise than as it usually is" and that Deleuze and Guattari define with much more chutzpah as the Body without Organs, "in other words, the unformed, unorganized, nonstratified, or destratified body and all its flows."[32] Nor, then, is form a metaphysical entity, no matter how much the consolidation of power might attempt to make it that. Form is the stylized rhythm of relationality—regular or not—given this movement of matter.

It should be clear that I do not intend the relation between form and substance to be thought of as one between controller and controlled, nor do I intend that relation to be considered one between container and contained. Rather, I mean to underscore the relation between form and substance as one of relative, although complex, disarticulation. And, I wish to propose, it is in this disarticulation that history emerges as potentiality. In the relative difference between form and substance, something else is being satisfied: a certain particularity that cannot be fully captured or signified, but is instead symptomatically pressed onto the flesh as the embodiment of this "something else" at the threshold of recognition, judgment, and identitary time. In the civilizing process, as much as the body becomes the support for a form of judgment by which it is evaluated, the body also becomes the locus for an unavoidable differentiation from that form. This differentiation can be suspended from the reasoning processes of consciousness, but it cannot be entirely disembodied—suspended, that is, from the "unconscious" thinking of the body.

The civilizing process posits as its primary mode of power a metaleptic form of expression based on the fold, on the folding of force in order to bring it to bear upon oneself as the condition for civility. For instance, toward the beginning of *The Book of the Courtier,* defining what I take to be the exemplary masculine pose of the Renaissance civilizing process, Lodovico proposes that a courtier's grace is determined by "a hidden seed" [*occulto seme*] given as a gift by Nature to those of "noble birth and good family" and is expressed in the actions of the body—strength, suppleness in battle, horsemanship, tennis, and so forth.[33] But Lodovico proposes this model only to reverse it. Soon after having made his first assertion, he admits that even if one does not have this hidden seed, one can make others think that one has it by imitating the grace of others, through what Lodovico considers to be theft: "Just as in the summer fields the bees wing their way among the plants from one flower to the next, so the courtier must steal this grace [*rubare questa grazia*] from those who appear to possess it and take from each one the quality that seems most commendable" (*BC,* 67/47). As Lodovico's circumlocution implies, and as he later makes explicit, because grace is hidden until expressed through the body, it is the act of expression, governed by what Lodovico calls *sprezzatura,* that is "the real source of grace" [*il vero fonte donde deriva la grazia*] (70/50). As it ends up, "natural" grace is not a cause. It's an illusion of civility, an effect of successful performances enacted within the civilized spaces that *sprezzatura* defines. The cunning of *The Book of the Courtier*—and what allows it in particular to become such a portable model for courtliness in the sixteenth century—is that it sublates this metaleptic stance into a general mode of judgment and recognition that posits the evacuation of cause as the basis for civilized subjectivity. *Sprezzatura* involves bringing the force of judgment to bear upon oneself as a preventative measure against the possible recognition that one is a graceless rube. Lodovico explains:

> I have discovered a universal rule which seems to apply more than any other in all human actions or words: namely, to steer away from affectation at all costs, as if it were a rough and dangerous reef [*e cioè fuggir quanto più si po, e come un asperissimo e pericoloso scoglio, la affettazione*], and (to use perhaps a novel word for it) to practice in all things a certain nonchalance which conceals all artistry and makes whatever one says or does seem uncontrived and effortless [*usar in ogni cosa una certa spressatura che nasconda l'arte e dimostri ciò, che si fa dice, venio fatica e quasi senza pensarvi*]. . . . To labor at what one is doing and, as we say, to make bones over it, shows an extreme lack of grace and causes everything, whatever its worth, to be discounted. So we can truthfully say that true art is whatever does not seem to be art; and the most important thing is to conceal it, because if it is revealed this discredits a man completely and ruins his reputation. [*(P)erò a po dir quella esser vera arte, che non appare arte; né più in altro si han do poner studio che nel nasconderla: perchè, se è scoperta, leva in tutto il credito e fa l'umo poco estimato.*] (67/47)

Since *sprezzatura* is by definition a practice of concealment, it demands to be read where there is nothing there to read. For this reason, *sprezzatura* posits a readership where there is not necessarily a material reader. That is, since "we" all know that *sprezzatura* is feigning, "we" also know that any performance of *sprezzatura* that seems effortless only seems so. The more effortlessly graceful one appears, the more one raises suspicions that one is hiding something. Because this aesthetic culture is defined by the practice of hiding practice, every performance of *sprezzatura* assumes a fold in the epistemological fabric of civilized, courtly space and a virtual reader for whom that fold raises suspicions.

Nevertheless, in the dehiscence of form and substance the civilizing process also commemorates, quite conservatively, the possibilities for a different sociality and a different relation to the flesh. In one of the opening anecdotes of Della Casa's *Galateo*, Count Ricciardo, a polite, pleasant, and well-mannered gentleman who has "one small fault in his deportment," is a guest of the bishop, Giovanni Matteo Giberti.[34] After Ricciardo leaves the court, the bishop has one of his courtiers, Galateo, speak to him:

> My lord, my lord bishop extends your lordship his infinite thanks for the honor you have bestowed upon him by entering and dwelling in his humble house. Furthermore, as recompense for all the courtesy you have shown towards him he has commanded me to present you with a gift on his behalf. This is the gift. You are the most graceful [*il più leggiadro*] and well-mannered [*il più costumato*] gentleman that the bishop thinks that he has ever met. For this reason, having carefully observed [*attentamente risguardato*] your manners and having examined them in detail [*essaminatole partitamente*], he has found none which was not extremely pleasant and commendable except for an unseemly motion that you make with your lips and mouth at the dinner table, when your chewing makes a strange sound which is very unpleasant to hear [*non atto difforme che voi fate con le labbra e con la bocca masticando alla mensa con un nuovo strepito molto spiacevole ad udire*]. The bishop sends you this message, begging you to try to refrain from doing it, and to accept as a precious gift his loving reprimand and remark, for he is certain that no-one else in the world would give you such a gift. (37–38/374)

What Galateo—as the bishop's proxy—offers is the gift of the fold. It is not enough that Ricciardo's body has been "encoded" by the values of decorum; Ricciardo must bring these values to bear upon himself by reforming his "unseemly" mouth and producing as his own the graceful face. This face, as the civilizing process's substance of expression, serves to index both that fold's failure and success: upon hearing this reprimand, Ricciardo blushes (38/374). On the one hand, this blush indicates the success of Ricciardo's conscription within the civilizing process by demonstrating an integration of civilized judgment. Insofar as the blush is a shameful admission to the propriety of the bishop's judgment, it demonstrates that Ricciardo has already introjected the judgment given. On the other hand, in reacting to the will asserted by aesthetic culture, this blush repeats the strange uncontrollability of the flesh that Ricciardo's mouth had previously demonstrated. Some troubled excess located in the defiles of the aesthetic culture is also endlessly repeated. Taking the two together, this blush indicates a relative dislocation between the form and substance of expression that splays Ricciardo between civilized sociality and "uncivilized" possibility.

The *Galateo* attempts to mend this dislocation by reading it out onto the "uncivilized" lower classes who stand in as forms of relationality around the flesh that civility repudiates, but in so doing, the *Galateo* also offers the possibilities of these other forms. After telling the anecdote about Ricciardo and Galateo, the book's narrator asks, "Now what do you think the bishop and his noble friends would have said to those we sometimes see who, totally oblivious like pigs with their snouts in the swill, never raise their faces nor their eyes, let alone their hands, from the food in front of them? Or to those who eat or rather gulp down their food with both cheeks stuffed out as if they were blowing a trumpet or blowing on a fire? Or to those who soil their hands nearly up to their elbows, and dirty their napkins worse than their toilet towels?" (38–39). This projection only partly forecloses "uncivilized" possibility by consolidating the demands for self-scrutiny that make up civilized sociality into the snobbish pleasure of distancing oneself from the "ill-mannered" social behavior of others.

If, as I proposed, matter is simply historical potentiality, then the translation of matter into formed substance always establishes a relation to exteriority through forgetting. This is not a forgetting that can easily be opposed to remembering. It is, rather, a forgetting that commemorates and refuses possibility in almost the same gesture. Of course, matter per se cannot be forgotten, but matter as absolute potentiality must be. Finally, however, the problem is not just a philosophical one. It is also a problem of history: how is the forgetting of absolute possibility manifest in other counter or minor forms of expression and content? It is to this extent, I shall argue, that war bears a crucial relation to the civilizing process. On the one hand, in its attempts to map a regulated and civilized psychic space, the double articulation of the body in the civilizing process aims quite explicitly to forget war. On the other hand, war as a mapping technique itself attempts to develop an aesthetic form outside the psychologistics of the civilizing process.

«

In the mid-fifteenth century, after the Peace of Lodi (1454) and the establishment of the Italian League (1455), the Italian peninsula achieved a fairly delicate balance of power between the Venetian republic, the duchy of Milan, the Florentine republic, the kingdom of Naples, and the papal states. But in 1494, Charles VIII of France marched through the Alps to claim Naples. Although Charles was defeated by an alliance of the pope, the Holy Roman Emperor, the king of Spain, the republic of Venice, and the duke of Milan, his successor, Louis XII, negotiated alliances with England, Spain, Venice, the Borgia family (and, therefore, Pope Alexander VI) that allowed him to reclaim Naples in 1501. Later that same year, however, the Spanish turned on the French and reconquered the city. The Italian League was destroyed, and, up though almost the first half of the sixteenth century, during the *calamità d'Italia,* the Italian peninsula underwent continued diplomatic and geographic unmapping and remapping. Upon his succession in 1503, Julius II, a self-styled warrior pope, immediately squashed the Borgia family, and in 1504 he negotiated a treaty with the French and the Holy Roman Emperor against the Venetian republic. Venice held out against its enemies, though, and even despoiled the Holy Roman Empire of Trieste, Gorizia, Pordenone, and Fiume and took some territories in Hungary. In 1508, Julius II and the Holy Roman Emperor established the Treaty of Cambrai, which allied the major powers of Western Europe in an attempt to repartition all of Venice's recent and ancient conquests. After three years of war and immense military losses, Venice had been all but defeated when Julius, contrary to the wishes of his allies, turned against the French and formed the Holy League, which included the papacy, the Spanish, and the Venetians—collateral agreements brought in the English and the Swiss. Venice switched sides once more in 1513, but that same year Pope Leo X, who succeeded Julius II, renewed the Holy League to include the Holy Roman Emperor, but not Venice. The French were forced to renounce their claims to Milan and, the following year, to reach a truce with the Spanish. However, in 1515, Francis

I succeeded Louis XII as king of France and, in alliance with Venice against the Holy League, retook Milan, and Venice reconquered its lost lands.

In 1516, Charles V, then governor of the Netherlands, was crowned king of Spain, and in 1518, because of his Hapsburg blood and Fugger money he was also elected Holy Roman Emperor. As king of Spain, he was already holding Naples, Sicily, and Sardinia, but he also resolved to take Milan, which he did in 1521, with the help of papal forces. Notwithstanding the formation of the League of Cognac in 1526, which ranged Francis I, Pope Clement VII, and the Venetian republic against him, Charles over the next four years conquered almost the entire Italian peninsula. After the infamous sack of Rome in 1527 and the papal alliance with the Holy Roman Empire two years later, and especially after a series of wars the 1540s, the Spanish effectively ruled most of the Italian peninsula, Venice being the main exception.[35]

Lauro Martines, rightly I think, cautions against reading nationalism too quickly into these events. "Italians—Neapolitans, Genoese, Milanese, Florentines, Mantuans, and others—fought for France, for the empire, and for Spain against one another, but without any sense of betraying a homeland. First they were Genoese, Milanese, Florentines or the rest, and next they swung to the other extreme to become cosmopolitan."[36] The logic of state formation thus cannot adequately address the shifting alliances and diplomatic remappings of the Italian wars. The participants' motives and, more generally, their relation to territory did not rely upon civility's consolidation of judgment and concurrent conservation of power through modes of discipline. Rather, the wars in the Italian peninsula promoted a series of locally delimited agreements and exchanges whose function was to remap almost continually the geography that state apparatuses would have sought to stabilize and pacify. To this extent, the Italian peninsular wars of the first half of the sixteenth century fall outside nascent European nation formation.

Nevertheless, as Martines also notes, one cannot avoid raising the issue of the nation when considering these wars, since during these events "France and Spain were edging toward a sense of nationhood."[37] Meanwhile, according to Machiavelli at least, the Italians were moving away from the possibility of one. The continued wars

made it evident that the humanist hope of resuscitating a hyper-
manly, hyper-disciplined republican ethics from the models offered
by ancient Rome in order to reunify the Italian peninsula was nothing
more than a pipe dream. It is perhaps most precise to assert, following
Deleuze and Guattari, that the logic of war bears an integral though
exterior relation to the civilizing process, that the logic of war offers
"a mode of a social state that wards off and prevents the State."[38]

The logistics of war—its practical, though symbolic logic—develops a version of force that exceeds the state's monopoly on violence.
When Charles VIII first invaded the Italian peninsula, he brought with
him forty or so bronze-barreled cannons from the port of La Spezia.
These cannons were light enough to be permanently attached to a
two-wheeled gun carriage and to be drawn by horses, not oxen, giving
the attacking French an astounding mobility. Moreover, instead of
firing smoothed stones as did most, much heavier cannons of the late
fifteenth century, these lighter cannons shot iron balls, which could
destroy fortified stone walls within a surprisingly short amount of
time. In the siege against Naples, for example, the French took only
eight hours to breach the frontier stronghold, Monte San Giovanni,
and to massacre its garrison, the same stronghold that had successfully
withstood a siege of seven years against older versions of artillery.
Owing to the mobility and force of their cannons, the French were
able to do pretty much the same at Capua (1501), Pavia (1527), and
Malfi (1528). As Franceso Guicciardini explains, the French

> placed [their cannons] against the rampart of a town with incred-
> ible quickness, and the interval of time between one shot and an-
> other was so little, that as much violence was done in a few hours,
> as beforehand in Italy, in a number of days. These, rather devilish
> than human instruments, were not only used in campaigns but
> also in field combat, and were used with others of a smaller size,
> which allowed for great dexterity and agility. This artillery made
> Charles's military exercises quite formidable to all of Italy.
>
> [*condotte alle muraglie erano piantate con prestezza incredibile; e in-*
> *terponendosi dall'un colpo all'altro piccolissimo intervallo di tempo,*
> *sì spesso e con impeto sì veemente percotevano che quello che prima*
> *in Italia fare in molti giorni si soleva, da loro in pochissime ore si*
> *faceva: usando ancora questo più tosto diabolico che umano instru-*
> *mento non meno alla campagna che a combattere le terre, e co'mede-*

*simi cannoni e con altri pezzi minori, ma fabricati e condotti, se-
condo la loro proporzione, con la medesima destrezza e celerità.
Facevano tali artigliere molto formidabile a tutta Italia l'esecito di
Carlo]*[39]

After being defeated by the French at Calabria in 1495, Spanish troops
began to rely more heavily on arquebuses, firearms that gave the Spanish land forces greater mobility than the French, who had to lug
around heavier artillery. Whereas the more prevalent *schioppo* required fire to be applied to the gun's touch hole by hand, these new
firearms had a trigger mechanism, which also afforded the Spanish
a more rapid firepower. At Cerignola (1503), the Spanish used the
arquebuses in conjunction with trench warfare to preempt the slower-
moving French artillery. Because the French didn't have time to set
up their cannons, they had to rely on their cavalry, which was unable
to cross the Spanish trenches. By the 1520s, the Spanish had added
muskets to their artillery. Although they were more difficult to carry
than the arquebuses, their heavier bullets, traveling at the same speed
as the arquebuses' rounds, had a stronger impact and were therefore
much more effective against cavalries.[40]

It is not in the practices of war per se, but through the logistics of
war's weaponry that an integral version of force external to the civilizing process's consolidation of judgment emerges. The double tactics
of quick mobility and local entrenchment, developed from the cannon
and arquebus, allowed for an aesthetic conception of force outside the
"pacified social spaces" that the state's "monopoly of force" creates in
its emphasis on discipline and its consolidation and abstraction of
judgment. In addition to their astounding technological creativity, Leonardo da Vinci's sketches of military machinery also present dia-
grams of a force whose two main functions are mobility and speed
(figs. 3 and 4). For example, Leonardo's "clean" drawing of a rapid-
fire crossbow offers an imaginative, response to the problem of how to
produce quick fire, an engineer's response. Nevertheless, particularly
when viewed alongside his more sketchy drawing of the same invention, it is clearly also concerned with how to express rapid motion as
a formative gesture by way of the line. In other words, it is concerned
with how the line as an instantiation of quick motion produces surrounding space. This motion is both a residual trace of the hand's

Fig. 3. Leonardo da Vinci, sketch of a horse-drawn tank, MS B, 59ʳ.
Bibliotèque Nationale, Paris.

gesture and a diagram of immanent force. Leonardo's drawings of
scythed cars and armored and horse-drawn tanks all address the same
problem: how to conceive of and diagram an immanent force that
refigures space as it moves through it. The shock value of these images
should not serve to confuse the difference between represented violence and the violence of representation. It is the latter that gives these
drawings their diagrammatic value: in thinking through weaponry,
Leonardo's drawing also uses the line to present a force whose mobility depends upon differentiation from itself.

If Leonardo's drawings of military machines figure the force of mobility, Michelangelo's studies of fortifications diagram the force of entrenchment. Michelangelo's drawings begin with a fragment of architectural fortification in order to diagram its "dynamic, attacking role,"
as John Hale puts it.[41] In these drawings, architectural fragments propose angled areas of force—possible lines of fire—whose delimitation
works to defend the architectural space that produces them (figs. 5
and 6). During the Italian wars, city-states tended to counter mobile
land forces by translating local entrenchment into a strategy of durable
fortification. By the mid-fifteenth century, rounded fortress walls
were being replaced by angled bastions. The problem with rounded

wall fortification was, first, the curvature made it difficult to aim more
than one cannon at a particular spot on the surrounding battlefield
and, second, a rounded wall inevitably had a surrounding territory at
its base that artillery from above could not reach. The straight edges
of the angled bastion solved both of these problems.[42] "Those besieged
would consider no protection better than the ingenuity and skill of
the architect," Alberti proposes in the middle of the fifteenth century.
"Should you examine the various military campaigns undertaken, you
would perhaps discover that the skill and ability of the architect have
been responsible for more victories than have the command and fore-
sight of any general."[43] But these bastions alone couldn't withstand the
force of French artillery, so city-states turned to military architecture.
Before the French and the Florentines attacked their city in 1500, the
Pisans dug ditches behind their fortress walls and also built ramparts
behind these ditches, so that when the walls fell, as the Pisans expected
they would, the jagged stones could serve as an outer buttress to the
interior ditch. In effect, the collapse of the first wall created a double
rampart system of defense. Upon discovering the Pisans' defensive
system, which came to be known as *retirara,* the French retreated and
Pisa withstood the siege. The Venetians used a modified version of
this strategy successfully in 1509 to defend Padua against the League
of Cambrai, as did Brescia in 1515 and Parma in 1521. As Machiavelli
writes in *The Discourses,* "the force of artillery is such that no wall can
stand it, not even the thickest, for more than a few days. Hence if those
within have not a goodly space in which to retire and dig trenches and
build ramparts, they are doomed."[44]

The main engineering question of Michelangelo's drawings appears
to be how to allow for a positioning of artillery so as to defend the
space behind the walls most effectively. In short, how can the architect
turn a wall into a weapon? But in posing this question, Michelangelo
also fractures the architectural apparatus, in a sense turning durable
fortification back into a local entrenchment whose function becomes
simply the nonce-configuration of possible lines of force in relation
to a flexible, fragmented, and mobile arrangement of space. Taken
together, Michelangelo's drawings of fortifications and Leonardo's
drawings of military machines extrapolate from military weaponry a
logic of force that, while it bears a relation to military tactics, does not
simply repeat those tactics' violent objectives. Rather, these drawings

Fig. 4. Leonardo da Vinci, sketch of a rapid-fire crossbow, Codex Atlanticus, 387ʳ. Ambrosiana Library, Milan. All rights reserved. Reproduction is forbidden.

reconfigure the weapons to express a force that cannot be equated with that of the civilizing process.

The civilizing process attempts to fold this force in order to formulate an interiority whose expression is the posed body, a folding quite evident in Bronzino's *Portrait of a Young Man* (fig. 7). In light of the drawings considered above, what's most striking about this painting is the hidden space between the two walls behind the poser, a space taken up and recited by the hidden space in the book the young man holds. Together, these two hidden spaces conspire to transfer an aura of interiority to the relation between viewer and poser. Is the poser showing himself to you, as his forward elbow would suggest, or withdrawing, as his shoulder would suggest? Is he staring at you, as one eye would make you think, or just beyond you, as another implies? Instead of the line whose immanent mobility depends upon differentiation from itself, this painting gives us the architectural space of the fold and its translation into an epistemology of secrecy through the

posing of the body. The point, however, is not simply that interiority is produced through a translation of architectural spaces. Rather, the point is that the civilizing process's production of interiority is an attempt to bend the differential exteriorization of war's logic such that one brings this force to bear on oneself.

This production of interiority is quite evident in the *Galateo*. Very much like the men at Urbino who in Castiglione's *Book of the Courtier* attempt to construct the ideal courtier, the *Galateo*'s narrator attempts to piece together a set of regulations for his interlocutor, "a young relative." The uneducated old man compares his project to that of the sculptor Chiarissimo [Clearest], who

> wrote a treatise in which he gathered up all the rules of his craft [*in quello raccolse tutti gli ammaestramenti dell'arte sua*] with the authority of someone who had known them very well. He showed how the limbs of the human body ought to be measured, each independently and each in relation to the others so that they

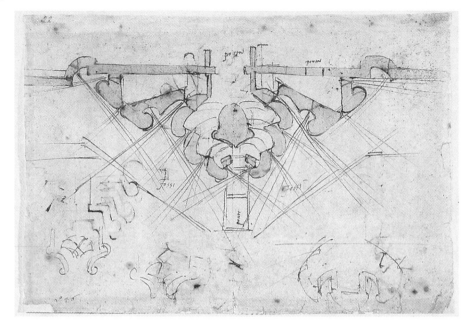

Fig. 5. Michelangelo, project for the arming of a door, MS, 22 A$^r$. Casa Buonarroti, Florence. Photo: Art Resource.

should be in proper proportion among themselves. He called the volume his Canon [*Il Regolo*], meaning that henceforth every master of the craft should shape and design statues [*dirizzare e regolare le statue*] according to it, just as beams, stones, and walls are measured with a standard ruler [*come le travi e le pietre e le mura si misurano con esso regulo*]. (82–83/424–25)

Moreover, the uneducated man continues, because most people learn better through examples and the senses rather than through abstracted rules, Chiarissimo also "carved a statue from [a block of marble] that was as regular in each of its limbs and in each of its parts as his treatise proposed in its rules" [*cosi regolato in ogni suo membro e in ciacuna sua parte come gli ammaestamenti de suo tratto divisavano*] (83/425). Just as Chiarissimo gives a set of rules and subsequently forms the sculptural body that proves these rules, so too does the old man give a series of rules—for example, "it is impolite to scratch oneself at the table" [*non istà bene grattarsi sedundo a tavola*] (92/435), or "one should not take off his clothes, and especially not his lower

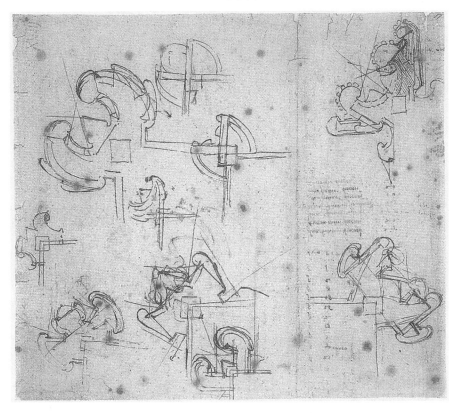

Fig. 6. Michelangelo, study for the fortification of a door, MS, 17 A<sup>r</sup>. Casa Buonarroti, Florence. Photo: Art Resource.

garments, in public" [*non si dee alcuno spogliare, e spezialmente scol-zare, in pubblico*] (95/438)—that he hopes his young relative will put into practice and in the process come to embody. Much as with Bron-zino's *Portrait of Ugolino Martelli*, the corporeal recitation of a statue enframed within pacified space is the project of the civilizing process (fig. 8). In the *Galateo*, the more the young relative follows the rules the old man puts forth, the more regulated, well-proportioned, and graceful he will become, until his body turns into a pure manifestation of the rules of manners that the old man elaborates. The old man's hope is that his interlocutor will become one with the rules of courtesy that he has passed along.

But the text of *Galateo* shows this graceful body to be strictly speak-

Fig. 7. Bronzino, *Portrait of a Young Man.* Metropolitan Museum,
New York.

ing uninhabitable, and it does so by forcing its readers *not* to take the
role of the young relative to whom the old man speaks. Because the old
man attempts to shape the well-mannered body by way of negation,
the experience of reading this treatise tends to contradict the construction of the graceful, well-mannered body that he wants to mold.

> Dirty, foul, repulsive, or disgusting things are not to be done in
> the presence of others, nor should they even be mentioned. And

Fig. 8. Bronzino, *Ugolino Martelli*. Staatliche Museen, Berlin.
Photo: Art Resource.

not only is it unpleasant to do them or recall them, but it is also
very bothersome to others even to bring them to mind with any
kind of behaviour. [*Perciocché non solamente non sono da fare in
presenza degli uomini le cose laide o fetide oschife o stomachevoli, ma
il nominarle anco disdice; e non pure il farle e il ricirdarle dispiace,
ma eziandio il ridurle nella imaginazione altrui con alcun atto suol
forte noiar le persone.*]

Therefore, it is an indecent habit practiced by some people
who, in full view of others, place their hands on whatever part of

their body it pleases them. Similarly, it is not proper for a well-mannered gentleman to prepare to relieve his physical needs in the presence of others. Or, having taken care of his needs, to re-arrange his clothing in their presence. And, in my opinion, when returning from nature's summons he should not even wash his hands in front of decent company, because the reason for his washing implies something disgusting to their imaginations [*Conciossiachè la cagione per la quale egli si le lava rappresenti nella imaginazion di coloro alcuna bruttura*].

For the same reason it is not a proper habit when, as sometimes happens, one sees something disgusting on the road to turn to one's companions and point it out to them. Even less should one offer something unpleasant to smell, as some insist on doing, placing it even under a companion's nose saying: "Now Sir, please smell how this stinks," when instead he should be saying: "Don't smell this because it stinks." (34/370–71)

The old man, who has no intention of stopping here, continues his theme by admonishing his young relative not to grind his teeth; not to cough or sneeze too loudly; and, if he must cough or sneeze, not to "spray those near him in the face." Nor should he "howl and bray like an ass" when he yawns—in fact, he should abstain from yawning altogether. Furthermore,

when you have blown your nose you should not open your hand-kerchief and look inside, as if pearls or rubies might have de-scended from your brain. This is a disgusting habit which is not apt to make someone love you, but rather, if someone loved you already, he is likely to stop then and there [*che sono stomachevoli modi ed atti a fare, non che altri ci ami, ma che, se alcuno co amasse, si disinnamori*]. The spirit of the Labyrinth, whoever he may have been, proves this: in order to cool the ardour of Messer Giovanni Boccaccio for a lady he did not know very well, he tells Boccaccio how she squats over ashes and coughs and spits up huge globs. (35–36/372)

While the old man exhorts the young relative not to call attention to these "dirty, foul, repulsive or disgusting things," throughout the en-tire treatise calling attention to dirty, foul, repulsive, and disgusting things is exactly what the old man does. At stake, though, is not simply the old man's "uneducated" and contradictory performance, his transgression of the rules of manners at the very moment of uttering them. Also at stake is the fracturing of readership. The proposition of the young relative invites us to assume a reader who takes these rules seriously—either out of respect for the rules themselves or out of respect for the old man, either because of a belief in the rules or because of a fairly conscious suspension of disbelief. But the specificity of that reader as well as the old man's contradictory performance produces a position eccentric to that performance, a position from which one can observe both the practice of manners by the uneducated old man and the transmission of those manners in his explicit attempts to mold the body of his young relative. In other words, the *Galateo* splits the epistemological field of reading between a naive acceptance of the rules and a critical response to their transmission.

The sign of this split is not so much "in" the text as it is in a kind of fleshiness produced by the text. While *Galateo* shows a serious narrator who assumes an equally serious interlocutor, the foregrounding of the contradictions involved in the transmission of this system of manners also opens up the possibility of a laughter that recognizes the bad faith inherent in such systems. That is, the particular kind of laughter that *Galateo* produces, laughter at the contradictions in the transmission of the rules of manners, seems to fly in the face of the very rules and customs by which one "makes other people's desires one's own" [*fare dell'altrui vogli suo piacere*] (45/382). Nevertheless, this laughter is not some carnivalesque subversion of the system. Indeed, its function is to strengthen critical judgment. It is, after all, if not the laughter of the courteous and elite, at least the laughter of those in the know. The reader who laughs also judges the old man's transgression using the very system that is being transmitted. Quite specifically, the reader's laughter isolates the moment of equivocation between an unintentionally rude, ill-mannered citation of the rules of conduct and submission to those very rules. And it isolates this moment in the embodied epistemological field of reading.

This laughter, I wish to propose, is the *Galateo's* sign of forgetting. For a number of contemporary writers, the Italians' commitment to manners in the first half of the sixteenth century is the flip side of the *calamità d'Italia* and the supposed failure of Italian military prowess. In his *History of the Sack of Rome,* Luigi Guicciardini, brother of Francesco, can only lament Italian cowardice:

In our common disaster everyone recognizes the cause of our
mortal wounds and of the death that seems to be waiting for us
and for our homeland. Nonetheless, held back by a long-term
habit of cowardice, people don't know how to prepare themselves
or persuade others to follow the glorious examples of the well-
constituted republics of Antiquity.[45]

From this point of view, an insistence on manners is simply complicit
with foreign domination as both a cause and sign of failed Italian
nationalism. What the narrator of the *Galateo* thinks of as the necessity of "[making] other people's desire's one's own" (45) is more accu-
rately making the customs and ceremonies of one's conqueror one's
own—an understanding this narrator both knows and attempts to
disown. Bowing, "giving . . . exquisite titles, and kissing each others'
hands" are customs and ceremonies about which the narrator is suspi-
cious, "certainly not native to us but . . . foreign and barbarous, only recently brought into Italy from where I do not know" (54). A few chapters later, though, the narrator shows his ignorance to be disingenuous,
since he admits that "such a meticulous distinction between degrees of
nobility" in fact has "been brought into Italy from Spain" (61). The
*Galateo* tenuously resolves the problem of failed nationalism by identifying the reader, through "his" body, with a masculine, epistemological space whose vanishing point is the Spanish conquest of the Italian
peninsula. The *Galateo* uses the icon of the civilized body and the
civilized judgment that forms alongside that icon's humorous presentation to rescript a geography destroyed by warfare and conquest into
an epistemological landscape unaffected by history. It is a project of
active forgetting through the positing of readership.

The "uneducated old man" who narrates *Galateo* only connota-
tively commemorates the Spanish conquest of Italy in a dream he describes. Messer Flaminio Tomarozzo, "a Roman gentleman, not at all
unlearned or thickheaded, but enlightened [*scienziato*] and sharp wit-
ted [*acuto ingegno*]," has a dream that the old man finds worth repeating, even though, as he enjoins, "one should not bore others with
such worthless things as dreams," since most are "not worth the
noise." Tomarozzo's is the exception:

In his sleep, he thought he was sitting in the house of his neighbor,
a very rich apothecary, and then, for one reason or another, the
mob went on a rampage and began to loot the shop [*levatosi il*

*popolo a romore, andava ogni cosa ruba*]. One took an electuary, another a confection, one man took one thing, another something else and swallowed it right there and then so that, in less than an hour, there was not a phial, a jar, a pot, or a box that was not empty and dry. A small flask remained, full of a very clear liquid [*e tutta piena di un chiarissimo liquore*], which many smelled but none would taste. In a short time he saw an old man of great stature and with a venerable appearance [*uomo grande di statura, antico e con venerabile aspetto*] come in and look at the poor apothecary's empty boxes and jars, spilled and scattered about, and almost all of them broken. Catching sight of the small flask I mentioned, he picked it up and drank all the liquid it contained to the last drop. Having done this, he left as everybody else had done. Messer Flaminio was much taken aback by this, so, turning to the apothecary, he asked: "Master, who was that man, and why did he drink so heartily the water in the flask that everyone else had refused?" And he thought that the apothecary answered saying: "My son, that was the Lord God. The water which he alone drank and which everyone else, as you saw, despised and refused was good judgment which, as you may have understood, no man is willing to taste by any means. [*l'acqua da lui solo benvuta e da ciascun altro, come tu vedusti, schifata e rifiutata fu la discrezioni la quale, sì come tu puoi aver conosciuto, gli uomini non vogliono assaggiare per cosa del modo*]"(49–50/387–88)

This otherwise inexplicable scene of looting resonates with the awful descriptions of the sack of Rome that stand metonymically as the event that proves the barbaric sadism of the Spanish conquerors. Take, for instance, Luigi Guicciardini's descriptions of looting and pillaging:

> [I]n a short time nearly everyone was taken prisoner, for they had no respect for the sacred places and (as always in such crises) many women, children, and frightened men had taken refuge. Divine things were treated no differently by them than profane ones. And rushing continually here and there like Furies from hell, they searched every sacred place and, with terrible violence, broke into any building they chose. Where they encountered resistance, they fought with ferocity; and if they could not overcome the defenders, they set the place on fire. Many priceless objects and many people who would not surrender themselves into their bestial hands were burned and consumed.

> How many courtiers, how many genteel and cultivated men,

how many refined prelates, how many devoted nuns, virgins, or chaste wives with their little children became the prey of these cruel foreigners! How many calixes, crosses, statues, and vessels of silver and gold were stolen from the altars, sacristies, other holy places where they were stored. How many rare relics, covered with gold and silver, were despoiled by bloody, homicidal hands and hurled with impious derision to the earth. (97–98)

According to Francesco Guicciardini, the absolute horror of this event exceeds even the most careful attempts to describe it. "It would be impossible," he writes, "not only to narrate but almost to imagine the calamity of that city" [*Però sarebbe impossibile non solo narrare ma quasi immaginarsi le calamità di quella città*].[46] Most appropriate, it might seem, were the generic *lamenti di Roma* that commemorated Rome's sack with imprecations against fate. In the *Galateo*, Tomarozzo's dream repeats this scene of looting without giving it its historical location. War remains only as a psychic residue. And dream interpretation deflects attention from this military location toward a program of promoting good judgment. According to the apothecary's interpretation in Tomarozzo's dream, when the stately [*grande di statura*] old man drinks the clearest [*chiarissimo*] liquid refused by the looting group, he comes to embody precisely the corporeal ethos that the elderly narrator imagines himself to be teaching—the ethics of good judgment embodied in good manners.

It is this ethics that Caravaggio, Marlowe, and Bacon will refuse. In relation to the civilizing process as a dominant social form, each develops a minor, sexed *poiesis* that develops different relations between judgment, the body, and the flesh. It is with these three thinkers in mind that we can begin to pose the question that a history of sexuality most urgently needs to ask: How, as the dominant social poetics of the Renaissance body, does the civilizing process negotiate the possibility of being otherwise?

# THREE

# History and the Flesh: Caravaggio's Queer Aesthetic

ॐ

## Spectatorship and the Queering of Form

Can sex be resolved by a historicist reading of sexuality? Can sex be determined by historicizing sexual practices, sexual ways of being? Can historicism delimit the space of sex? The time of sex? The polemical force of these questions concerns sex and the ego. Is sex a concern for the ego—the posed or practicing ego that is the object of historical and critical inquiry, or perhaps even the ego of the historian or critic? If so, what, if anything, does sex communicate? And if not, to whom, if anyone, is sex addressed?

I shall develop some responses to these questions by reading some poses in a number of Caravaggio's paintings. My thesis is that sex is central to Caravaggio's aesthetic and historical project insofar as it doesn't signify. For this reason, any attempt to make the sex of Caravaggio's aesthetic meaningful, to make it communicate, ends up being anachronistic—not just historically inaccurate, but also out of step with the temporality of the flesh. While, as I argued in chapter 2, the civilizing process produces and enforces a masculine psychic space around the problematicization of the flesh, here I will argue that Caravaggio traverses this space by effecting a shift within the historical that mobilizes the erotic flesh as what history does not comprehend. This does not mean that Caravaggio remembers what the civilizing process wants to forget. Rather, in this traversal, Caravaggio establishes a different relation with the unhistorical.

In essence, I shall argue that Caravaggio turns typology against itself. As many scholars have demonstrated, typology is a Christian hermeneutics, introduced by Paul and subsequently developed by Augustine and later reformers such as Luther and Calvin, that attempts to read Christianity's Hebrew past as the prefigurement of Christianity's decisive historical moments—the incarnation, passion, and resurrection of Christ—and in so doing to enact the formation of a Christian spiritual community that transcends a Hebrew sense of sociality based on genealogy. One main purpose of Paul's epistles is to transcend Hebrew genealogy and kinship through the allegory of Christ's body so that Judaism can become a world religion, in Weber's sense of the phrase.[1] Paul explains this project most clearly in his Epistle to the Galatians: "For all of you are children of God, through faith, in Christ Jesus, since every one of you that has been baptised has been clothed in Christ. There can be neither Greek nor Jew, there can be neither slave nor freeman, there can be neither male nor female—for you are all one in Christ Jesus. *And simply by being Christ's, you are that progeny of Abraham, the heirs named in the promise*" (Gal. 3:26–29, emphasis mine). If through the practice of baptism you partake in the Christic incarnation, then you are part of Abraham's seed, even if genealogically you aren't—so Paul's reasoning goes. This reasoning depends upon a Hellenistic separation of spirit and flesh. Because spirit is separate from and has precedent over flesh, being a child "by faith" supersedes the limits of fleshy genealogy and its corporeal inscriptions, most famously circumcision (Rom. 4). To support the formation of this spiritual community and to secure for it a sense of historicity, Paul produces a typological reading of the story of the birth of Abraham's two sons, "one by the slavegirl" Hagar, "one by the freewoman" Sarah (Gal. 4:22). Paul asserts that the birth of Hagar's son is a figure for birth under the law and the old covenant, whereas the birth of Sarah's son is a figure for birth under the promise and the new covenant. In this reading, the birth of Isaac figures the "spiritual" seed of Abraham of which Christians are a part through baptism and identification with the body of Christ, but of which the Jews who are bound by the law are not.

Paul's universalism is limited, however, because it establishes itself in dialectical tension with Jewish particularity and carnality. Although the Israelites of the Hebrew Bible can stand as prototypes for Christianity, the contemporary presence of the Jews signals something unassimilable to the truth of Christianity. As Julia Lupton puts it, "on the one hand, the Old Testament represents the heroic yet naive ground of modern faith that provides Christianity with its historic prototypes and patriarchs; on the other hand, the modern Jews who resist incorporation into the new covenant instantiate the unrighteous [and, it is crucial to add, carnal] remnant of the historical process who threaten to give lie to its story of progress."[2] The post-Pauline Jews become the main figure of what Lacan calls an auto-differential mark, an unassimilable and carnal difference around which Christian identity and claims to historical domination are constituted. As Daniel Boyarin and Jonathan Boyarin have argued, Paul's "very emphasis on a universalism expressed as the concern for all of the families of the world turns very rapidly (if not necessarily) into a doctrine that they must all become part of our family of the spirit with all of the horrifying practices against Jews and other Others that Christian Europe has produced." The result is that in European Christianity "the place of difference increasingly becomes the Jewish place, a place configured as undeniably fleshy, as Augustine puts it."[3]

However, it would be a mistake to think that typology is simply motivated by anti-Semitism. Typology obtains as a hermeneutics that converts history because it functions primarily as a palliative for Christianity's difficulties in dealing with the problem of evil in the world. In *De libero arbitrio,* Augustine accords man free will, but he does so in order to make man and not God responsible for evil. Evil is not a worldly substance, he argues; it is rather an effect of a bad choice motivated by *libido,* lust. "The movement which, for the sake of pleasure, turns the will from the Creator to the creature belongs to the will itself."[4] Therefore, Augustine argues, God is entirely just in punishing evildoers because man is responsible for all the ills of history. Augustine makes this argument in order to salvage the concept of the world. Once the New Testament located the basis for salvation in the individual's faith in Christ's resurrection, the created world threatened to become disappointingly irrelevant—a line of thinking most radically developed by Gnosticism.[5] Arguing against the Manichean Gnostics' thesis that the created world is defective in its creation, Augustine proposes instead that the created world is defective in its history. The deficiencies of the world are not the failure of creation; they are due to the failures of human free will. As Hans Blumenberg has argued, with Augustine "the original eschatological pathos directed against the *existence* of the world was transformed into a new interest in the *condition* of the world."[6] Once Augustine posits world history as the turning of humanity against God's will, he must also posit a concurrent hermeneutics reorienting the faithful Christian's relation to that history—exactly the function typology serves. Christianity's unconvertible Jew figures the problem of choosing libido over choosing the Christian God.

Caravaggio's paintings take typology as their starting point. Only, rather than simply repeating it, these paintings introduce a difference into the difference that is Jewish identity and embodied in Jewish carnality, producing it as a kind of sexual *jouissance* that is neither contained nor reduced by the civilizing process's organization of sexual difference. The civilizing process attempts to avoid the flesh through its arrangement of psychic space, but Caravaggio, in traversing that space, introduces a different, ethical relation to the flesh. When Caravaggio turns typology against itself, he refuses to posit an ideal community that will exist at the supposed end of history. Rather, focusing on the moment of reception, Caravaggio's aesthetic produces in its spectators an erotic openness to a future that resists eschatology.

The problem with many current discussions of sex and sexuality in relation to Caravaggio's paintings is that a number of these discussions' participants tend to collapse the appeal of the posed body with the sense of meaningfulness that a group compresses onto that pose and, in so doing, have misread the place of the sex in Caravaggio's paintings. In 1971, Donald Posner argued that the coy poses of Caravaggio's early boy-paintings are homoerotic and that these poses worked as a "homosexual appeal" to his early, supposedly homosexual patron, Cardinal Francesco Maria Del Monte. In order to lay the groundwork for his argument, Posner also asserted that Caravaggio was a homosexual. To a large extent for Posner, the evidence lay in the pose. To take one example, what Posner found remarkable, and remarkably homosexual, about *The Boy Being Bitten by a Lizard* was "the squeamishness and effeminacy of his reaction. His hands do not tense with masculine vigor in response to the attack; they remain limp in a languid show of helplessness" (fig. 9).[7] If, as Baglione describes in his *vita* of Caravaggio, this painting is done with such diligent work that "you could almost hear the boy scream" [*parea quella testa vera-*

Fig. 9. Caravaggio, *Boy Being Bitten by a Lizard*. National Gallery, London.

*mente stridere*], then what Posner hears is the squeal of the sissy-boy, the shriek of the nelly queer.[8] Recently, in 1995, Creighton Gilbert has attacked Posner's thesis on the basis that it reads homosexuality from the perspective of mid- to late-twentieth-century group formation. Without a doubt, Gilbert's charge is correct. There is no homosexual ego formation before the mid-nineteenth century. Only, this assertion doesn't exactly mean that these poses aren't homosexual; it means that the temporality of this "homosexual appeal" remains unthought. Must every appeal be to the ego? Can't there be poses that appeal to groups not yet formed?

Instead of addressing these questions, Gilbert continues to argue that, given the lack of Renaissance male homosexual ego formation, the poses of Caravaggio's boys aren't homosexual at all. Rather, they are as much a part of normative Renaissance male heterosexuality as are twentieth-century athletes "hugging [their] teammates," or "happy wrestling between two baseball players"—an assertion whose contemporary examples belie the security of its historical force.[9] The problem with Gilbert's argument is that he takes for granted male heterosexual ego formation in the Renaissance. It is also a mistake to assume, as Gilbert does, that contemporary male heterosexuality isn't affected by homoeroticism, even if the relations of modern male heterosexuality to this homoeroticism aren't the same as those of male homosexuality.

It is fairly easy to assert that the discursive mechanisms out of which twentieth-century male homosexual and heterosexual egos are formed did not exist in late-sixteenth- and early-seventeenth-century Italy, and that in their accounts of sexuality in Caravaggio's paintings both Posner and Gilbert quite unproblematically rely on discourses that, for Caravaggio, would have held little sway. This is a line of argumentation that David Carrier takes up. Pitting a vulgar Foucauldian "archeology" of Caravaggio criticism against the search for *the* narrative of Caravaggio's aesthetics and identity that informs much of this criticism, Carrier argues, among other things, that the question of Caravaggio's homosexuality is simply an invention of twentieth-century art criticism, a "code" by which this criticism can sustain its own inquiry.[10] Because homosexuality is a kind of ego formation that postdates both Caravaggio's sexual practices and self-identity—whatever these may have been—homosexuality tells the truth neither about Caravaggio nor about his aesthetic. (Of course, one wonders if egos ever tell the truth. For psychoanalysis, the answer is that, as much as one trusts the ego's confessions of its truths, one will never find the truth of the ego. And what is this "truth"?—the truth that the ego is, structurally speaking, a defensive liar.)[11]

But we still must ask, What is it about these poses that demands interpretation? What is it about these poses that so strongly appeals? My answer is this: Caravaggio's poses are appealing precisely insofar

as they oddly embody a demand that resists easy recognition and conscription by a group who wants to read them as transmitting its sense
of identity and value. These poses are appealing precisely insofar as
they are formally, aesthetically, and historically queer.

By queer I mean, with Eve Sedgwick, that Caravaggio's poses refer
to a dehiscence in the symbolic order in which "the open mesh of
possibilities, gaps, overlaps, dissonances and resonances, lapses and
excesses of meaning when the constituent elements of anyone's gender, of anyone's sexuality aren't made (or *can't be made*) to signify
monolithically." While Sedgwick makes it clear that she is interested
in expanding the dissonances and resonances of "queer," the lapses
and excesses of meaning to which it refers, so that queer attaches itself
among other things to the "fractal intricacies" of race, ethnicity, and
postcolonial nationalities, she also asserts that to wrench the term's
"definitional center" from same-sex sexual expression "would be to
dematerialize any possibility of queerness itself." Now, this assertion
should lead Sedgwick to interrogate the materiality of homosexual
sexual expression as a kind of resistant differential that threatens the
irresistible analogies by which groups construct and enforce communal identity. But instead, when Sedgwick turns to analyze the specificity of queer, she locates its material particularities in the performing
and performative ego. "'Queer,'" she writes, "seems to hinge much
more radically and explicitly on a person's undertaking particular,
performative acts of experimental self-perception and filiation. A hy-
pothesis worth making explicit: that there are important senses in
which 'queer' can signify only *when attached to the first person*." When
*attached* to the first person, perhaps; but Sedgwick immediately continues with a "possible corollary" that conflates queerness *with* the
first person: "[W]hat it takes—all it takes—to make the description
'queer' a true one is the impulsion *to* use it in the first person."[12]

It is the control of this impulse toward queerness by the ego's poses
that I want to resist. Queerness isn't about the ego; it's about history.
Moreover, the fall of the historically queer into the identificatory logic
of self-representation marks the end of queerness per se. While I do
want to insist on the formal queerness of the poses in Caravaggio's
boy-paintings, nevertheless I will argue that we can't read sexuality
into the pose as such. What makes these poses "sexual" is the way in
which they determine a space between painting and viewer that opens

up a fantasy scene that enacts as sexual practice the epistemological and communal organization of this aestheticized space. To this extent, I am very much in agreement with Leo Bersani and Ulysse Dutoit's recent, quite nuanced readings of Caravaggio's paintings, readings predicated upon the thesis that "Caravaggio resists the reduction of the sensual to the sexual." The effect of this resistance, Bersani and Dutoit argue, is that Caravaggio moves from the erotic to "another mode of connectedness between bodies."[13] As I shall argue, rather than reinforcing the ego formation of either the poser or the viewer, these paintings open up an erotic and aesthetic space in history through their traversal of typology and a queering of form into which emerges a *jouissance* that shatters ego identity.

⊷

In much the same way that a number of twentieth-century art historians interpreting Caravaggio's paintings have tended to fantasize an overly homosexual scene of artistic production, so too did a number of Caravaggio's contemporaries fantasize an overly theatrical scene of artistic production, and in so doing, misread his formal project. Specifically, Caravaggio's contemporaries read in his posed figures an excess of theatricality, which they translated as a deficiency in the paintings. For instance, in his early-seventeenth-century *Considerazioni sulla pittura*, Guilio Mancini writes that Caravaggio's style "is closely tied to real life." But "since it is impossible to put in one room a multitude of people acting out the story," especially when it comes to the poses in narrative painting, Caravaggio's style leads to failure. His "figures, though they look forceful, lack movement, expression, and grace."[14] In his later-seventeenth-century *Vite di pittori, scultori, e architetti moderni*, Giovanni Bellori is more general in his criticism. In Bellori's account, Caravaggio "lacked invention, decorum, design, and any knowledge of the science of painting. The moment the model was taken from him, his hand and mind became empty."[15] In a culture in which *sprezzatura* marks class savoir-faire, these aesthetic judgments more or less condemn Caravaggio as a rube.

But we need not accept these critical judgments. Caravaggio's paintings effectively modulate the aesthetic culture of the Renaissance by distressing formal expectations, mostly surrounding genre paintings, thereby introducing a more visible dislocation between substance and form in which the expression of formal innovation distorts and expands the implications of content. With Caravaggio, the expression of form depends quite strongly on recognition. Form doesn't pretend simply to shape some inchoate appetite that exists outside formal constraints; form articulates a fundamentally transferential relation between viewers and painting that modulates and refashions an aestheticized desire not to know. The function of Caravaggio's formal innovations is to aggravate and estrange this desire not to know by pushing at the aestheticization of that desire. Hence, as Arnold Hauser has shrewdly noted, the ideological ire of Caravaggio's contemporaries is primarily supported by an extended misreading of Caravaggio's formal project from the old-fashioned perspective of Renaissance aesthetic culture.[16] Let me take Hauser's observation one step further. Encouraging this misreading in order to secure as old-fashioned an aestheticized class formation based on imitation *is* Caravaggio's formal project.

Caravaggio's paintings insist on a relation between spectator and canvas that differs from the one that Vasari theorized in his writings on *designo*. *Designo*, "parent of . . . Architecture, Sculpture, and Painting," is "like a form or idea of all the objects in nature . . . cognizant of the proportion of the whole to the parts and of the parts to each other and the whole." Vasari argues that this form is both prior to and an effect of looking at paintings:

> [Since from the knowledge of *designo*] there arises a certain conception and judgment, so that there is formed in the mind that something which afterwards, when expressed by the hands, is called design, we may conclude that design is not other than a visible expression and declaration of our inner conception and of that which others have imagined and given form to in their idea.[17]

Moreover, in his *Lives of the Artists*, Vasari considers the manifestation of *designo* as historical process. In his preface to part 3, for example, Vasari explains that artists of the first period like Cimabue and Giotto did not posses the qualities of *designo*; artists of the second period possessed this quality "but failed to realize [its] full potential"; and artists of the third period not only realized its full potential, but also realized it so strongly that they (especially Michelangelo) "triumphed over later artists, over the artists of the ancient world, and over nature herself."[18]

With Caravaggio, the formalism of a *designo* prior to the act of painting turns into a theatrical space of reception that insists on a sense of unknowingness on the part of the spectator. The effect of this unknowingness is to reorient the spectator's relation to history. Take, for instance, *The Lute Player* (plate 1). If we read the score from which the young boy plays, we can see that it is a popular madrigal by the French composer Jacques Arcadelt, whose lyrics begin, *Voi sapete ch'io v'amo* (You know that I love you). This phrase hails "you" both as the object of love and as the one who knows that you are the object of love. Without the presence of the singing boy, we could argue that if you identify with this virtual "you," then what allows you to ignore the split between you and "you," what allows you to pretend with some certainty that you are sincerely loved, is the lack of a split in the "I" who loves you. However, the boy's pose gives this phrase an embodied enunciative position and, in the process, translates this knowledge into something more complex: *I know* that you know that I love you. This pose doubles the place from which knowledge is imputed to occur—"you know"/"I know that you know"—and in so doing exacerbates the uncertainty of the viewer who identifies with this "you." You may think that you know that I love you, so this pose asserts, but once you know that I know, the certainty of your knowledge is compromised.

In effect, this pose establishes an epistemological field that splits its virtual, viewing "you" in a desire for certainty, a desire that is routed through a longing for voice. In the painting, the unused violin and the bottom score marked *Bassus* can stand as coy invitations to its spectators to join in the music making. But if you are lured into the invitation of the painting and find yourself in the odd position of wanting to sing the bass part along with the boy, then what exactly are you supposed to sing? Because that score is closed, you are faced with a conundrum. To understand oneself as the addressee of this painting's solicitation is to confront an inarticulateness that is directly proportional to the coyness of the boy's pose. If there is a coyness in the pose of the boy, it is matched by the inarticulate unknowingness of the virtual spectator, the "you" whom this painting hails.

Fig. 10. Caravaggio, *Rest on the Flight into Egypt.* Galleria Doria-Pamphili,
Rome. Photo: Art Resource

Caravaggio's early paintings do not structure their reception
through the meaningfulness of the images on the canvas. Rather, they
structure their reception through a sense of unknowingness sustained
through the viewer's inability to say what it is the painting seems to
want its viewer to say—like the awkward and dumbstruck figure of
Joseph in *Rest on the Flight into Egypt,* doubled by the head of an ass
(fig. 10). Within the epistemological space that they construct, these
paintings present the subject's interior split as materialized dumbness.

The unknowingness that this theatrical space produces is not something that one could fill out with more historical or psychological information. Instead, this unknowingness marks a heterogeneity to the
space of posing that, if you take the portrayed singing as an expression
of the boy's desires, turns the painting into a lure to catch you as a
spectator and forces you to identify with a structural muteness, a lack
of what Lacan calls the "vociferated signifier," in both the subject and

the Other.[19] In other words, these paintings attempt to procure an epistemological pose from their viewers, in the process procuring interpretations that will never quite overcome or assuage this loss of voice. If I identify with that virtual "you," I find myself not so much at a lack of words as at a lack of voice. *I cannot say what it is that this painting drives me to want to say, but*—so the painting appears to promise—*if I study the painting long enough, maybe I will be able to say it.* This experience of lack isn't a problem that the painting can solve; rather, identification with the loss of voice is the "guarantee" that this painting is meant for you.

These paintings procure less a confirmation of Vasari's *designo* and more an "agitation" that Descartes will describe some forty years after Caravaggio as wonder: "[W]hen the first encounter with some object surprises us, and we judge it to be new or very different from what we formerly knew, or from what we supposed that it ought to be, that causes us to wonder and be surprised."[20] Descartes continues by arguing that the body wants very much to sustain this sense of newness, so much so that it will attempt to change itself in order to commemorate this wonderful object:

> [Wonder] is thus primarily caused by the impression we have in the brain which represents the object as rare, and as consequently worthy of much consideration; then afterwards by the movement of the spirits, which are disposed by this impression to tend with great force towards that part of the brain where it is, in order to fortify and conserve it there; as they are also disposed by it to pass thence into the muscles which serve to retain the organs of the sense in the same situation in which they are, so that it is still maintained by them.[21]

While I do not wish to assimilate Descartes's scientism to Caravaggian aesthetics, I do wish to propose that in procuring this structural muteness, Caravaggio's paintings attempt to excite this sense of newness that comes with the experience of wonder and to keep their spectators open to the future through an erotic, corporeal attachment to the posing boy.

Caravaggio's paintings also imply a relation between representation and embodiment that differs from Alberti's *istoria*. As I briefly discussed in the chapter 2, *istoria* is primarily a technique for rendering

the body in painting such that "all [its] members should fulfill their
function according to the action performed, in such a way that not
even the smallest limb fails to play its appropriate part." The body
submitted to *istoria* becomes a functional narrative unit. But Alberti
also uses this technique to articulate his larger politico-aesthetic project of forming a community based on embodied, mimetic grace. Alberti first divides *istoria* into its discrete parts. "Parts of the *istoria* are
the bodies, part of the body is the member, and part of the member
is the surface." Subsequently, Alberti expands from the surface of the
canvas toward an aesthetic regime that connects the well-composed
body to the beautiful. "From the composition of the surface arises
that elegant harmony and grace in bodies, which they call beauty." In
addition, Alberti suggests that this model of aestheticized embodiment should modulate into a standard for paintings' reception. He
expresses the hope that observers charmed by *istoria* will be taken over
by a sympathetic identification with actions performed by the bodies
represented on the canvas. "A '*istoria*' will move spectators when the
men painted in the picture outwardly demonstrate their own feelings
as clearly as possible. Nature provides . . . that we mourn with the
mourners, laugh with those who laugh, and grieve with the grief-
stricken. Yet these feelings are known from the movements of the
body."[22] While *istoria* explains to the painter how to compose a body
on the surface of the canvas, it also becomes a model for an idealized
version of aesthetic reception in which the spectator properly imitates
the grace, beauty, and elegant harmony of the bodies represented on
the canvas.

Clearly, in Caravaggio's paintings as well as in Alberti's aesthetic,
the body gets caught up in a system of representation, but in Caravaggio's corporealizations, the moment of representation pushes the
courtly class system of Alberti's aesthetic theory to its breaking point.
No longer is the body the site of an *istoria* to be imitated with *sprezzatura* by a community of viewers. Rather, Caravaggio's paintings tend
to break the functional organization of the body that *istoria* demands.
Caravaggio's poses freeze and ex-pose, if you will, an interruption that
suspends identity based on mimetic group identification.

A number of Caravaggio's religious paintings mobilize the topos of
conversion against the courtly aesthetic. However, these paintings do
not simply repeat this religious topos. Instead, they arrest their central

figures in poses that exacerbate the distinction between being and call-ing that conversion narratives produce in order to allay. These paint-ings show posed bodies that tend *not* to follow the voice that impels group formation, and in the process, they reconfigure that impelling voice into something potentially disruptive of group formation, some-thing materialized as eccentric to the diegetic space afforded by the canvas. Think of *The Raising of Lazarus* (fig. 11). In the biblical version of the story, Jesus cries, "Lazarus, come out!" and immediately follow-ing, Lazarus walks out of his tomb, alive (John 11:44). But Caravag-gio's painting freezes the moment between Jesus' call and Lazarus' res-urrection. Lazarus is posed between life and death, one hand falling corpselike toward a skull lying on the ground, the other raised toward a light just behind Jesus' head. The weeping mourners who look di-rectly at Lazarus don't seem to recognize that he is coming to life, while others in the painting do appear to recognize that something odd is going on, somewhere off the space of the canvas. What counts here is not just the hailing of Lazarus, but something heterogeneous to Jesus' command.

Think also of *The Calling of St. Matthew* (fig. 12). All three gospels that tell this brief story present Jesus' voice as irresistible. Jesus sees Matthew and says, "Follow me." Immediately thereafter, in the next sentence, Matthew gets up and follows him (Matt. 9:9; Mark 2:14; Luke 5:28). In contrast, Caravaggio's painting captures the moment between the call and Matthew's understanding that he is the one being called. Far from being self-evident and compelling, the voice he hears is opaque. The painting shows Matthew pointing—to himself? to the seemingly drunk adolescent sitting next to him?—posed as if to say, "Who? Me?" This sense of opacity in the voice is underscored by the young boy sitting toward the front of the painting whose back is turned to us. Like some of the figures in *The Raising of Lazarus*, this boy focuses on something eccentric to Jesus' command, something heterogeneous to the scene of Matthew's calling.

Not only do Caravaggio's religious paintings tend to configure voice as both opaque and eccentric to what narrative would present as a self-evident command; they also present the opacity of voice as something that produces longing for an illicit, unarticulated enjoy-ment, a longing embodied in the pose of the one who is being called. Think, finally, of *The Conversion of St. Paul* (fig. 13). Paul describes the events on the road to Damascus as follows:

Fig. 11. Caravaggio, *The Raising of Lazarus.* National Museum, Messina.
Photo: Art Resource.

It happened that I was on that journey and nearly at Damascus
when in the middle of the day a bright light from heaven shone
suddenly round me. I fell to the ground and heard a voice saying,
"Saul, Saul, why are you persecuting me?" I answered, "Who are
you, Lord?" and he said to me, "I am Jesus the Nazarene, whom
you are persecuting." The people saw the light but did not hear

Fig. 12. Caravaggio, *The Calling of St. Matthew.* Contarelli Chapel, Church
of San Luigi dei Francesi, Rome. Photo: Art Resource.

the voice which spoke to me. I said, "What am I to do, Lord?"
(Acts 22:6–10)[23]

Following Paul's story, Caravaggio's painting arrests Paul in the very
moment of embodying his question: "What am I to do?" We see Paul
hearing the voice that no one else hears, that everyone else sees as
light. Surely, Caravaggio's Paul is posed *in the process of* being drawn
toward the absent voice calling him to be something else. But also
note, this pose of being in process is deeply erotic. Paul's supine body,
open-armed and open-legged, encourages us to trace out the absent
voice as that of a lover whose spatial outline the quietude of both
the old man and the horse block out.[24] A visual example of Freudian
negation, this quietude, along with the placement of the old man and

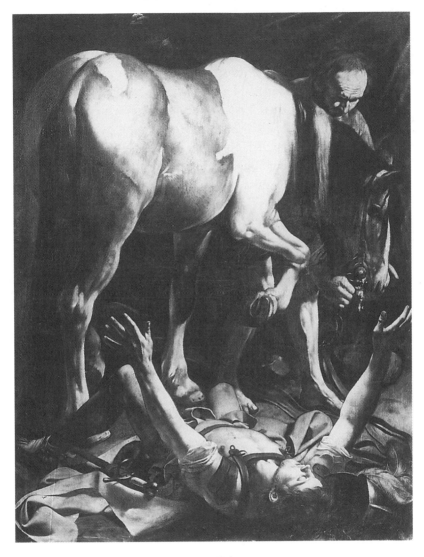

Fig. 13. Caravaggio, *The Conversion of St. Paul.* Cerasi Chapel, Santa Maria
del Popolo, Rome. Photo: Art Resource.

horse, stands as a bulwark that denies the particularly illicit material-
ization of this voice that Paul's body appears to encourage.[25] This pose
resuscitates the flesh that Paul relinquishes (Gal. 1:16), and it resuscitates it in the psychic space of spectatorship.

The voice that these paintings isolate is not the one that compels

a historic "progression" from the religion of the ancient Hebrews to
Christianity. Even *The Conversion of Paul* doesn't simply reenact Pauline historiography in which the spiritual life of the Christian transcends the carnality of the Jews. Rather, these paintings present us
with a voice that is opaque and heterogeneous to the diegetic space of
the canvas—a voice, then, that isn't so much presented as historical
demand as it is materialized *in its absence* by the posed male body
demanding a particularized, absolute, and corporeal satisfaction of
being. These bodies, caught up within the symbolic networks of Caravaggio's paintings, demand a certain vocalization that is eccentric to
the call of the historical, of narrative progression, and of *istoria*—a
vocalization that has no discernible content. In Lacanian parlance,
these bodies present us with a demand for voice as *objet a*.

In Lacanian theory the *objet a* is not the desired object. Quite the
reverse. The *objet a* is desire's cause, and, if anything, desire's objective
is to obscure that cause. The *objet a* is the object of the drive. What
does this distinction mean? While desire sustains itself by repeatedly
searching for some illusory, impossible object that, were it to exist,
would offer a satisfactory end to desire, the drive aims to satisfy itself
by continually returning to its circuit. Hence, although desire can
never achieve satisfaction, the drive achieves satisfaction through the
repetition of its own aim.[26] And, in the process, the drive traces out
some object—some *objet a*—that agitates desire and serves as desire's
inexplicable cause. As Lacan puts it, the *objet a* "is the cause of desire,
and this object that is the cause of desire is the object of the drive—
that is to say, the object around which the drive turns."[27] Even though
the drive has a distinctly historical dimension, in that it traces out
what a history that takes for its end some utopian communalism
wants not to know, the drive is nevertheless also tied to the flesh. Desire attempts to avoid the object of the drive by rendering it meaningless, dissatisfying, disgusting. But the drive, clinging to its enjoyment,
renders this object an intrusive and fleshy surplus in the space of
desire.

Voice as *objet a* stands in relation to group formation. For the good
of the group, we sacrifice particularity to some general history and to
the practices that support it. But in the enunciation of history, something veers away: a voice that exceeds or even contradicts its idealized
meaning. It's the heterogeneity, the eccentricity of this voice, and not

some sense of meaning or knowledge that it carries with it, that demonstrates its incompatibility with group formation. Rather than being filled with meaning, voice as *objet a* is filled out with an enjoyment that indexes a "particular absolute" of *jouissance,* as Joan Copjec puts it.[28] It is the *plus-de-jouir,* the surplus enjoyment, both in excess of the knowledge afforded by desire and against which desire defends.[29]

The voice as *objet a* is not unrelated to the work of angels. Ceaselessly extending the moment beyond the confines of history, opening new identities and new universes, angels "circulate," as Irigaray writes, "as mediators of that which has not yet happened, of what is still going to happen, of what is on the horizon."[30] Nor are angels unrelated to the flesh: they announce its miraculous incarnation to barren women and virgins. But just as soon as an angel will extend the moment beyond the confines of history, it returns the moment back to the historical and its strictures. Even the angel in Revelation who comes to announce the end of history gives in to the desire for history as he commands John to eat the book. And eat it at the cost of the flesh: "I went to the angel and asked him to give me the small scroll, and he said, 'Take it and eat it; it will turn your stomach sour, but it will taste as sweet as honey.' So I took it out of the angel's hand, and I ate it and it tasted sweet as honey, but when I had eaten it my stomach turned sour" (Rev. 10:9–10).

This voice as *objet a* can't allay the spectator's sense of unknowingness produced by Caravaggio's aesthetic, theatricalized space of reception. Its effect is exactly the opposite. Voice as *objet a* guarantees a gap between the future and any attempt to make it mean before its time. By sustaining this gap in the face of all attempts to close it, Caravaggio's aesthetic remains formally, historically (and angelically?) queer.

## Sublimation and Social Fantasy

The drive need not be obscured by desire. It can also change its aim from one that is primarily sexual to one that is primarily social. As is well known, Freud calls this change in aim sublimation, and he tends to make two seemingly contradictory statements about it. On the one hand, Freud asserts that when the drive changes its aim from the sexual to the social, it still retains its primarily erotic purpose of establishing a "tendency to unity." In either case then, sexual or social, the drive attempts to master stimuli by forming the flesh into a coherent body and by projecting onto the external world whatever parts of that flesh the ego "regards as hostile."[31] On the other hand, Freud asserts that when the drive is sublimated, its "erotic component no longer has the power to bind," so that sublimation also carries with it a certain "inclination to aggression and destruction" located in the created object. Sublimation forms a community that doesn't *just* project what it regards as hostile onto some external source. This hostility also returns to affect members of that community in one way or another.[32]

The example that Freud gives to support this antinomy is the idealized law—"the dictatorial 'Thou shalt.'" While this law attempts to establish unity and group identification through what Freud calls "desexualized libido," nevertheless, this same law displays a "general character of harshness and cruelty" that threatens group unity by reintroducing a libido that is now sadistic.[33] Sublimation can lead to an introjection of the super-ego—an internalization of the law in order to avoid becoming the object of the harshness and cruelty, the sadistic *jouissance* that motivates the law. In this case, sublimation reinforces a collective desire not to know the libidinal occupations from which that desire is built. But, for psychoanalysis, cultural artifacts need not only reinscribe the subjectifying mechanisms of social demands, of political norms. Sublimation also affords the possibility of formulating a different communal arrangement, "a different criterion of another, or even the same, morality," as Lacan puts it.[34]

It is through this antinomy that Guy Hocquenghem defines what he calls "homosexual desire." On the one hand, homosexual desire relies on "an ascent towards sublimation, the superego and social anxiety" that converts *jouissance* into a homosocial, between-men symbolic order. The particular sexual aim of *jouissance* is translated into a social aim on the condition that *jouissance* is desexualized. On the other hand, homosexual desire emerges as such in a desublimating "descent towards the abyss of non-personalized and uncodified desire," what Freud calls "a sexualization of social instincts" that have previously been desexualized.[35] In Hocquenghem's definition, homosexual desire isn't prior to sublimation; it's an effect of this very process. And insofar as homosexual desire is linked to the inclination toward aggression and destruction that Freud argues is part of the created object, the sexuality of homosexual desire stands as a threat

to the very sociality out of which it emerges. This sexuality is, as Hocquenghem rather brazenly puts it, "the killer of civilized egos"—including, I should add, civilized homosexual egos.[36]

At stake in this assertion is the relation of homosexual desire to
social fantasy and to *jouissance,* a relation that Hocquenghem reads
through the philosophical loci of the phallus and the anus. A society
that invests *jouissance* in unity around one significant organ (the phallus) must also divest the *jouissance* articulated through other organs
of their possible significances and various modalities. Hence, although
the anus is one of the first sites for educating some soon-to-be-
civilized ego about bodily control through submission to the demand
of the Other ("Make a poopy for Mommy and Daddy!") and about
social discomfort over the gift that exceeds social expectation ("Here's
a poopy you didn't even ask for!"), that education is completed when
the anus is no longer the locus of social relations, when "your excre-
ment is yours and yours alone."[37] The anus becomes the philosophical
locus for thinking a *jouissance* that no longer serves a social function.

The reason that this anus isn't simply philosophical is that the *jouissance* for which it comes to stand translates into a social fantasy about
homosexual desire in which this *jouissance* is conflated with a "homosexual practice" that restores to the anus a social and sexual function:
coming together through anal sex. Whether or not gay men are having
anal sex is beside the point. As Hocquenghem writes, "homosexuality
is always connected with the anus, even though—as Kinsey's precious
statistics demonstrate—anal intercourse is still the exception even
among homosexuals."[38] The social fantasy of homosexual desire translates the philosophical anus into a site of obscene dread insofar as it
expresses an aspect of desire—a relation of desire to useless *jouissance*—that "is not merely the accomplishment of the sexual act with
a person of the same sex."[39]

Leo Bersani names this obscene dread, this useless *jouissance,*
"homo-ness," and in his trenchant critique of queer theory's trust in
ego-identity, he argues that homo-ness is the somewhat paradoxical
foundation for homosexual identity. Historically preceding the invention of "the homosexual," this homo-ness is a "self-shattering" *jouissance* intrinsic to homosexuality, an "anti-identitarian identity" that
defines homosexual sociality through the confrontation of that identity with antirelationality.[40] In other words, homo-ness is a specific

version of a more general kind of confrontation with the absolute particularity of a *jouissance* that serves no social use, that threatens all social bonds. Moreover, this *jouissance* can't be read simply by reference to social practices or by reference to the egos that emerge from these practices. As we shall see, it can only be read in the subject's relation to social fantasy. Exactly how the subject relates to social fantasy and, thereby, to this useless *jouissance* depends on that subject's relation to sublimation.

At stake in sublimation is the production of objects that bear the burden of communal reality testing. It would be easy to test reality if there were a simple distinction between an internal world of imagination and an external world of real objects. For better or for worse, though, this simple distinction does not hold. Nor is there any simple correspondence between objects in psychic space and objects in material reality. Material objects exist differently in our psychic space than they exist externally; sometimes they exist only in our psychic space; and sometimes they exist only externally. To acknowledge and to account for the complexities of these distinctions, Freud introduces both the pleasure principle and the reality principle. While the pleasure principle attempts to bind the ego with whatever offers pleasure by expelling and avoiding those things that are dissatisfying, the reality principle sustains the recognition of those things that aren't satisfying and, in so doing, allows the subject to recognize the world. For psychoanalysis, this ability to recognize a world that is not simply of one's making is *not* more or less theologically grounded in some magical, though absent signified. Rather, this ability is grounded in an initial expulsion of what is dissatisfying, what is kept at bay by rendering it "bad, alien, and external."[41] Hence, Freud writes, "the first and immediate aim in the process of testing reality is not to discover an object in real perception corresponding to what is imagined"—this would simply be a narcissistic conscription of the world—"but to re-*discover* such an object, to persuade oneself that [reality] is still there."[42] It is precisely through an encounter with avoided dissatisfaction that one comes to recognize and sustain a distinction between psychic space and material reality.

Following Freud, Lacan calls the stuff of this initial expulsion "the Thing" (*das Ding*), and he characterizes it by its absence, its strangeness, and even its hostility toward the ego. This Thing is what one

PLATE 1. Caravaggio, *The Lute Player.*
The Hermitage, St. Petersburg.
Photo: Scala/Art Resource, NY.

PLATE 2. Caravaggio, *Victorius Cupid.*
Gemäldegalerie, Staatliche Museen, Berlin.
Photo: Nimatallah/Art Resource, NY.

PLATE 3. Caravaggio, *The Sacrifice of Isaac.*
Uffizi, Florence.
Photo: Scala/Art Resource, NY.

PLATE 4. Caravaggio, *David with the Head of Goliath.*
Borghese Gallery, Rome.
Photo: Scala/Art Resource, NY.

must avoid if one wants to follow the egoistic pathways of pleasure and desire. But also, this Thing is what one must negotiate and rediscover in the testing of reality. Here lies the importance of Lacan's definition of sublimation as that which "raises an object to the dignity of the Thing."[43] To say that sublimation raises an object to the dignity of the Thing and not to some social ideal is to say that in the process of sublimation some object—any object—becomes the Thing by which a group gets and sustains its sense of reality.

The social value of sublimation is that, in "giving . . . fantasies bodies," as Freud puts it, sublimation can satisfy society's demand to reproduce itself.[44] For instance, in *The Four Fundamental Concepts of Psychoanalysis,* Lacan proposes that the social value of an icon is that it allows for the fantasy that the god it represents is also looking at it. The icon is there to please God, to "arouse the desire of God." Even iconoclasm preserves this organization, since it declares that God doesn't care for certain images precisely because they give pleasure either to other humans or to other gods. The artistic production of icons and even iconoclastic backlashes allow a group to participate in a fantasy that sustains it in its relation to the desire of the Other. In order to elaborate a survey of art history organized primarily by the myth of the murder of the father in *Totem and Taboo,* Lacan continues by interrogating the social value of the paintings in the great hall of the Doges' Palace. In these paintings, the social function of establishing the viewer in relation to the desire of the Other stays the same, only here the fantasy shifts from paternal toward oligarchic organization. "What do the audiences see in these vast compositions? They see the gazes of those persons who, when the audiences are not there, deliberate in this hall."[45] In both cases, sublimation produces the fantasy of a particular, fundamental representation of social organization within the aesthetic space that these artifacts solicit.

In other words, the social value of sublimation is that it allows a group to sustain its sense of reality by reinstating desire and seeming to ignore this threatening Thing. But, as I keep suggesting, sublimation can serve a function that doesn't simply reinscribe group reality, a group's organization of desire. Sublimation also allows for the elaboration of a *jouissance* that serves no social function and about which society wants to know as little as possible. Take, for example, Caravaggio's *Victorious Cupid* and its companion piece, *The Sacrifice of Isaac*

(plates 2 and 3). (I say the two are companion pieces in part because in *The Sacrifice of Isaac*, Caravaggio uses the same boy model that he used in *Victorious Cupid*.) Caravaggio's Cupid straddles highly iconographic objects that signify the world of knowledge and power: astronomy (the globe with the stars on it), the military (the armor), intellectual production (the book and quill), kingship (the crown and scepter), and fame (the laurel wreath). But the straightforward signification supposedly promised by this iconographic mode is immediately complicated by the drape that, in partially covering certain objects and surely hiding others, turns them into objects of desire. The placement of this drape asks us to imagine even more objects of this world over which Cupid rules. Moreover, what invests or cathects these objects with a sense of desire is Cupid's pose. In this painting then, objects of power and knowledge do not shine with the lure of satisfaction *objectively;* they shine insofar as they are invested with the coyness encouraged by this boy's pose. That is, these objects of knowledge and power are invested with desire through the youthful male body. As with this painting's presentation of iconography, with Cupid's pose what might at first seem like straightforward exhibitionism turns quickly into a coy withdrawal. While the boy projects his right side forward, he withholds his left side, draws it back into the shadows, hiding his left arm and the lower half of his left leg, a dynamic of exhibitionism and withdrawal most forcefully located in his exhibited genitals and shadowy perineum.

It isn't just the pose, however, but also the status of Cupid as poser that emphasizes this dynamic. After all, this Cupid is not a celestial Cupid. Caravaggio paints him as a young boy dressed up as Cupid (note, for example, his dirty toenails)—a move that led Baglione to paint a rival *Divine Cupid* "in competition with [this] *Earthly Cupid* by Caravaggio," as Orazio Gentileschi explained in the famous trial of 1603.[46] Years later, still trying to contain and negate the "earthiness" of Caravaggio's Cupid, Baglione describes him as a Cupid who "subjugated the profane."[47] Rather than subjugating the profane, though, Caravaggio's boy dressed up as Cupid stands in as a metonymy of desire—as a metonymy that *is* desire—for profane, worldly objects.

And not just a desire for objects. Since this Cupid takes the same pose as does Michelangelo's St. Bartholomew in the Sistine Chapel, one could argue that Caravaggio's repetition attempts to recall a past

paganism supplanted by Christianity and thus that this painting reverses the familiar Christian topos. However, given the theatricality of Cupid's pose, I would suggest that the painting accomplishes something more radical. It creates a rift in that topos by inciting the desire for a history Christianity has prevented, and it does so precisely through the erotic and coy body of a contemporary boy. In other words, this young boy's pose forces an opening in a familiar Christian topos the effect of which is to incite the desire for a history of the flesh, a history of sex, a history that in the early seventeenth century has yet to be written.

Whereas *Victorious Cupid* uses visual metonymy to engage our desires for knowledge, power, and history through the youthful, theatrical male body, *The Sacrifice of Isaac* uses substitution to present us with a gap in knowledge, power, history. We can see this process in the two dominant movements of this painting. First of all, there is the downward motion from Abraham's arms to Isaac's head. The biblical narrative would encourage us to extend this movement so that it would culminate in the eagerly acquiescent ram in the painting's lower right-hand corner. As we know from Genesis, the angel prevents Abraham from sacrificing his son and has him sacrifice this ram in Isaac's stead. Certainly, the painting shows us the ram that will serve as Isaac's substitute. But between Isaac's head and the ram's neck this painting insists on a gap, a void of absolute darkness that momentarily interrupts the painting's otherwise smooth movement toward substitution. Second, there is the crosswise movement from the angel's finger to the city and lighted sky in the background (a background rarely found in Caravaggio's paintings). This movement suggests that civilization, in particular the generic representation of European civilization common to Italian Renaissance painting, is itself a substitute for the sacrifice that Abraham is about to enact. And this movement, too, is interrupted by a visual gap. The same darkness that separates Isaac's head from the ram's neck also separates the scene of sacrifice from the promised civilization that will come to replace it.

This painting thus presents substitutions that project forward in chronological time, attempting to secure the scene of Western European civilization in the background as the effect of what is enacted in the foreground. Nevertheless, through the fantasy scene that organizes the aesthetic communities the painting solicits, these very acts of sub-

stitution encourage us to see in the painting the presentation of a historical past. Not only do the relative positions of Abraham and Isaac
analogically suggest that this act of sacrifice is itself a substitute for
*coitus a tergo* between a man and a boy, but also, if we reverse the
movement that the painting encourages from Abraham to Isaac—
more specifically from Abraham's hands, one holding down his son,
the other holding a strikingly erect knife—the retroactive movement
in the cloaked and voided engagement between Abraham's lower front
and Isaac's lower rear suggests anal sex. When the angel grabs Abraham's arm and blocks the knife that he is about to use to slice his son's
neck, this prohibition strengthens the fantasy construction the poses
suggest. It is as if the angel were offering civilization and its sacrificial
economies instead of, as a replacement for, pederastic anal sex. In
effect, this painting introduces a schism in the Pauline historiography
that would have us understand the origin of Christianity in a conversion from Jewish carnality to Christian brotherhood. Through its
structuring of fantasy, this painting introduces an erotic, homosexual,
pederastic, and anal carnality *alongside* the Jews, which the angel of
God attempts to terminate.

We can, I think, draw an analogy here between the angel's voice
and the lute, L-square, and compass that Caravaggio's Victorious
Cupid *doesn't* straddle: the angel's voice, like music, allows us to enter a constructed space that attempts to avoid—to render unknown,
even—that other space between boys' legs. That is, both the angel
pointing to civilization and the Cupid not straddling musical instruments offer us an opposition between the constructed and aestheticized space of civilization on the one hand and the fantasmic scene
of pederastic anal sex on the other. What renders this opposition dynamic is the history *The Sacrifice of Isaac* isolates and the desire for
history the *Victorious Cupid* incites. Taken together, these two paintings introduce a conceptual difference into the carnality that is for
post-Pauline Christianity the fleshy embodiment of the Jew, give historical priority to this difference, and encode it through the fantasy of
anal sex. To the extent that Caravaggio's *Cupid* coyly and erotically
imposes the history to which *The Sacrifice of Isaac* points, another
name for it might be *The Angel of History*.

Please understand, though: I do not with any certainty take this
fantasy scene to be the unconscious articulation of Caravaggio's sexual

experiences. To do so would be both misleading and, finally I think, irrelevant. I do, however, take this fantasy to be the primal scene of Caravaggio's boy-paintings, the primal scene of the social and theatrical space of desire that these boy-paintings establish. To put it bluntly, this scene of pederastic anal sex *is* the social fantasy that Caravaggio's aesthetic assumes.

Remember that for psychoanalysis fantasy isn't the space of wish fulfillment, the scene in which we imagine our desires to be fulfilled. On the contrary, fantasy is the scene that stages our desires as such, and that in the process represents the barriers to *jouissance* that constitute the subject as split. To this extent, fantasy allows a group to keep the Thing at bay. But in this act of representation, the subject establishes a relation with the *objet a* as surplus enjoyment. Hence, the importance for psychoanalysis of the construction of the fantasy scene: this construction allows us to specify the coordinates of our desire, the relation of our desire to its object-cause. The purpose of fantasy construction is to locate this *objet a* by reading in the habitual posturing of desire a relation to the drive toward *jouissance* that endless desiring unwittingly satisfies. To underscore this function, Lacan designates fantasy with the following equation: $\$ \diamondsuit a$, the subject in some relation to the object-cause of desire. The psychoanalytic point of constructing fantasy is to effect its reversal, to foreground the object-cause of desire in relation to the subject's willful misapprehension of it: $a \diamondsuit \$$.

To stop analysis here would be, basically, to reinvest authority in the fantasy about which the subjects of Caravaggio's early boy-paintings want not to know. In order to effect a reversal of the fantasy scene of pederastic anal sex that we see in *The Sacrifice of Isaac*, we must understand that the acts of substitution by which this fantasy is constructed make fantasy itself a screen that sustains subjects' desires. But in its particularity, this fantasy also demonstrates a repeated relation to surplus enjoyment that the solicited subjects of Caravaggio's paintings enact in endless attempts to grab hold of whatever these paintings encourage us to think we want. This fantasy may or may not tell some truth about Caravaggio, but it does stage for us in a precise and specific form a barrier to *jouissance* around which the Caravaggian aesthetic is formed. If the knife is a substitute for the penis with which Abraham is (not, as it ends up) about to puncture his son, then Isaac's open mouth stands most forcefully as a substitute for the gaping darkness that blurs the engagement of Isaac's rear and Abraham's lower front. This open mouth is not some metonym for the practice of pederastic anal sex that has been substituted out of consciousness into fantasy. Rather, sexual fantasy, as a model for aesthetic practice, stands in relation to an object that opens up onto a void. To this extent, Isaac's open mouth operates as what Tim Dean, following Catherine Clément, calls a syncope, an obfuscation in an aesthetic *and* sexual field of desire that, in introducing an ego-annihilating *jouissance,* has the potential to change that ego's relation both to itself and to group formation.[48] This open mouth serves as a kind of erotic ex nihilo around which history happens. In *The Sacrifice of Isaac,* this syncope doesn't continue to sustain us in an inarticulate desire for knowledge. Instead, it reveals emptiness as the emptiness for which voice as *objet a* previously stood. I should add that this presentation of emptiness doesn't make things any more comfortable. After all, when it comes down to it, anal sex isn't that scary; opening up onto a void that threatens corporeality, that divests the body of its meaningfulness, at least potentially is.

## Traversing History through Paint

There's no pretense in Caravaggio's paintings that masculinity exists outside fields of desire, history, and the logics of civility. But by putting masculine posing in relation to the voice as *objet a,* Caravaggio is able to open a gap in the desire for an aestheticized and civilized masculine community. He is able to open a moment of unknowingness upon which that community's epistemological formation depends. Rather than filling out this epistemological void with something meaningful, though, rather than filling out this void with some narrative that takes the role of master-narrative, some history that turns into History, Caravaggio's later paintings substantiate the unknowingness that results from obscuring the voice as *objet a* in the libidinality of paint.[49]

This libidinal substantiality of paint makes a double mark: It marks Caravaggio's traversal of the identificatory mechanisms of Renaissance aesthetics and, in effect, "presentifies" the voice as *objet a* around which the space of spectatorship in his paintings is formed. In the same gesture, it also translates unknowingness—primarily a form of

temporality—into a local logic of self-representation that particular-
izes the opening of history that Caravaggio's paintings engage. Since
this voice as *objet a* serves as a future contingent that exceeds the positing of any community, the force of particularization is in no way
salvific. It makes no pretenses toward transcending history.

We can see these two moves in Caravaggio's *David with the Head of
Goliath* (plate 4). Given the parallel movements of David's left arm
and his sword, one might argue that this painting presents us with a
young boy whose pose brags about his having evaded the cut of castration. It is as if, by taking this pose, David were announcing that in
beheading the Philistine giant who threatened to subject all the men
of Israel, he has supplanted Goliath's hyper-masculinity without sacrificing his own youth. *Who cares*, the nonchalance of the sword's placement suggests, *if the sword comes so close to my penis? I already have
the phallus.* Certainly, this interpretation follows the nationalist and
masculinist movement of the biblical narrative. You will remember that before slaying Goliath, David was the "well spoken, good-
looking" young harpist whose music soothed Saul whenever he was
plagued by evil spirits (1 Sam 16:14–23). It is only after the slaying of
Goliath that David gains Jonathan's love, becomes the object of Saul's
intense envy, and sets out on the road that will eventually lead him to
become Israel's popular warrior king. Having evaded castration, David poses as if on the way to becoming what the history of the Hebrew
nation will have him be.

But there is more to this painting than that. There is also the dark
void out of which David emerges to pose as an emblem of imaginary
masculine wholeness. This void isn't simply the space in which David
fought Goliath, the space in which David cut off Goliath's head. Indeed, this void literally avoids that historical space with the darkness
of paint, signaling something more horrible than even beheading,
*more unspeakable* than even castration. Compare this painting with
the more generic representations of David and Goliath—for example,
Pesellino's *Story of David and Goliath*; or the representation of the
story in Ghiberti's ninth panel for the third door of San Giovanni; or
even Michelangelo's painting of David beheading Goliath in the Sistine Chapel. In each of these examples, the function of the background
is to work in tandem with the pose in the foreground in order to give
the story of David slaying Goliath its historical fullness. By contrast,

in Caravaggio's painting the dark void of the background creates an opening in the historical narrative. To attempt to say exactly what the background is would simply situate us once more at the position of the virtual "you" solicited by *The Lute Player*. We would find ourselves again identifying with the inexpressible, the absent voice as desire's objective, not its cause.

But, as it ends up, this painting does not encourage that identification. Rather, *David with the Head of Goliath* shows us what we cannot say as paint. First, by reiterating the darkness of the background in Goliath's open mouth in the foreground, this painting identifies the absent voice of the earlier boy-paintings with the void from which masculine posing emerges. And second, this painting presentifies this absent voice in the substance of paint. When David thrusts the severed head into the foreground, he shows an absent voice that traces out the hostile, alien, and overpowering Thing.

In a sense, *David with the Head of Goliath* accomplishes a historiographic move similar to that of *The Sacrifice of Isaac*. Both paintings portray a certain carnality in their representations of stories from the Hebrew Bible, though neither locates this carnality in the ethnicity of the Jews, as Paul does. Instead, these two paintings each translate that carnality into an eccentric eroticism about which the spectator can say nothing meaningful. The difference between the two paintings is that in *David with the Head of Goliath* Caravaggio also substantiates carnality as paint. When David displays the sullen head, red paint oozes out of the structural muteness of the menacing Thing. This paint *is* the substantiation of voice metastasized on the canvas.

Doubtless, this is a standard move in Caravaggio's beheading paintings. In *Judith Beheading Holofernes* and in *Medusa* as well, the open mouth signals an absent voice, cut off by the act of decapitation, that materializes on the canvas as red, splattered paint (figs. 14 and 15). Only in the *David with the Head of Goliath*, the red paint is precisely what engages David, what *appeals* to him, in the moment of his showy pose. Note David's red ear: it's the same red as the paint that drops from Goliath's neck. It is precisely the materiality of this voice—and not its significance—that appeals to David, that demands his attention, that catches his ear.

If Caravaggio's interest in the theatrical space of the pose is that, when the body is posed, something escapes and slips out, then in this

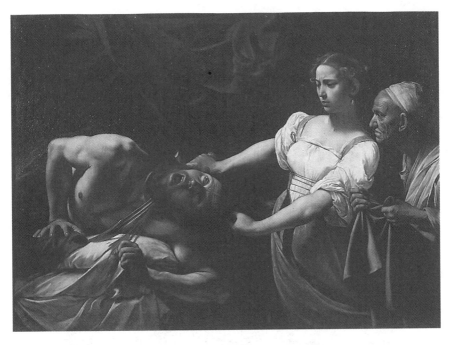

Fig. 14. Caravaggio, *Judith Beheading Holofernes*. Galleria Nazionale
dell'Arte Antica, Rome. Photo: Art Resource.

painting we can say that this something returns, appeals, and trans-
fixes the body of the posed boy. If this something were only a gap,
then David could simply avoid it with imaginary identifications—so
many masculine poses. But in its substantiality, this something opens
up a rift in the imaginary universe of "civilized" masculinity. It sub-
stantializes the threats to imaginary masculinity in something other
than castration. It grounds these threats in paint.[50]

To put it differently, this painting shifts economies. We move from
narrative, a choice of meaning and history, to the drive and *jouissance,*
a choice of being. As I have argued, the poses in Caravaggio's early
boy-paintings work to solicit a viewer who takes these poses as significant, a viewer who supposes these posed boys know something
meaningful about desire that we ourselves can't articulate. But if
choosing meaning is a strategy to keep the Thing at bay, then drive is
the mechanism that brings it back, that lets the Thing rematerialize,
metastasized as paint, as a consistent and agitated imposition that disturbs this choice of narrative meaning and history.

Fig. 15. Caravaggio, *Medusa*. Uffizi, Florence. Photo: Art Resource.

As a substance, paint stands in as the *jouissance* that serves no function, that short-circuits an aesthetic community based on *istoria*, narrative, history. To whom is this *jouissance* addressed? It may appeal to some, catch the ears of others, but fundamentally it can be addressed to no one at all. This is not to imply that Caravaggio's paintings attempt to be ahistorical. Far from it: these paintings are deeply historical, but in a way that is radically oriented toward the future. And they will remain so as long as we can watch in them the elaboration around this useless *jouissance* of an ethic that drains the body of its narrativized and grand historical significance.

As a kind of coda, let me point out that at the end of a Lacanian psychoanalysis, this *jouissance* becomes, oddly enough, the site of

Fig. 16. Caravaggio, *The Beheading of St. John*. Pro-Cathedral of Saint John the Baptist, La Valletta, Malta. Photo: Art Resource.

identification. Against the notion that analysis should end either with an introjection of the analyst's supposedly healthy ego or with an acceptance of Freud's infamous "bedrock" of castration,[51] Lacan argues that throughout analysis the analyst must embody the *objet a* in its ectopic distance from the idealized positions of knowingness that the analysand demands the analyst incarnate. "It is from this idealized identification that the analyst has to fall, . . . crossing the plane of identification" until the analysand comes to recognize the particular surplus enjoyment that her or his fantasy has repeatedly attempted to screen out.[52] In so doing, the analyst allows the analysand to recognize this surplus enjoyment not behind but *on* the screen of the fantasy. The analyst introduces a piece of the Thing back into the symbolic order so that the analysand can traverse fantasy as an organizer of desire and begin to experience it as a way to make present the drive against which it has hitherto defended.

For Caravaggio, this crossing translates the historical opening produced by his paintings into an identificatory logic that situates the aestheticized body in relation to a violence of representation. As is well known, the head of Goliath that David shows us is Caravaggio's self-portrait. And if, as critics have noted, the letters on David's sword that read M A C O stand for *Michel Angelo Caravaggio Opus*, then we could speculate that the sword suggests the work of painting cuts the painter from his body, turns him into paint.[53] What Caravaggio's self-portrait as Goliath realizes is that the painter doesn't have the voice either. The substantialized voice also oozes from his own neck. But rather than sustaining a relation to the ex nihilo of history, this painting translates that ex nihilo into a point of identification. Caravaggio presents himself as senseless paint, specifically as paint trapped in the body of a man. To support this interpretation, let me conclude by pointing to just one more painting: *The Beheading of St. John* (fig. 16). Notice the old woman standing above the younger woman who is holding the platter. She's looking at the act of beheading and covering her ears, preventing herself from hearing some obscene noise that doesn't seem to bother anyone else. In 1955 and 1956, when this painting was restored, an obtrusive detail came to light. The blood pouring out of St. John's neck turns into Caravaggio's signature. It is the only painting that Caravaggio ever signed.

# "The Forme of Faustus Fortunes": Knowledge, Spectatorship, and the Body in Marlowe's *Doctor Faustus*

❦

## Malediction and Jurisprudence

In this chapter, I shall argue two theses about Marlowe's *Doctor Faustus*. The first concerns the play's thinking about the literary. When in 1927 T. S. Eliot asserted that the blasphemy so crucial to Marlowe's work necessarily implies some sort of belief (a felicitous link of signs with what they signify, as C. L. Barber put it in 1964), Eliot quite perspicuously located the stakes of Marlowe's play. However, in a fashion perhaps to be expected, he also contained what is most disturbing about that insight.[1] Specifically, in asserting that this blasphemy implies and is contained by Christian belief, Eliot could not recognize that Faustus's blasphemy develops a sense of language that completely reformulates theological belief. Hence, my first thesis: What makes the *Tragicall History of the Life and Death of Doctor Faustus* tragical is less Faustus's renunciation of God and pact with Lucifer than the relation it establishes between Faustus and the literary, a relation that makes the literary, as the site of what Eliot calls blasphemy, tragically inescapable. My second thesis is that, in its reformulation of theological belief, this literary language develops the grounds for sexual knowledge. *Doctor Faustus* is, I shall argue, inextricably bound to a hermeneutics of sodomy. Stephen Greenblatt has argued that Marlowe's fictions "echo in the void" with both a "playful energy" and a "haunting sense of unsatisfied longing," and Jonathan Goldberg, with a great deal of panache, has argued that what gives name to this void is sodomy.[2] In what follows, I shall argue that this void-as-sodomy is the mediating force for the forms of relatedness that *Doctor Faustus* posits—not just

relations between characters on stage but more forcefully relations between the play and the modes of spectatorship that it solicits and produces.

What I mean by the literary is a language that is performative, a
language based neither on a one-to-one correspondence between
words and things (what Sidney, for example, thinks of as the language
of historians) nor on a one-to-one correspondence between words
and concepts (what Sidney thinks of as the language of philosophers).
As Sidney puts it, the poet "nothing affirms, and therefore never lieth."
To put it less tersely and more prosaically, literary language simply
cannot be judged by the protocols of referentiality. Sidney writes, "We
see we cannot play at Chesse but that wee must giue names to our
Chesse-men; and yet, mee thinks, hee were a very partiall Champion
of truth that would say we lyed for giuing a peece of wood the reuer-
end title of a Bishop."[3] What distinguishes literary language are the
modes of recognition that it posits, modes that assume a sense of *disbelief,* which nonliterary language attempts to suspend. "What child
is there," Sidney famously and quite cagily asks, "that, coming to a
play, and seeing Thebes written in great letters upon an old door, doth
believe that it is Thebes?" Over and against the apparent intentions of
Sidney's speaker, this question points to a dynamic relation between
two modes of recognition. To see the sign "Thebes" in a theater is both
to know that you are not in Thebes and to suspend that knowledge, *to
act as if* you do not know that you are not in Thebes. Moreover, since
the stage-prop sign "Thebes" itself is the precondition for the dynamic
relations that emerge between the sustainment and suspension of disbelief, it points to textuality, to what Joel Fineman calls the "lan-
guageness of language," as an emblem that allows for the sustainment
of disbelief over and against the suspension that Sidney's apparently
intentional version of spectatorship demands.[4] That is, Sidney's example invests textuality with an emblematic capacity to unravel the
suspension of disbelief by which a theatrical epistemology of spectatorship is sustained.

Act 3 of *Doctor Faustus* gives an example of this suspension and
sustainment of disbelief in relation to language when Faustus, on stage
supposedly invisible, beats the pope's friars while they attempt to exorcise him by saying the *maledictat dominus.* Because Faustus continues to beat the friars even after they say the *maledictat dominus,* the

play demonstrates the performative force of this phrase over and against its magical, ritual function. That is, Faustus's comic violence demonstrates that the phrase itself is not invested with the protective power of some extraliterary signified assumed by the friars. Rather, the phrase has a protective power only because the friars can suspend a prior disbelief that the phrase as theatrical utterance assumes. One could argue that this example only serves to prove Faustus's evil—his ability to counter the magic of the *maledictat dominus* with his own demonic magic—except that in the scene (in the B-text) immediately following, when Robin calls forth Mephostophilis, he uses a bastard-ized Latin, *O per se, o,* mocking Faustus's incantations in act 1.[5] If the *maledictat dominus* is not invested with the power of the signified, neither is the language that Faustus uses to call forth Mephostophilis. Neither Faustus's incantations nor Robin's *O per se, o* call forth Meph-ostophilis because they are invested with power from some evil signi-fied. These words call forth Mephostophilis because of Robin's and Faustus's suspension of disbelief.

But I do not want to suggest that the play's thinking about the liter-ary and its positing of an epistemological situation is somehow simply a matter of how language de facto works. After all, in this example, how language works is also historically situated. The divestment of the authority of ritual performance and concurrent investment of the force of textuality that *Doctor Faustus* presents in part repeats Protes-tantism's iconoclastic breaking of Catholic control. In the above ex-ample, the relation between Catholic authority and Faustus to some extent repeats the relation that John Foxe proposes in *Acts and Monu-ments* between Catholic authority and his own historical project. In his dedicatory letter to Queen Elizabeth, Foxe asserts that the Roman Church has denied history through what amounts to the manipula-tion of the literary and of theatrical performance. The Catholics, who "altogether delight in untruths, . . . have replenished the whole church of Christ with feigned fables, lying miracles, false visions, and miser-able errors, contained in their missals, portuses, breviaries, and sum-maries, and almost no true tale in all their saints' lives . . . ; yet not-withstanding, as though they were a people of much truth, and that the world did not perceive them, they pretend a face of zeal and great verity."[6] For Foxe, writing the history of Protestant martyrs divests the Catholic Church of its disingenuous, theatrical authority by proving the "difference between the Church of Rome that now is, and the ancient Church of Rome that then was" (*AM*, 1:2) in the very vituperation of the Church when confronted with its own internal contradiction.[7] Addressing the Catholic Church, Foxe writes, "Behold your own handy work! consider the number, almost out of number, of so many silly and simple lambs of Christ, whose blood you have sought and sucked; whose lives you have vexed; whose bodies you have slain, racked, and tormented. . . . ; whose wounds, yet bleeding before the face of God, cry vengeance! . . . See therefore, I say—read, and behold your acts and facts; and when you have seen, then judge what you have deserved" (1:xii). Through its assertions of the literary, *Doctor Faustus* too insists on the contradiction upon which an authority whose force is ritual depends, and the play also tends to locate that contradiction through aggression. However, *Doctor Faustus* isn't simply a Protestant version of, say, the mid-sixteenth-century pro-Catholic play *Respublica*. Instead of simply repeating Protestantism's iconoclastic gesture as a reversal of Catholic satire or saint's life, *Doctor Faustus* reoccupies the position afforded by this iconoclastic gesture in its relation to worldly authority, formally repeating Protestantism's functional power relation to Catholicism, but also effectively asserting a sense of literariness and its concomitant modes of recognition.

At stake in this reoccupation is the body. As Calvin points out, the central issue of idolatry is always the flesh: "Daily experience teaches that the flesh is always uneasy until it has obtained some figment like itself in which it may fondly find solace as an image of God."[8] For Paul, idolatry is an externalization of the "unclean" lusts of the heart, an egoistic projection that offers the heart a "foolish" comfort whose backlash formation is self-defilement and the defilement of others: "[T]hei turned the glorie of the incorruptible God to the similitude of the image of a corruptible man. . . . Wherefore also God gaue them up to their hearts lustes, unto unclenes, to defile their owne bodies betwene themselves" (Rom. 1:21–24).[9] *The Acts and Monuments* extends this logic of idolatry and the flesh, asserting a history of the tormented, vexed, and martyred flesh as proof, if not symptom, of Catholic authority's constitutive idolatry. *Doctor Faustus* does not simply repeat this hatred and distrust of the flesh. Rather, reconfiguring the body through a hermeneutics of disbelief, the play develops a sense of corporeality split between the performative body and the textualized flesh.

In *Doctor Faustus,* the assertion of literary modes of recognition and the concurrent development of corporeality are underwritten by Tudor sodomy laws. When the Parliament of 1533–34 passed its "act for the punishment of the vice of buggerie," it claimed ecclesiastical jurisdiction to prosecute sodomy in order to turn that jurisdiction against the authority of the Catholic Church. As Bruce Smith has noted, this statute "is carefully worded so as to exclude 'benefit of clergy,' an ability to read Latin, as a means of escaping punishment."[10] Once sodomy was under the jurisdiction of civil law, it became possible for Henry VIII to produce the scandal of this clerical vice as an ideological cover—one among many—for the dissolution of the monasteries. But when in 1563 Elizabeth's Parliament reinstated the Henrician act—after its alteration by Edward VI and repeal by Mary—its justification wasn't even implicitly a local politics. Instead it carried the necessity of moral law: "Sithens which Repeale so hadd and made dyvers evyll disposed persons have been the more bolde to comitt the said most horrible and detestable Vice of Buggerie."[11] As Goldberg explains, because sodomy has no clear referent but instead enforces an epistemological communality in which "we" all "know" what "it" means, once the adjudication of sodomy comes under civil jurisdiction, sodomy comes to locate the place where the disciplinary power of law gives way to a mesh of social forces. Hence, the sodomitical is both the place of extraordinary possibility as well as the place of raw injustice.[12] Indeed, I shall argue that, through its relation to the literary, *Doctor Faustus* responds to this potentiality by positing forms of judgment—kinds of aesthetic and imprudent jurisprudence—that can read the sodomitical outside the disciplinary strictures of law but within aesthetic expressions of form.

Before I begin my argument proper, though, I wish to put forth three hypotheses about this literary language and its relations to disbelief and to material culture:

1. *What Doctor Faustus proposes as literary language is unthinkable without books, writing, and print culture.* In the diegesis of the play, Faustus's renunciation of God is prompted by the reading of books. "Negromantike bookes are heauenly" (78), Faustus says, establishing

a seeming paradox in which necromantic books are signified by precisely their opposite, "heauenly." When, before turning to necromantic books, he renounces theological interpretation ("What doctrine
call you this? *Che sera, sera:* / What wil be, shall be? Diuinitie, adieu"
[75–76]) and later charges that hell is nothing more than a literary
genre ("I thinke hell's a fable" [559]), in effect Faustus renounces the
primacy of the signified in favor of a world that emphasizes metaphor
and making. Even if Faustus's announcement that "negromantike
bookes are heauenly" implies some sort of belief, "negromantike
bookes" cannot be contained by the Good Angel's subsequent advice,
"[L]ay that damned booke aside. . . . Reade, reade the scriptures, that
is blasphemy" (98, 101). What Faustus has read cannot be contained
because once he renounces the seemingly obvious and straightforward signified that necromantic books call forth, he becomes so powerfully committed to the literary that he cannot escape its hold, even
when, after exhausting all other possibilities, he cries somewhat belat-
edly, "Ile burne my bookes" (1477).

However, I do not want to suggest that books and, more generally,
print culture somehow drained theological substance and alienated
readers from theological meaning. Books, writing, and print culture
do not here serve as a historical cause of so-called secularization; they
serve instead as a means of comprehension offered by a social imaginary. In this social imaginary, the suspension of disbelief that literary
language asserts appears—but only appears—to depend on a fairly
rigid shift from oral performance to written performative.

2. *The shift that literary language asserts may be used to encode social
and historical change, but more significantly, it is also a way to think the
body as a device for communication.* Here, I rely on the interdepen-
dence that Harry Berger, Jr., finds between a communication shift and
a semiotic shift. Berger argues for a heuristic scheme in which changes
in media directly affect the production of surplus meaning, or "meaning unbound by intention." Berger argues that the superimposition of
the written performative onto oral performance "progressively broad-
ens the range of communication and extends its power, but at the
same time it progressively abstracts the means of production from the
control of the body and thus alienates the production of meaning." [13]
This abstraction from means of production ultimately to modes of
recognition and valuation, characterized as it is by shifts in communi-

cations media, is precisely what allows for suspension of disbelief in an oral performance that appears both more confined and less alienated than the written performative. To put the point a different way, Faustus begins with a textual exegesis that makes any movement back toward an authoritative diegesis impossible because his world has been reterritorialized by the regime of the book. Instead, I shall argue, Faustus moves toward a sexuality unbound by intention.

3. *In a world of literary language, all kinds of objects—including Faustus's soul—become signs of disbelief.* Literary language—a language that is performative and that relies on the suspension of disbelief—is the condition for the transformation of objects into commodities. This relation between commodification and a mode of representation is perhaps best expressed by a detour through Elaine Scarry's *The Body in Pain.* In discussing the Old Testament God in his relation to the bodies of the Hebrew people, Scarry argues that "the agonizing labor of sustaining belief (that is, sustaining over endless days the unobjectified mental object of imagining within one's own psyche) is modified by the external existence of material and verbal artifacts that themselves take over the substantiating function of the sentient body." Hence, the extraordinary investment among the Hebrews in objects (especially the altar, the well, and the pain and suffering of the body) that appear to substantiate (literally, offer the material that gives body to) a disembodied deity of their own making.[14] For a discussion of the Renaissance, I would emend Scarry's sentence to read as follows: "The agonizing labor of *suspending disbelief* modifies the external existence of material and verbal artifacts." Think back to Sidney's chess piece: naming that object a "bishop" underscores the difference between the name and the object and, in so doing, underscores naming as a mode of representation. While sustaining belief in what cannot be seen intensifies relations between believers and the material world, suspending disbelief both deintensifies and re-encodes the objects of that world, making these objects both fetishistic and what Douglas Bruster calls "objects of farce."[15] Literary language is the apparatus upon which this latter process depends.

## Faustus, Form, and Subjectivity

To say that Faustus cannot escape the literary is to say that Faustus is a subject of literariness, as the opening lines of the play insist. The play begins with a Chorus that comes on stage to announce what the play is not about:

> Not marching in the fields of Tracimene
> Where Mars did mate the warlike Carthaginians,
> Nor sporting in the dalliance of loue,
> In courts of Kings where state is ouerturnd,
> Nor in the pompe of prowd audacious deedes,
> Intends our Muse to vaunt his heauenly verse:
> Onely this (Gentles), we must now performe,
> The forme of Faustus fortunes good or bad.
>
>                                              (1–8)

The forms that the Chorus announces as *not* being the setting of the play are rendered indeterminate by what does get performed in them. In the formal setting of the military "fields of Tracimene," the troops perform not fighting but mating;[16] in the formal setting of courtly "dalliance," not love but political upheaval is enacted; and finally, although not in the formal, pompous setting in which proud and audacious deeds are usually performed, "our Muse" nonetheless vaunts the play *Doctor Faustus*.[17] In each case, the performance of the form differs from the form itself.[17] This is also the case with Faustus himself. Because the Chorus renders the performance of Faustus's fortunes *either* good *or* bad, we know that Faustus (whose name in Latin means "the fortunate one") gets his being, as it were, when his name becomes a signifier for another signifier, "good or bad," and not for the signified "fortunate." That is, rather than giving stable value or meaning to the name "Faustus," in the prologue fortune is valued as possibility, "good or bad."[18] Because the opening of the play announces possibility as the ground of subjectivity, because this possibility is expressed in and given form by a language that tends to eschew simple referentiality, the character Faustus cannot be understood as a simple, allegorical instantiation of a particular virtue or meaning. Instead, he must be understood through the difference that inheres in the relation of his name to itself.[19] When Faustus bids *on cai me on* farewell (Greek: being and non-being), in effect he renounces an entire philosophical tradition in which particular beings are nourished through the contemplation of being itself. Perhaps most striking about Marlowe's play, though, is the way that Faustus's renunciation fails. The play reabsorbs the question of being that Faustus renounces within the domain of the literary in such a way that being de facto becomes eccentric to meaning. If, as Thomas Aquinas asserts (in almost commonplace philosophical fashion), form is the principle of being, then in *Doctor Faustus* performativity is the form of a being that is always someplace else.[20]

In a certain sense, then, *Doctor Faustus* assumes the character of Vice from late medieval drama as its figure for literary subjectivity. However, to say this is not to say enough, for the performativity of language locates the being of subjectivity in the objects to which this being is attached. In the B-text, Adrian asserts his proper and orthodoxical right to be pope instead of Bruno, the nominee of the Holy Roman Emperor, by raising a question, "Is not all power on earth bestowed on vs?" (B-text, 952). The answer that he gives immediately thereafter not only assumes that the question is a rhetorical one, that the answer is always and already yes; it also demonstrates the rhetorical mechanism by which orthodoxy operates. Adrian responds to his question as if it had already been answered: "And therefore tho we would we cannot erre" (B-text, 953). Instead of answering the question "Is not all power on earth bestowed on vs," Adrian makes clear the circular logic of orthodoxical propriety. Because he is the pope, he cannot err. Any mistake that he makes is always and already not a mistake because he is vested with "all power on earth." Thus, when he claims to be the pope, he cannot be wrong (even if, indeed, he is wrong) because he is the pope. As John Foxe writes, "[T]he pope, under hypocrisy, maketh a face of the spiritual sword, which is the word of God; but, in very deed, doeth all things with the temporal sword; that is, with outward forcement and coaction" (*AM*, 1:58). In its hypocrisy, papal authority works solely by force of will, even as it pretends otherwise.

While revealing the performativity and undermining the inherence of his claim to the papacy, Adrian's tautology does not guarantee his being pope. Rather, Adrian's claim to have a felicitous relation with the signified that would secure his apostolic authority is supposedly guaranteed by the showing of certain objects: "Behold this Siluer Belt whereto is fixt / Seuen golden seales fast sealed with seuen seales" (B-text, 954–55). He argues that he can be the signifier that stands under the signified "seuen-fold power from heauen" (B-text, 956) because he wears the objects that traditionally and symbolically guarantee this position. However, since the signifier of the signified "seuen-fold power from heauen" is precisely what the play has put into question by having two contenders for the papacy, Adrian's recourse to these objects only serves to underscore the rhetorical force of his assertion. Being pope does not just mean ignoring any evidence to the contrary since, as it ends up, all evidence is already potentially to the contrary. Much more forcefully, being pope means having one's being staked in objects that could, potentially, also be one's undoing.

Adrian's assertion reveals, first, that the logic of orthodoxy can appear logical only insofar as it literally excommunicates, suspends, or renders silent any disbelief in the authority of that orthodoxy. Second, this argument reveals that disbelief is logically prior to belief. In order to make the argument that he is the signifier of the signified "seuen-fold power from heauen," Adrian must suspend disbelief by making his question "Is not all power on earth bestowed on vs?" into one that is purely rhetorical. In the process, Adrian proposes a temporal structure that itself assumes (even as it dismisses) the possibility of disbelief: "And therefore tho we would we cannot erre." Third, and finally, the failure of Adrian's rhetorical claims to produce as anything other than rhetorical the signified that would prove him pope results in certain objects, specifically his belt and its trappings, standing in as evidence that guarantees apostolic authority. These objects do not evidence clear and perspicuous ontological propriety, however. Instead, they underscore the rhetorical nature of Adrian's claims even as they stand in as evidence that attempts to guarantee the signified that proves him pope. The play makes this point most powerfully with the "triple Dyadem" (B-text, 981) that Adrian takes from Bruno, only to have Faustus and Mephostophilis, dressed like cardinals, steal it. The very object that should stand as perspicuous and determinate evidence of who is pope is instead caught within a network of theft and fraudulence so intricate that the object cannot indicate its proper owner. That is, the crown can be taken as an ontological indicator of its proper owner only on the condition that one ignores the fraudulence of the network in which it emerges as property.

To the orthodoxy that maintains itself by suspending disbelief, the play puts forth a heterodoxy that operates by sustaining the disbelief that orthodoxy attempts to suspend. For example, in one of the comic scenes, Faustus sells a horse to a horse courser with the warning that the horse courser must not ride the horse into the water. The courser, "thinking some hidden mystery had beene in the horse" (B-text, 1138–39), rides the horse into the water, after which the horse disappears. Faustus plays a joke on the horse courser very much like the famous Jewish joke that Freud tells in *Jokes and Their Relation to the Unconscious,* in which one Jew says to another, "I am going to Cracow." The other Jew responds, "If you say you're going to Cracow, you want me to believe you're going to Lemberg. But I know that in fact you're going to Cracow. So why are you lying to me?"[21] Like the Jew going to Cracow, Faustus tricks his interlocutor not by lying, but by telling the truth. Telling the truth does not prove Faustus to be a truth teller; rather, it demonstrates that because words can mean something different than what they say, they can appear to convey a hidden meaning, a mystery that, once revealed, disappears. Thus, while the heterodoxical assumption of "some hidden mystery" belies the ontological propriety of the orthodoxical "always already," by definition the heterodoxical can in no way become an orthodoxy (an insight crucial to *The Jew of Malta,* which begins with Barabas wishing for "Christian Kings, / That thirst so much for Principality" [1.1.172–73] and ends with Barabas's downfall, which occurs only after he is made governor of Malta). If, as William Empson has argued, Marlowe makes the improper, "the unmentionable sin for which the punishment is death," into "*the proper thing to do,*" then *Doctor Faustus* is perhaps the most improper (and, therefore, proper) of Marlowe's plays, because it is marked by the failure of the improper to sustain its most powerful function—its ability to destabilize and disrupt.[22] To be sure, in *Doctor Faustus* the improper is the trope for the proper, but the proper must maintain its propriety for the improper to work.

Because the trope for the proper is the improper, the maintenance of an orthodox signified is nothing more (or less) than a desire for a signified. This desire includes Faustus's turn to magic. Although the play begins with Faustus's renunciation of the signified, being "glutted" with the signified is exactly what Faustus wants, to be "swolne with cunning, of a selfe conceit" (20), which would, as Faustus says, "[r]esolue me of all ambiguities" (108). Faustus would be an instantiation of a signified whose significance he would subsequently act out, were it not for the fact that every potential signified that Faustus

considers (logic, medicine, law, and theology) is marked by insufficiency. When Faustus chooses necromantic books as what he "most
desires"—"Lines, circles, sceanes, letters, and characters" (79–80) that
will resolve him of ambiguities—he unwittingly chooses signifiers
whose materiality mark his desire for a signified as his own ontological insufficiency. Hence, when Faustus answers Cornelius's question,
"What shal we three want?" by saying "Nothing Cornelius. O this
cheares my soule" (177–78), that answer can be taken as a desire to
be fully satisfied. At the same time, it must also be taken as an affirmation that this desire for full satisfaction results in an ontological
emptiness that is nonetheless quite material. The character O that interrupts the purely blissful "nothing" that Faustus cheerfully anticipates is itself a material manifestation of the nothingness that Faustus
gets. Toward the end of the play, right before Faustus dies, one of
the Scholars comments on his melancholy, "tis but a surffet sir, feare
nothing" (B-text, 1366), to which Faustus answers, "A surffet of deadly
sinne that hath damnd both body and soule" (1367). Immediately
thereafter, Faustus locates the cause of this surfeit of nothing within
the domain of the literary: "O would I had neuer seen Wertenberge,
neuer read booke" (1376–77). In desiring to be glutted by the signified, Faustus becomes nothing in the same way that the horse courser's
"hidden mystery" becomes nothing once revealed. Because it is governed by signifiers and not by a signified, the literary always promises
more and delivers less.

The formal, political heterodoxy belies the fullness but not the materiality of the ontological object once Faustus's desires are constrained and determined by the literary. Michael Goldman makes a
similar point in his discussion of what he calls Marlowe's "histrionics
of ravishment":

> Initially, Marlowe's heroes present themselves to us as ravished by
> referring to an object, a prop, to which they transmit their energy
> of impersonation and from which, in turn, they receive further
> energy. . . . At the same time, however, the hero further defines
> himself in some sense by rejecting the prop. The prop is a source
> of bliss, but it is also—in some part or aspect—trash. Out of this
> double-valued attack on the prop emerges the audience's sense of
> character as definite . . . intensely appetitive, restlessly in motion,
> both in love with, and curiously out of, this world.[23]

Insofar as the double valuation of this object in *Doctor Faustus* relies on the uncanny relation between orthodoxy and heterodoxy, what gives Faustus a sense of being is the object around which the form of his fortune is performed. If there is, as the play asserts, "danger in words" (1262), it is not exactly because words can be "anagrammatiz'd" (243), because, as Marjorie Garber puts it, words can "go either way."[24] The danger of words is that, in going either way, words cathect an object that indicates the place of being around which subjectivity arises.

In *Doctor Faustus,* the performativity of a heterodoxical difference that inheres in and speaks against an orthodox form is put forth as a critical issue of audience reception. The play constructs two audiences. When Faustus comes on stage to mock the pope's "solemne festiuall" (B-text, 1034), Mephostophilis has rendered him invisible "[t]hat no eye may [his] body see" (B-text, 1025). Either Faustus cannot be seen, in which case an audience can come into being as an audience who suspends disbelief by not seeing what is so obviously there, or Faustus can be seen by an audience who sustains disbelief on the condition of being "no eye," of coming into being through negation around ontological emptiness.

The Chorus explicitly makes this issue of reception a problem. Faustus returns home, having "with pleasure tane the view / Of rarest things" (905–6), and uses his art to show Charles V his "progenitors": "The royall shapes and warlike semblances / Of Alexander and his beauteous Paramour" (B-text, 1021–22). "What there he did," the Chorus says, "in triall of his art, / I leave vntold, your eyes shall see performd" (920–21). However, exactly what our eyes see performed here is the problem. On the one hand, at least Charles believes what he sees, so much so that he forgets Faustus's warning—"demand no questions of the King [Alexander the Great] / But in dumbe silence let them come and goe" (B-text, 1103–4)—and tries to approach the "shadowes" (B-text, 1112), his thoughts being "so rauished / With sight of this renowned Emperour" (B-text, 1113–14). Of course, Charles has good reason to believe what he sees because what he sees, Alexander the Great establishing himself as emperor, guarantees Charles's own authority as Holy Roman Emperor. On the other hand, hungover Benvolio watches Faustus from a window above but does not believe what Faustus says: "Bloud [Faustus] speakes terribly: but for all that, I doe not greatly beleeue him, he lookes as like a Coniurer as the Pope to a Coster-monger" (B-text, 1079–81). Soon thereafter, before Faustus presents his show, Benvolio says that he does not believe what he sees: "I could eate my selfe for anger, to thinke I haue beene such an Asse all this while, to stand gaping after the deuils Gouernor, and can see nothing" (B-text, 1094–97). And finally Benvolio compares Faustus's presentation and reception to literature: "[A]nd thou bring Alexander and his Paramour before the Emperour, I'le be Actaeon, and turne my selfe to a Stagge" (B-text, 1106–8), to which Faustus answers, "And Ile play Diana and send you the hornes presently" (B-text, 1109–10). The play shows two audiences, responding to what their eyes "see performd." On the one hand, we have Charles V, who sees and then suspends disbelief, forgets that what he sees "are but shadowes, not substantiall" (B-text, 1112), while on the other hand, we have Benvolio, who when he sees and sustains disbelief, sees Faustus's fraudulence.

The various responses of Charles V and Benvolio to Faustus's show are the same possible responses to Marlowe's play. Either one can suspend the belief that the play is a fiction and accept the actors on stage not as actors but as characters whose psychologies speak to larger issues of good and evil, or one can sustain the disbelief that these actors are actors and that this play is a piece of literature that can enforce its own reality, that Faustus does have the magic he claims, by reference to another piece of literature, Ovid's *Metamorphoses*. Of course, one could argue that Faustus forces Benvolio to suspend his disbelief (in a way much less delightful than Charles V) when he makes Benvolio act out the story of Actaeon and Diana. However, since that story itself is about belief and disbelief, Faustus's actions only serve to intensify the issue of sustaining disbelief. In Ovid's famous version of the story, Actaeon has just finished hunting with friends when he accidentally stumbles into Diana's grotto, "as fate would have it" [*sic illium fata ferbant*], and sees her naked and disarmed.[25] Had Diana had her arrows ready, she would have killed Actaeon. Instead she flings water onto his face and says, "Now you are free to tell that you have seen me unrobed—if you can tell!" [*si poteris narrare, licet!*] (3.192–93). Actaeon turns into a stag, and, though "his mind remains unchanged" (203), he cannot speak. He is then hunted by his own dogs, who finally catch him and rip apart his body while his friends watch.

Whatever it is that Actaeon knows after he sees Diana "disarmed," subsequent interpretations of this story make it into an analogy for the relations between rulers and their subjects. For instance, George Sandys writes in his 1632 *Ovid's Metamorphoses Englished* that "this fable was invented to shew us how dangerous a curiosity it is to search into the secrets of Princes, or by chance to discover their nakednesse: who thereby incurring their hatred, ever after live the life of a Hart, full of feare and suspicion: not seldome accused by their servants, to gratulate the prince, unto their utter destruction." Thus, Sandy's moral: "Guard we therefore our eyes; not desire to see, or knowe more than concernes us: *or at leaste dissemble the discovery.*"²⁶ Sandys's interpretation is almost a verbatim repetition of Bacon's interpretation of the same myth in his *Wisdom of the Ancients:* "For whoever becomes acquainted with a prince's secrets without leave and against his will, is sure to incur his hatred: and then, knowing that he is marked and that occasions are sought against him, he lives the life of a stag; a life full of fears and suspicions. Often too it happens that his own servants and domestics, to curry favor with the prince, accuse and overthrow him. For when the displeasure of the prince is manifest, a man shall scarcely have a servant but will betray him; and so he may expect the fate of Actaeon."²⁷ What Actaeon sees that Diana cannot let him speak is the fraudulence of her own authority—Diana disrobed and unarmed—just as what Benvolio sees is the fraudulence of Faustus's authority. Moreover, this fraudulence that disrupts Diana's chaste authority is given a very material embodiment: Diana's tribadism. As Sandys comments, Juno implies to Latona that Diana changed Actaeon into a stag "for feare he should divulge her deformity: and not out of modesty; being so farre from a Virgin, as continually conversant at the labours of women, like a publicke midwife."²⁸

So too with the fraudulence that *Doctor Faustus* presents to its audiences: the only way for an audience to believe that Faustus forces Benvolio to believe in his abilities is for that audience to ignore the very obvious fraudulence in the play itself. The two most powerful pieces of evidence for suspending disbelief are the horns that grow on Benvolio's head while he is leaning out of a window asleep—horns that, as Faustus points out, are so large they prevent Benvolio from pulling his head back inside the window—and the false head that Benvolio cuts off Faustus in his attempt to get vengeance for the shame. The only way to get the horns on Benvolio's head would be to have them put on while the audience's attention, along with Charles V's, is diverted by the spectacle of Alexander the Great, and the cutting off of false heads was so commonplace in the Elizabethan theater that an audience could not help but recognize it as a stage trick—a kind of Brechtian *Verfremdung* that depends upon a specific, material sign of fraudulence and that results in a peripeteiac movement that the audience experiences as a split between the literary and the nonliterary, between the sustainment and suspension of disbelief. This fetishistic sign of fraudulence around which the audience turns is precisely what locates Marlowe's audience in relation to its being.

## Sodomy and Exnomination

The textual history of *Doctor Faustus* itself plays out the antiphrastical mechanism that I have been describing. Critics have inherited two versions of the play—the 1604 A-text, which is chronologically closer to Marlowe's life but seems truncated and unsatisfying as a tragedy to be performed, and the 1616 B-text, which is filled with comic scenes that many readers find un-Marlovian. As Leah Marcus has argued, it is the difference between the two that keeps what she calls the "Marlowe effect" alive. Each version, in relation to the other, situates its readers on a "ravishing razor edge between exaltation and transgression."[29] What is interesting about these two versions of the play is the way in which together they construct two audiences: (1) an audience that sustains disbelief and is, therefore, acutely aware of the play's textuality and textual unfoldings; and (2) an audience that suspends disbelief and is, therefore, unaware (or densely aware) of the play's textuality and textual unfoldings. As I discussed in the section above, the difference between these two modes of reading is in a strong way motivated by issues of power. Since the latter tends to reinforce an authority that the former questions, the audience that suspends disbelief has very good political reason for doing so, whether or not that audience recognizes these motives.

I shall argue that the difference between these two modes of reading is the condition for the emergence of the sodomitical in the play. *Doctor Faustus* concludes with the Chorus and the Scholars attempting to bring an end to the play by asking us not to think about Faustus's body. We are asked quite literally to suspend the disbelief for which

Faustus has stood, to be complicit in a mode of judgment that would interpret Faustus's body as that which must remain unthought. But, I shall argue, the play also allows for the construction of a different mode of judgment, one that reads this exhortation to stop thinking as motivated by the representational logic of sodomy in which the Scholars and the Chorus participate and about which they want to know nothing at all. Moreover, as I shall demonstrate, in his desires for the literary Faustus himself falls prey to this representational logic and its insistence upon the suspension of disbelief. To this extent, Marlowe's play locates sodomy at the limit of the literary and the forms of subjectivity produced by it.

At the end of the play, the Scholars and the Chorus attempt to allay the anxieties that accompany the sustainment of disbelief by providing for an ending that interprets Faustus's torn body as precisely what Christianity would rather leave unthought. "Faustus end be such / As euery Christian heart laments to thinke on" (B-text, 1490–91), one of the Scholars pronounces. The Chorus is more explicit:

> Faustus is gone, regard his hellish fall,
> Whose fiendful fortune may exhort the wise,
> Onley to wonder at vnlawful things,
> Whose deepenesse doth intise such forward wits,
> To practise more than heauenly power permits.
> (1481–85)

For these interpreters, the torn body of Faustus becomes the endpoint of thought, of representation, and of disbelief. This interpretation is a response to the sense of endlessness the play provokes, a response to what Greenblatt calls Faustus's "struggle against *theatrical* [i.e., diegetic] time."[30] In many ways, the entire play can be characterized as Faustus's refusal to make an end of things. Witness the way the play begins with Faustus's repeated claims that he has reached "the end of euery Art" (32); the way he begins his contract with Mephostophilis by repeating Christ's words on the cross, "*Consummatum est,* this Bill is ended" (506); or the way he discovers at the conclusion of the play that his end is endlessness, "no end is limited to damned souls"— almost, finally, a piece of literature destined to be reread. Moreover, the text of *Doctor Faustus* makes this endlessness a problem not only for its characters, but also for its author. *Terminat hora diem, terminat*

*Author opus:* so the play ends, calling forth an ending, midnight, that is also unavoidably another beginning.[31] Given the play's emphasis on endlessness, the Chorus's interpretive strategy becomes clear: if the eccentricity of being is produced by the endlessness of meaning, then the only way to solidify Faustus's being is to stop thinking, specifically, to translate what thinking can never meaningfully articulate into what must not be thought because "we" all know what "it" means. In other words, the Chorus translates Faustus's "fiendful fortune" into a metonym for what should not be thought (because "we" all know it) in order to return the play and its audiences to the confines of the theological. Thus, instead of recognizing the fiendfulness of "fortune" announced at the beginning of the play, the Chorus submits Faustus and his "fortune" to some unthought, yet "fiendful" signified.

The Chorus and Scholars attempt to substantiate this interpretation by reference to the body of Faustus:

> SCHOLAR 2: O help vs heauen, see, here are *Faustus* limbs, All
>             torne asunder by the hand of death.
> SCHOLAR 3: The deuils whom *Faustus* seru'd haue torne him
>             thus.
>
>                                             (B-text, 1483–85)

This torn body, rhetorically presented as "a body-image of power and presence," is what Berger describes in a different but related context as "a kind of preventative immunization against the spectre of textuality."[32] It is the point at which the Chorus and Scholars wish to stop interpretation. However, this immunization fails precisely because of textuality. The Scholars' and Chorus's interpretation is not only countered by Mephostophilis's threat that if Faustus *refuses to revolt against God,* he will "in peece-meale teare thy flesh" (1306), but also relies on a certain refusal of literary history. The ripping apart of Faustus's body repeats another version of the Actaeon story, the version in which Actaeon is "devoured . . . by his favorites," as Sandys puts it,[33] or, as Bacon would have it, by "his own servants and domestics." This version of the Actaeon story specifies what remains unthought as the sodomitical to which the play so strongly points. While Ovid's version of the Actaeon myth points to an epistemological excess for which Actaeon is devoured, Plutarch's version, explained in his *Moralia,* refers to what would be characterized by the Renaissance as an excess of male friendship.

> Melissus had a son named Actaeon, the handsomest and most modest youth of his age, who had many lovers [*Erostai*], chief among them was Archais, of the family of Heracleidae, in wealth and general influence the most outstanding man in Corinth. Now, when he could not gain the boy by persuasion, he determined to carry him off by force. So he got together a crowd of friends and servants, went as in a drunken frolic to the house of Melissus, and tried to take the boy away. But his father and friends resisted, the neighbors also ran out and pulled against the assailants, and so Actaeon was pulled to pieces and killed.[34]

Although Faustus forces Benvolio to act out Ovid's version of the Actaeon myth, Faustus and the devils act out a version of the myth much closer to Plutarch's. Just as Actaeon's refusal to give himself over to his lover Archais results in his body being ripped apart, so too does Faustus's refusal to give himself over to Mephostophilis result in his body being ripped apart. The endlessness called forth by the play's literariness (the sustainment of disbelief) and the terminus whose term the Scholars and Chorus insist must remain unthought (the suspension of disbelief) both join in the sodomitical—an "abominable sin," a sin both everywhere and nowhere because "amongst Christians not to be named," as Edward Coke infamously puts it.[35] More aptly, given the importance of magic in *Doctor Faustus*, it is recognized in the words of Macbeth's witches as "a deed without a name" (4.1.49).

Reading this moment as sodomitical is difficult only because what gives sodomy its forcefulness in Renaissance England is the capability of that term to revise an exnominated semiotic into evidence of sodomy. Moreover, while sodomy charges rely on metaphor, exnomination, and renomination, these charges are also deeply metonymic and connotative. As Alan Bray has argued, the execrated figure of the sodomite doubles "in an uncanny way" the universally admired figure of the male friend, the sodomite standing in for the "specter," "phantom," or "shadow" inherent in the idealized, intensely homosocial world of Elizabethan male friendship. Hence, in his analysis of *Edward II*, Bray argues that the most disturbing aspects for an Elizabethan audience of the relationship between Edward and Gaveston would have little to do with what twentieth-century audiences could recognize as homosexuality, a term of course inconceivable to Elizabethans. Instead, the two most disturbing aspects of that relation would have been Gaveston's "base" birth and the mercenary nature of his intimacy with the king, both of which would be recognizable to an Elizabethan audience as deviations from the cultural tropes of idealized male friendship. The relation between Gaveston and Edward emerges as transgressive of the economic order that cultural tropes of male friendship secured as natural. These transgressions, Bray argues, conjure up "the profoundly disturbing image of the sodomite, that enemy not only of nature but of society and the proper kinds and distinctions within it."[36] It is not Edward's quite obvious solicitations of his favorites to let him play the boy that makes these relations sodomitical. They are sodomitical insofar as they conjure "the sodomite" as a way to avoid knowledge and recognition.

*Doctor Faustus,* with its disruptions of and deviations from the orderly world of theology and idealized male friendship, also conjures this disturbing image *as precisely what the Chorus wants to remain unthought.* What more mercenary a servingman than Mephostophilis? What more transgressive economic transaction than selling one's soul to the devil? Let me be as clear as I can about this point. I am not arguing that these two literary characters "did it," which, of course, would be no guarantee whatsoever of sodomy. As it ends up, sexual acts themselves are never proof of sodomy. Sodomy designates sexual acts that need not have "actually happened." Allegations of sodomy in Elizabethan England turned not on any real evidence of a sexual relationship, but rather, as Jonathan Goldberg puts it, "on a sharp-eyed recognition that the public signs of male friendship—open for all the world to see—could be read in a different and sodomitical light." But these signs can emerge into visibility as *signs* of sexual acts "only when those who are said to have done them can also be called traitors, heretics, or the like, at the very least, disturbers of the social order that alliance—marriage arrangements—maintained."[37] Instead of arguing that any of the characters in *Doctor Faustus* is a sodomite, I am arguing that the version of being that *Doctor Faustus* offers is inextricably bound up in the representational logic of sodomy.

One of the more striking consequences of Bray's and Goldberg's analyses is that, given the antiphrastical nature of any piece of evidence that could retroactively be judged to prove sodomy, the judgment of sodomy established an identitary time that relied on a very particular logic of representation. Freud calls this logic *Verneinung,* or negation, the creation of a symbol of negation that allows for the performance of judgment.[38] Freud proposes two sorts of decisions fundamental to the performance of judgment, first, a decision of meaning, the evaluation of a thing's particular properties, a decision about whether a thing is "good" or "bad." The decision of meaning establishes the boundaries (male friend/sodomite) by which the "good" (male friendship) can be recognized as such. Second, Freud proposes the decision of being, the decision to affirm or dispute the existence of a particular image, or *Vorstellung,* that has been rendered alien or bad. Freud insists that this second aspect of judgment does not exactly aim at discovering an object in perception that corresponds to a particular *Vorstellung;* rather, the aim of this process is "to *re-discover* such an object, to convince oneself that it is still there."[39] The trick, for Freud, is that in the creation of a symbol that could denote what is alien or external to the "I," the "I" rediscovers that alien object as already inside. This second decision denotes as the being of the "I" precisely what the "I" assumed as excluded, meaningless, unassimilable.

To expand the representational logic at work here, I wish to turn to Lacan's "Logical Time," where Lacan elaborates an almost syllogistic three-step logic of culture and masculine recognition. I turn to this essay in order to propose that the spatialization of sodomy upon which both Bray and Goldberg focus—sodomy's peculiar relation to a sense of normativity secured and regulated mostly by visibility—is conditioned by sodomy's temporal structure of recognition. The ontological "void" of sodomy relies on what Judith Butler might call sodomy's "social temporality."[40] Steps one and two of Lacan's essay develop Freud's decision of meaning. In these steps, Lacan asserts in commonplace fashion that group recognition depends on exclusion: (1) a man knows what is not a man, and (2) men recognize themselves to be men among men. For homosocial male friendship to be in any way meaningful, it relies on the recognition and exclusion of what it encodes as "not a man"—here, "the sodomite." It is with step three that the excommunicated becomes the locus of being, when one member of the group articulates the following: *Je m'affirme être un homme, de peur d'être convaincu par les hommes de n'être pas un homme.* (I assert myself to be a man for fear of being convinced by men that I am not a man.)[41] Recognition as a man within the conventions of male friendship is conditioned by the logically prior anxiety of the infelicitous performance of these conventions. In step three, the subject of the group finds its being denoted by what the group is already defined against.

Given Bray's and Goldberg's analyses, I propose that the ideal recognition of men among men is conditioned by the term "sodomy," the identification as a man invoking the prohibition of sodomy as the very measure of that identification. The effect of this prohibition is to denote as sodomitical the failure to be recognized fully and perspicuously as a man among men—a failure to which all performance of the masculine is open.[42] The prior exclusion of sodomy from the world of Elizabethan male friendship is precisely what allows Bray to argue for what he terms an "uncanny" relation between cultural images of idealized male friendship and execrated sodomy: while the latter is rendered alien, unfamiliar, and abhorrent to the former, nevertheless the latter is evidenced only by the infelicities of the former. When the reassuring conventions of idealized male friendship falter, precisely at that moment allegations of sodomy arise. As Jean Hyppolite argues in his highly influential and nuanced discussion of Freudian *Verneinung*, negation produces "an appearance of being in non-being," which accounts for the seeming paradox of sodomy.[43] There could be in Elizabethan England no self-identifying sodomites; by the same token, as John Rainolds put it in *Th'Overthrow of Stage-Playes*, sodomy is a "monstrous sin against nature" to which "men's natural corruption and viciousness is prone."[44] Strictly speaking, it is sodomy as a symbol of negation in the Freudian sense that allows for the appearance of being a sodomite, or more precisely of a sodomitical spirit that is both everywhere and nowhere.

While Faustus's resistance to and desire for being in literature is exactly what makes him a subject of literariness, the being of this subjectivity relies on the representational logic of sodomy, the inherence of sodomy within the tropes of high homosocial exchange. It is the ability both to resist and desire being in literature that allows for the sodomitical to emerge. To put the point in its strongest form: In *Doctor Faustus* sodomy emerges not as the name for certain acts abhorrent to a homosocial culture, but out of the insight, however dim, that homosocial gender roles are being performed, as a kind of mediator between the naturalization of theatricality and the infelicities to which all performatives are of necessity open. In the famous Helen of Troy speech, which Faustus gives as a weak attempt to forget his own literary destiny—as Marlowe writes in *Hero and Leander*, "Loue is too full of faith, too credulous, / With follie and false hope deluding vs" [2.221–22])—Faustus explains how he will escape his story by becoming a literary figure in another story:

> I wil be Paris, and for loue of thee,
> Insteede of Troy shal Wertenberge be sackt,
> And I wil combate with weake Menelaus,
> And weare thy colours on my plumed Crest:
> Yea I wil wound Achilles in the heele,
> And then returne to Helen for a kisse.
>                                   (1335–40)

Faustus begins this speech to Helen with the famous question, "Was this the face that launcht a thousand shippes? / And burnt the toplesse Towres of Ilium?" (1328–29), a very good question that by the next line goes unanswered: "Sweete Helen, make me immortall with a kisse" (1330). The rhetorical force of this response is to refuse the question that comes before by making its answer an assumed "Yes, this is that face." However, all evidence in the play is to the contrary. When Faustus asks Mephostophilis to give him a wife, what Mephostophilis says that he gives Faustus and what Faustus gets are two very different things. After Mephostophilis brings Faustus his wife (*stage directions:* "Enter Mephostophilis with a diuell drest like a woman" [579]), Faustus asks, "What sight is this?" (B-text, 579) and refuses Mephostophilis's offering. What Faustus sees is that this woman is not a woman. Nor is this sight exactly a man. Rather, Faustus sees what fifteenth- and sixteenth-century manuals on magic call a succubus, a devil that takes on female morphology in order to procure a man's semen: "The divell plaieth *Succubus* to the man and carrieth from him the seed of generation, which he delivereth as *Incubus* to the woman,"

as Reginald Scot writes in his *Discoverie of Witchcraft* (1584). As the
*Malleus Maleficarum* (1486) explains, the devils turn themselves into
incubi or succubi so that "through the vice of luxury they may work
a twofold harm against men, that is, body and soul, that so men may
be more given to all vices." Perhaps not surprisingly, the *Malleus Maleficarum* names these vices as follows: "[W]e do not speak only of
sodomy, but of any other sin whereby the act is wrongfully performed
outside the rightful channel."[45] The wife that Mephostophilis brings
demonstrates that marriage is no signified that can stabilize the performance of gender. Instead of producing a signified that stabilizes
the performance of gender, the play replaces this wife with a series of
courtesans in an economy of homosocial exchange:

> Marriage is but a ceremoniall toy,
> And *if thou louest me, thinke no more of it.*
> Ile cull thee out the fairest curtezans,
> And bring them eu'ry morning to thy bed.
> She whome thine eie shall like thy heart shal haue,
> Were she as chaste as Penelope,
> As wise as Saba, or *as beautiful*
> *As was bright Lucifer before his fall.*
> (583–59, emphasis mine)

Mephostophilis replaces the succubus with a highly homosocial economy, barely legible as male friendship because the objects of exchange
between Faustus and his servant are women whose beauty depends
on their being like men.

In light of this scene, and of Valdes's earlier comment that one of
the services the devils provide is appearing "[s]ometimes like women,
or vnwedded maides" (156), I wish to assert that Faustus's refusal to
answer the question that he raises about Helen—"Was this the face
that launcht a thousand shippes?"—is motivated by a certain desire
*not to know* that this is the face of a succubus, a desire to suspend
disbelief that can be designated by the term sodomy. This suspension
may work for Faustus, but it certainly cannot work for us, since after
showing Faustus ignoring the gender slippages in his attempt to take
this particular devil in a dress to be Helen of Troy, the play has these
very slippages reemerge when Faustus designates himself first as Semele and next as Arethusa to Helen's Jupiter.

O thou art fairer than the euening aire,
Clad in the beauty of a thousand starres,
Brighter art thou then flaming Iupiter,
When he appeared to haplesse Semele,
More lovely than the monarke of the skie
In wanton Arethusaes azurde armes.

(1341–46)

The referent of Faustus's sure assertion that concludes this speech, "[a]nd none but thou shalt be my paramour" (1347), is rendered peculiar in the extreme since what we can know for certain is that, whatever that "thou" may be, it is not what Faustus thinks it is. Precisely this uncertainty alongside Faustus's particular desire not to know alleges the relation between Helen and Faustus as sodomitical.

## On the Soul

The objectification and exchange of Faustus's soul is probably what is most historically disturbing about Marlowe's play, specifically insofar as this exchange locates Faustus at a point of formal rupture. In that *Doctor Faustus* asserts the primacy of the soul, the play remains committed to a morality tradition that mobilizes allegory in order to contain the implications of theatricality. But the play also transgresses almost all of that tradition's transumptive urges. For example, in the scene after Faustus signs his soul over to the devil, and in order to put Faustus in the appropriate state of mind, Beelzebub stages a brief scene generic to the morality tradition in which Faustus watches a pageant of the seven deadly sins. This scene doesn't lead Faustus to identification, self-condemnation, and conversion; it leads him to sardonic enjoyment. "Now Faustus, how dost thou like this?" Lucifer asks; to which Faustus replies, "O this feedes my soule" (780–81). The complexity of this enjoyment—this feeding rather than chastening of Faustus's soul—is that he is nourished by a tradition his own actions subvert.

The residual after-effect of the play's threshold relation to theology and a morality tradition is the polysemous nature of Faustus's soul.[46] Faustus's soul acts as an odd surplus that binds together the various economies operative in the play. For instance, most striking about the Helen of Troy incident is that, in order to forget his contractual obligations to Mephostophilis and Lucifer, Faustus participates in a

highly eroticized exchange of his soul with a succubus. Both structurally (in its homosocial exchanges) and thematically (in its self-
characterization), this exchange registers exactly the anxieties over
sodomy that the homosocial wants to deny and exactly the commodification and exchange of the soul that Faustus has claimed he wants
to forget.

> Sweete Helen, make me immortall with a kisse:
> Her lips suckes forth my soule, see where it flies:
> Come Helen, come give mee my soule againe.
> Here wil I dwel, for heauen be in these lips,
> And all is drosse that is not Helena.
>
> (1330–34)

It would be a mistake to read this moment as one that simply replays
the theological, as does C. L. Barber, for instance, when he argues that
the emphasis on eating and consumption in *Doctor Faustus* rehearses
a theology of communion.[47] I don't deny that there is much to be
made over the modulations of Faustus's body from eating to being
eaten. One can point, for example, to the movement from Faustus's
wanting to be "glutted now with learnings golden gifts" (24) to his
consumption by a somewhat phagocytic hell; to his attempts to escape
damnation by entering the "intrailes" of "yon labring cloude" so that
his body can be vomited from its "smoaky mouthes" and his soul
ascend to heaven (1446–48); and to the series of meals that mark the
play, from Faustus's dinner with Valdes and Cornelius, to his devil-
ment at the pope's banquet, to his last meal at Wittenberg. At stake in
these transactions, though, is the way that Faustus's soul is constructed through the various modulations of the body as an object
traded within a highly erotic economy of consumption, a barely contained homosocial economy in which the "women" exchanged between Faustus and Mephostophilis serve essentially as instruments to
keep the exchange going.

Faustus's first agreement to exchange his soul for knowledge controverts a whole philosophical and theological tradition that runs
from Aristotle up through high Italian humanism in which the soul
is an organ of thought, the instrument by which thinking is attached
to the sensations and perceptions of the body. "It is doubtless better
to avoid saying that the soul pities or learns or thinks, and rather to

say," Aristotle writes in *De Anima,* "that it is the man who does this with his soul." Thus, Aristotle argues that the soul is analogous to the hand since each is a tool of tools, an instrument for the use of instruments. Following Aristotle, Aquinas argues that the soul is a noncorporeal organ, a substantial form that "contains the body and makes it one."[48] For Aristotle, Aquinas, and later for Pomponazzi, the soul is the noncorporeal instrument of thinking that, because noncorporeal, can comprehend and contain all corporeal things. As Pomponazzi notes:

> For I who am writing these words am beset with many bodily pains, which are the function of the sensitive soul; and the same I who am tortured run over their medical causes in order to remove these pains, which cannot be done save by the intellect. But if the essence by which I feel were different from that by which I think, how could it possibly be that I who feel am the same as I who think?[49]

This tradition more or less assumes a felicitous link between the act of thinking and its representation as thought; however, once the soul becomes an object of exchange, a commodity, it is no longer attached to thought. Rather, the soul attaches the body to the unthinkable. This is the thesis of Marx, to be sure, when he explains in almost commonplace Aristotelian fashion the way that the laborer formally reproduces his or her labor power as a commodity to be exchanged. The trick is that this exchange subjects the laborer not to his or her thoughts but to the "cunning reason" of the market—for Marx, the production of surplus value, the process by which the capitalist, who produces nothing, gets paid for it. Hence, the laborer is "like one who is bringing his own skin to market and has nothing to expect but—a skinning."[50] For Marx, the condition of the laborer is precisely what Pomponazzi finds unthinkable. Instead of a linkage between the "I who feels" and the "I who thinks," Marx proposes that the "I who feels" is emptied out by a thought process not its own, becoming an automated motor in the machinery of the market.[51]

*Doctor Faustus,* too, examines the effects of commodification, although the play conceptualizes exchange and its effects not entirely by way of the cunning of the market, but also through its considerations of the literary. When Faustus renounces theology for the literary, he

also renounces the theo-logic of the gift and replaces it with the logic
of endless exchange.

> *Stipendium peccati mors est:* Ha, *stipendium et cetera.*
> The reward of sinne is death: thats hard.
> *Si peccasse negamus, fallimur, et nulla est in nobis veritas.*
> If we say that we haue no sinne,
> We deceiue our selues, and theres no truth in vs.
> Why then belike
> We must sinne, and so consequently die.
> I, we must die an euerlasting death:
> What doctrine call you this, *Che sera, sera,*
> *What wil be, shall be? Diuinitie, adieu.*
>
>                                           (67–76)

*Stipendium peccat mors est.* As many readers have noted, if Faustus
had continued reading the verse that he quotes from Romans, he
would have discovered the theology of the gift. However, by replacing
this theology with a gesture toward endlessness—*Stipendium, et cet-
era*—Faustus remains caught within the logic of endless exchange.

   Endless exchange controverts the semiotics of a morality tradition.
A play like *Everyman,* for example, attempts to palliate the pressures of
market exchange through that tradition's insistence upon allegorical
conversion. In order to escape the implications of endless debt, *Everyman* attempts to convert the love of money into a love of community as expressed through charity. As Dethe explains,

> He that loveth richesse I will strike with my darte, His sight to
>     blinde, and fro heven to departe—
> Excepte that almes be his good frende—
> In hell for to dwell, worlde without ende.[52]

However, since the play addresses quite specifically a merchant audience, Dethe's initial condemnation of riches, even with his qualifica-
tion, is too bald a statement to suffice. To accomplish the ideological
conversion of merchant ethics into Christian culture, the play resigni-
fies the version of merchant ethics that accounting books generically
assume. In the preface to his *Maner and Fourme How to Kepe a Perfecte
Reconyng,* James Peele proposes that a bad record keeper lives in continual fear that "he hath been deceiued, when that he is not throughly

hable to saie (with a cleare consience) whether he haue been deceiued
of any thyng at all, or not." On the other hand, good record keepers
"frendly maie conferre their reconynges, and therby to staie suche
variances, as els maie ensue."⁵³ In short, good records make good
neighbors. Good records also make for inner peace. As Hugh Oldcastle explains, a good merchant must "dispose all his marchandises
in due order, whereby readily hee may haue knowledge of everything,
as well that concerneth his Debitors as his Creditors" because "without a due order to writing, his minde coulde not be quieted."⁵⁴ When
in *The Pathe Waye to Perfectnes* Peele associates merchant ethics
with Christianity, he relies on topoi of diligence, care, the law, and
withholding:

> Eche man that holdeth a howsholde in charge,
> Whose hope is to haue Gods bountie at large,
> With dilligent care, and studious paine,
> Must still be mindfull, his state to maintaine;
> His howshold alwaies, therewith to defend,
> As those which on God, do onlye depend,
> His secrets conceale, (for marke what I saye)
> Two will kepe counçell if one be awaye.
> Thus in thy callinge if warely thou walke,
> Of promisse be iust confirminge thy taulke,
> Wainge before hand with whome thou doest deale,
> Let diligence seke all doubtes to reueale:
> For Credit once crackt that maintaines the state,
> Then dame repentaunce will come verie late.⁵⁵

Beginning with the fundamental requirement of bookkeeping—"a
diligent marchant" must "bee prompt and readie in reconing, and to
make well and readie his accompt"⁵⁶—*Everyman* translates a detailed
attention to inventory and material goods, which "blotte[s] and blin-
de[s]" Everyman to his supposedly true "accounte" (419–20), into a
detailed attention to "the bokes of . . . workes" that Good Dedes keeps
(503). After this translation, Everyman undergoes an analogous process of cleansing and purification through confession and penitent
mortification of the flesh whose net imaginary effect is to posit the
erasure of the book as the sign of clean interiority. "Now thy soule is
taken thy body fro," the Angel explains, "Thy rekeninge is crystall
clere" (897–98). Merchant self-control converts into Christian rites of

purification, and concurrently attention to inventory converts into the giving of alms. However, it isn't just that its main figure must give alms, which he does before he dies; more precisely, the resignification of merchant ethics of accountability reformulates mercantile self-control as the grounds for salvation.

In contrast, by sending Divinity to God (*à Dieu*) and renouncing the theological and the morality tradition that supports it, Faustus is situated both in the world of the literary, in which the signified is subordinated to the signifier ("Diuinitie adieu"), and in the world of capital, the world of goods valued for their exchange and not by their relation to the Good, the "world of profit" (81) promised not to "Emperours and Kings" (85) but to "the studious Artizan" (83). Quite generally, then, just as the literary suspends the primacy of the signi-fied that would secure meaning and stabilize language, so too, the lit-erary suspends any good outside the production of goods by which one could sufficiently judge the value of the goods.[57] More specifically, given the folk etymology of Mephostophilis (*mefistof:* Hebrew for "de-stroyer of the good") as well as the particular relation to the literary that Mephostophilis admits at the end of the play ("[W]hen thou took'st the booke / To view the Scriptures, then I turn'd the leaues / And led thine eye" [B-text, 1426–8]), the subordination of the signi-fied to the signifier and the schism between the good and the goods are the two sides of the same very troublesome literary coin.

Moreover, the homosocial network in which Faustus's soul is ex-changed ensures that what is rendered illegible within these exchanges comes to be designated as sodomy in the second exchange with Helen—the "sucking forth" of Faustus's soul by the succubus. If, once Faustus rejects the theology of the gift, there is no good outside the production of goods by which one can sufficiently judge the value of goods and commodities, then this second exchange forces the thesis that there is no extraliterary good or felicity that can stabilize the ex-changes that comprise gender. Or, as Lacan puts it, "the sexual relation does not exist." We are left with overlapping economies of exchange whose very conventions allege the sodomitical to be at the heart of the performativity of gender.

For some time now, critics have read *Doctor Faustus* as a kind of morality play for humanists that emphasizes the dangers of overreach-ing the bounds of human knowledge and underscores the dire consequences of this act.[58] Much more forcefully, I have tried to argue, the play registers Faustus as a subject of literariness—a subject whose imaginary identification is to be a character in a story not his own, whose symbolic identification is to burn his books, and whose being locates him by the representational logic of sodomy. It is a form of subjectivity that finally Faustus cannot escape, not because he has overreached the bounds of humanism, but because he is inescapably committed to the literary. Near the end of the play, after his call to God for mercy fails, Faustus discovers the reason. "Why wert thou not a creature wanting soule?" he asks himself (1459). If only Faustus lacked a soul, or if the soul were given a certain materiality that would allow for its destruction or dissolution, then he would not be subject to the literary, which has displaced a merciful God. "O soule, be changde into little water drops, / And fal into the Ocean, neer be found" (1472–73). The commodity remains, its signified no longer an extraliterary good but instead the literary itself, "The forme of Faustus fortunes good or bad."

# Sexuality at the Epochal Threshold: Baconian Science and the Experience of History

ॐ

### Conversion and Queer History

It appears from a number of accounts that Francis Bacon had sexual relations with other men. John Aubrey speculates that Bacon was a "pederast" and that "his Ganimeds and favourites took bribes." Sir Simonds D'Ewes writes that Bacon was a sodomite and that even after his political fall he kept "still one Godrick a very effeminate faced youth to be his catamite and bedfellow." And Bacon's mother complains in a letter to another of her sons that Bacon retained a particular servant "as a coach companion and bed companion."[1] These accounts may or may not be accurate reports of Bacon's sexual relations; in any case, they are not where I shall locate the sexuality of the Baconian project. Rather, I shall argue that Baconian science traces out sexuality as an impasse of time. While Bacon's writings repeatedly express the desire for an epochal shift, sexuality continually emerges at that shift's threshold, problematizing the shift in a history of knowledge and judgment that the Baconian project attempts to effect.

It should be clear that I do not here mean sexuality in terms of object choice. I intend sexuality to denote an insistent and repeated relation between corporeality, oneself, others, and the complexities of representation implied by the cluster of terms "body," "oneself," and "others." In order to use sexuality to think a history beyond sexuality, queer history proposes considering sexuality as a subject's relation to discursive fields that implicate the body in the social and the political through specific corporeal practices. Insofar as the word "sexuality" is nowadays used to express some common identity, David Halperin asserts that it "represents the *appropriation* of the human body and of its erogenous zones by an ideological discourse."[2] Rather than taking this understanding to be the grounds for the continuity from which a history of sexuality might arise, though, Halperin argues for a queer history that traces the often discontinuous and particular implications and appropriations of the body and its erogenous zones within social and political discourses. In this understanding, it is important to add, the appropriations of the body that sexuality represents are most often indirect. It is society that "haunts" sexuality, Halperin argues, and not the other way around.[3] Thus, sexuality as a set of corporeal practices is not a direct reflection of social or political discourse. Rather, sexuality links the subject to these discourses in ambiguity.

I propose that this ambiguity is doubly articulated. This does not mean that ambiguity simply points to incoherence or to some messy proliferation of meaning. Rather, ambiguity points to a specific relation to discursive formations. The expression of an enigma on the level of discourse is substantiated in particular corporeal practices as a problematicized differential that meaning can neither entirely control nor deplete. As Lacan argues, the subject, constituted in relation to meaning, will inevitably confront the general problem of the Other and of desire. "A lack is encountered by the subject in the Other, in the very intimation that the Other makes to him by his discourse. In the intervals of the discourse of the Other, there emerges in the experience of [the subject] something that is radically mappable, namely, *He is saying this to me, but what does he want?*"[4] In Lacan's argument, sexuality is a particular (albeit generalizable) set of practices that respond to this interval in a way that returns the enigma of desire back to the Other. Sexuality does not make this enigma meaningful; it "communicates" this enigma in nonce-coordinated movements that, by repetition, trace it out.[5]

Sexuality is thus not synonymous with desire. It is not an attempt to make one's "true desires" known. As a particular, embodied response to the enigma of desire qua enigma of meaning, sexuality incarnates the problematic place an individual occupies in order to be a subject. In this precise way, sexuality "has the function of being for the Other, of situating the subject in it, marking his place in the field of the group's relations, between each individual and all others."[6]

Thus, when Foucault writes a history of sexuality, he does so in terms of problematicization rather than in terms of some vulgar Freudian version of repression. Problematicization accounts for the double ambiguity by which sexuality implicates the body in the order of discourse by historicizing the experience of the subject in relation to discourse's historical limit. Foucault explains: "Problematicization doesn't mean the representation of a preexistent object, nor the creation through discourse of an object that doesn't exist. It's the set of discursive or non-discursive practices that makes something enter into the play of the true and the false, and constitutes it as an object for thought." The question that sexuality raises is this: "How is an 'experience' formed where the relation to the self and to others is linked?"[7] An enigmatic "something" that enters the "play of the true and the false" is doubled as a problematicized experience by which the subject establishes relations to others and to itself through corporeal practice. And through this double articulation, this enigmatic "something" positivizes or "presentifies" a limit of discourse as an object for thinking to negotiate.

In his early fragment *The Masculine Birth of Time*, Bacon promises his interlocutor a scientific methodology that will result in a new, hyper-masculine epoch to "stand up against the ravages of time" [*pellendas injurias temporis*], an epoch of "dominion" [*imperii*] over nature in which "one bright and radiant [*clarum et radiosum*] light of truth [will shed] its beams in all directions and [dispel] all errors in a moment [*errores universos momento dispellat*]."[8] Evelyn Fox Keller has pointed out that this domination is not "simple violation," but is instead "forceful and aggressive seduction."[9] As Bacon elsewhere puts it, "Man, being the servant and interpreter of Nature, can do and understand so much and so much only as he has observed in fact or in thought or in the course of nature. . . . Nature to be commanded must be obeyed" [*Homo, Naturae minister et interpres, tantum facit et intelligit quantum de Naturae ordine re vel mente observaverit. . . . Natura enim non nisi parendo vincitur*] (*NO*, 4:1.1.3/1:1.3).[10] Moreover, as Keller argues, throughout his works Bacon underwrites the seduction of Nature with a homosocial seduction of the male audience that his writings assume. "My dear, dear boy" [*fili suavissime*], Bacon writes, explaining the future epoch that he promises to his hypothetical interlocutor, what I purpose is to unite you with *things themselves* in a chaste, holy, and legal wedlock; and from this association you will secure an increase beyond all the hopes and prayers of ordinary marriages, to wit, a blessed race of Heroes or Supermen who will overcome the immeasurable helplessness and poverty of the human race, which cause it more destruction than all giants, monsters, or tyrants, and will make you peaceful, happy, prosperous, and secure.

[*Ego . . . tibi sanctum, castum, et legitimum connubium cum rebus ipsis firmabo. Ex qua consuetudine (supra omnia epithalamiorum vota) beatissimam prolem vere Heroum (qui infinitas humanas necessitates, omnibus gigantibus, monstris, et tyrannis exitiosiores, subacturi sunt, et rebus vestris placidam et festam securitatem et copiam conciliaturi) suscipies.*] (*MB*, 72/3:538–39)

This promised epoch is organized around an extremely homosocial version of sexual difference from which "subsequent generations of scientists extracted a more consistent metaphor of lawful sexual domination."[11] The seductive promise of supercession, routed through a chaste wedlock that amounts to domination over female nature, serves to strengthen relations between men.

I do not disagree with Keller's account, but I do disagree with attempts to adduce sexuality directly from it. Keller speculates that this homosocial structure fends off the recognition that "the scientific mind must be, on some level, a hermaphroditic mind."[12] That is, the Baconian project represses the scientific mind's fundamental bisexuality. And, following Keller, Mark Breitenberg argues that when Bacon attempts "to draw a distinct line between the aristocratic, masculine subject and the 'vulgar' or the 'feminine,'" he also reveals "an anxious masculine prerogative."[13] In Bacon's writings, Breitenberg proposes, "the dissemination of knowledge between men is secured by female chastity. But what emerges from this figuring of female chastity . . . is of course an increased anxiety on the part of men." It is the "of course" that I find troublesome. There may be homoeroticism in Bacon's writings, but, Breitenberg argues, it is "of course" anxiously heterosexual through and through.[14]

What Breitenberg's account ignores is Bacon's insistent temporal pose. Bacon never gets to his promised future world governed by science. Rather, in his style as well as in a set of corporeal practices, Bacon

consistently positions himself at this promised world's epochal threshold, "like a seer with two faces, one looking towards the future, the
other towards the past" [*bifrontes vates sint, quamque et futuras et
praeteritas coram sistant*] (*MB*, 68/3:535)—a veritable Moses of science, as Abraham Cowley later suggests, who "Did on the very border
stand / Of the blessed promised land."[15] Moreover, Bacon attempts to
position his interlocutor at this epochal threshold as well. "Take heart,
then, my son," Bacon writes at the end of *The Masculine Birth of Time*,
"and give yourself to me so that I may restore you to yourself" [*Con-
fide (fili), et da te mihi, ut te tibi reddam*] (72/3:539). It will be my
argument that this positioning locates the sexuality of the Baconian
project in response to the problem of historical change. While the
seductive promise of the Baconian project is supercession, the experience—including the erotic experience—of the Baconian corpus is
that of the threshold never absolutely traversed.

    This experience is, first of all, a problem concerning knowledge and
the senses. In *The Advancement of Learning*, after considering that the
mind isn't "a clear and equal glass, wherein the beams of things should
reflect according to their true incidence" but is instead "like an en-
chanted glass, full of superstition and imposture," Bacon concludes
that "it is not possible to divorce ourselves from these fallacies and
false appearances, because they are inseparable from our nature and
condition of life; so yet nevertheless," he continues, "the caution of
them . . . doth extremely import the true conduct of human judgment" (*AL*, 3:395–97). The iconic tendencies of the human mind
teach the necessity of iconoclasm in the establishment of human judgment. The problem is that "we falsely admire and extol the powers of
the human mind" (*NO*, 4:1.9). Like Adam and Eve, Bacon argues, the
mind wishes to be like God, only more so: "For we create worlds, we
direct and domineer over nature, we will have it that all things *are* as
in our folly we think they should be, not as seems fittest to the Divine
wisdom, or as they are to be found in fact; . . . we clearly impress the
stamp of our own image on the creatures and works of God, instead of
carefully examining and recognizing in them the stamp of the Creator
himself" (*HN*, 5:132, emphasis Bacon's). For the mind, then, a sustained, iconoclastic attitude is the "true conduct" of reason and
judgment.

    But this experience is also one that speaks to issues of pedagogy and rhetorical presentation. In *The Masculine Birth of Time* Bacon enacts a spirited attack on the ancient authorities of science in order to disturb his young reader's secure and certain understanding of them and thus to prepare his reader for transition to the new epoch. Bacon explains the necessity of this procedure: "On the waxen tablets you cannot write anything new until you rub out the old. With the mind it is not so; there you cannot rub out the old until you have written in the new" [*In tabulis nisi priora deleveris, non alia inscripseris. In mente contra: nisi alia inscripseris, non priora deleveris*] (*MB*, 72/3:539). Therefore, Bacon urges, his reader needs to undergo an experience of destabilization before he can enter the age of experimental science: "My son, if I should ask you to grapple immediately with the bewildering complexities of experimental science before your mind has been purged of its idols [*si te jamjam animo ab idolis non repurgato vertiginosis experientiae ambagibus committerem*], beyond a peradventure you would promptly desert your leader. Nor, even if you wished to do so, could you rid yourself of idols by simply asking my advice without familiarizing yourself with nature" (72/3:539). What is needed before science is an epistemological and pedagogical experience of purging, an experience that in the *Advancement of Learning* Bacon argues must occur on the level of rhetorical presentation with a deferral of "present satisfaction" that prompts "expectant inquiry" (*AL*, 3:404). As Stanley Fish and Charles Whitney have argued, Baconian science necessitates a hermeneutic experience of doubt that disrupts both intellectual and historical certainty. The preparatory move of Baconian science is to critique various fragments of a cultural order that science wishes to supersede so its readers will be encouraged to doubt the straightforward and uncomplicated relation to meaning that these fragments might otherwise sustain. The effect is to produce as experience an uncertain relation to the future and an eccentric, out-of-synch relation to signification and to the past.[16]

Finally, this experience is a problem of health. For an inquiry into sexuality and the Baconian corpus, Bacon's epistemological elaborations of experience as the "purging of the idols of the mind" must be taken along with Bacon's insistent regime of enemas. In his diary, Bacon elaborates the series of enemas that he hoped would cure him of painful body heat and gas. He took his "familiar cooling glyster" [*clyster*] twice a day four or five days in a row, once in the afternoon and once before going to bed, "for that the one styrreth the more viscous humour and the other carry it away" (*LL*, 11:78). Bacon also took purging pills. But the problem with both was that "after certain inward pleasure" Bacon "found great vapourousnesses and disposicion *ad Montus mentis*, much wynd, great and glowing and sensible heat sub hypochondrus, wth some burning and payne more than usuall, besides wynd and rasping" (*LL*, 11:80). The homosocial and homoerotic seduction that promises an epoch of science is underwritten by the temporality of the enema, which promises a new ease but only returns Bacon to the old burning.

I would not encourage taking the experience of these enemas to be the authoritative grounds for Bacon's knowledge about the world or about himself in relation to the world. It is, rather, the temporality of the enema that makes it queer in relation to Bacon's desire for an epochal shift within the history of knowledge. In order to effect a shift from a science whose truthfulness is determined by the "external" authority of Aristotle to a science whose truthfulness is based on submission to formal method and experimentation, Bacon insists upon the necessity of repeatedly purging the "idols" of the mind. The main function of this purging is to prepare human understanding for a new historical enterprise—the collection of unlimited scientific experiments, all of which will be organized into "a natural history such as can serve as the foundation on which to build a new philosophy" (*PW*, 24). Purging prompts and sustains curiosity as the grounds for an epochal shift. But Bacon's enemas point to a *poiesis* of the body that frustrates the smooth movement that curiosity might otherwise admit. The analogies between Bacon's style, the problem of the senses, and these enemas assert a nonce-coordinated movement that responds to the desire for an epochal shift.

At stake in this *poiesis* is conversion. Hans Blumenberg has characterized the modern age as an attempt to readdress the Christian problematic of time in such a way that cancels out a theological conception of history. Blumenberg argues that New Testament eschatology was at odds with the persistent passage of time. Conversion to Christianity "tears the individual free from even the historical interests of his people and presses upon him his own salvation as his most immediate and pressing concern. . . . It makes an absolute lack of interest in the conceptualization and explanation of history a characteristic of the acute situation of its end."[17] Subsequent Christian thinking tended to compensate for the problem of historical time by locating the decisive events for salvation—the birth, death, and resurrection of Christ—firmly in the past, thus emphasizing faith in these events over action in history. The result was what Anthony Kemp has called an "ideology of time" based on a transcendence that cancels the passage of time in order to substitute for it "the immediate [and imaginary] presence of the Saviour one was born too late to know, too early to see come in glory."[18] It was Augustine who in *The Confessions* most forcefully accounted for the problem of time by locating this transcendental presence in memory as the recollection of an authentic, metaphysical origin forgotten through sinful actions. Augustine thereby transformed the "eschatological pathos directed against the *existence* of the world . . . into a new interest in the *condition* of the world" as a result of "original sin."[19] In Augustine's hands, the conversion to Christianity also necessitated the conversion of history through allegory into a sign of the existence and omnipotence of a Christian deity.

The modern age, Blumenberg argues, readdresses the problem of eschatology and historical time by turning a logic of conversion against Christianity's historical allegory. The modern age breaks with a theological revision of history by proposing an existential program of self-assertion "according to which man posits his existence in a historical situation and indicates to himself how he is going to deal with the reality surrounding him and what use he will make of the possibilities that are open to him."[20] One of the earliest and clearest examples of this existential program, one that Blumenberg does not discuss but that is important for Bacon, is Machiavellian republicanism. In the *Discourses,* Machiavelli replaces allegorical history and a concurrent notion of original sin with a model of history as the force of decay and disintegration opposed by the exertion of political will. In order to substantiate this will, Machiavelli imputes a theoretical subject whose capacities for doing evil precede the unfolding of history.

> All writers on politics have pointed out, and throughout history there are plenty of examples which indicate, that in constituting and legislating for a commonwealth it must needs be taken for granted that all men are wicked and that they will always give vent to the malignity that is in their minds when opportunity offers [*tutti gli uomini rei, e che li abbiano sempre a usare la malignità*

*dello animo loro, qualunque volta ne abbiano libera occasione*]. That
evil dispositions often do not show themselves for a time is due to
a hidden cause [*e quando alcuna malignità sta occulta un tempo,
procede da una occulta cagione*] which those fail to perceive who
have had no experience of the opposite; but in time—which is
said to be the father of all truth—it reveals itself. (*D*, 111–12/81)

Most striking about this account is the way in which an "evil disposition" deduced from historical time, "the father of all truth," contextu-
alizes the historical such that history is simply the proof of a malignant
"hidden cause" that the politically wise impute to all. In this modern gesture, as Blumenberg proposes, human freedom is burdened
not by original sin but by a "responsibility for the condition of the
world as a challenge relating to the future." This gesture thus cancels
a cosmodicy conditioned by theodicy by "basing its anthropodicy on
the world's lack of consideration of man, as its inhuman order."[21] In
Machiavelli's account, to refuse to choose evil is worse than choosing
evil because to refuse the choice is to give oneself over to the inhuman
order of history. As Gérald Sfez writes, Machiavelli's ethics involves
"making a leap from evil committed in indecision to a decision upon
evil. This leap is that from the apprehension of time as *chronos* to
time as *kairos:* not two different times but time relinquished and time
seized again."[22]

This existential program of self-assertion is predicated upon the
experience of history as fragmentation. Machiavelli forces this experience in order to urge an identification with his subject that supersedes
history in political terror. I do not mean to suggest that this experience
is outside the order of language. It is, rather, an effect of historiographic form. In the *Discourses* Machiavelli cuts up the consistent succession of events of both Livy's Rome and of contemporary Italian
history into small segments, examples—what Bacon in *The Advancement of Learning* will call Ruminated History, "a scattered history of
those actions which [some grave and wise men] have thought worthy
of memory, with politic discourse and observations thereupon; not
incorporate into the history, but separately, and as the more principal
in intention" (*AL*, 3:339). In so doing, Machiavelli modulates the protocols of early-fifteenth-century humanist historiography initiated by
Leonardo Bruni's *Historiarum Florentini Populi Libri XII* (presented to
the Florentine republic in 1449, five years after Bruni's death). Bruni

combined a two-hundred-year-old chronicle tradition, which had served as an instrument for the expression of city pride, with a humanist theoretical division of history into ancient, medieval, and modern. This reorganization of history through humanist modes of historical periodization allowed Bruni to endow historiography with the didactic function of teaching political wisdom. And it was through this political wisdom that Bruni in effect produced a narcissistic identification between Florentine urban magistrates (called "the Florentines") and the Roman republic. After Bruni, historiography could express civic pride not simply through the recording of successive events, but also by determining the causes of past events in order to help contemporary governments to similar results in the future.[23]

Instead of offering a straightforward point of identification, Machiavelli translates this historiographic and formal cutting up into the geopolitical effects of the church in the Italian peninsula in order to urge a political teleology that formally repeats the church's founding gesture. The church, Machiavelli argues, has made Italians "irreligious and perverse" [*sanza religione e cattivi*] (*D,* 144/96) because, through its irresponsible politics, it "has kept, and keeps, Italy divided" [*ha tinuto e tiene questa provincia divisa*] (145/96). The founding gesture of the church was to abolish pagan institutions, rites, and theologies that emphasized worldly glory and ferocious actions and substituted in their stead Christian rites that reinforce notions of sacrifice. The renaissance of the church, then, which Machiavelli locates with St. Francis and St. Dominic, repeated this founding gesture by persuading the people that "it is an evil thing to talk evilly of evil doing [*è male dir male del male*], and it is a good thing to live under obedience to such prelates [as confessors and preachers] [*bene vivere sotto la obedienza loro*], and that, if they did wrong, it must be left to God to punish them [*se fanno errore, lasciargli gastigare a Dio*]" (389/196). The repercussion is the corruption of the prelates, who fear nothing. In response to this state of affairs, Machiavelli counsels deciding upon evil in order to reverse the history of the church and, ultimately, revitalize Italian nationalism. But this decision formally repeats the church's founding gesture in a spectacle of masculine violence that attempts to control history's forces of fragmentation and decay. In his *Discourses,* Machiavelli argues that in the founding of a city, some amount of aggressive violation, the impression of *virtù* upon the unruly materiality out of which the city is built, is unavoidable. And when a republic becomes corrupt, as for Machiavelli it inevitably will, it becomes necessary to reintroduce the aggression of the founding moment through a spectacular act of terror, a cathartic purging of civic corruption. For a republic to "reconstitute" [*rigligliare*] itself, those entrusted with the care of the republic must "[instill] men with that terror and fear [*quel terrore e quella paura*] with which they had instilled them when instituting it" (388/196). The most infamous expression of this philosophy is chapter 25 of *The Prince*, where Machiavelli argues for the efficacy of impetuousness over circumspection in controlling change. As he puts it, "fortune is a woman and if she is to be submissive it is necessary to beat her" [*la fortuna è donna, ed è necessario, valendola tenere sotto, batterla e urtarla*].[24]

Science plays a central role in Blumenberg's analysis, insofar as scientific thinking relies on curiosity as a mode of orientation toward the future. Augustine opposes curiosity to "authentic" memory, arguing in *The Confessions* that curiosity—"making experiments by help of the flesh; which is masked under the title of knowledge and learning"—is an example of the world's seductiveness away from Christianity's eschatological program, at best an interruption of one's endless praise of God:

> What shall I say, whenas sitting in mine own house, a lizard catching flies, or a spider entangling them in her nets, oftentimes makes me attentive to them? Because these are but small creatures, does it make any difference? I proceed hereupon to laud thee the wonderful Creator and Disposer of all: but that is not the occasion of my beginning to be attentive to them. One thing it is to get up quickly, and another thing not to fall at all.

> [*Quid cum me domi sedentem stelio muscas captans vel aranea retibus suis inruentes inplicans saepe intentum me facit? Num quia parva sunt animalia, ideo non res eadem geritur? Pergo inde ad laudandum te, creatorem mirificum atque ordinatorem rerem omnium, sed non inde intentus esse incipio. Aliud est cito surgere, aliud est non cadere.*][25]

To fend off this seductiveness, this entanglement in the world, Augustine repeatedly insists upon the distinction between use and enjoyment, arguing that authentic enjoyment is in God and that everything else must be used for that purpose.[26] Scientific curiosity controverts Christian eschatology in that it results not simply in the accumulation of discrete novelties but also in an epistemological topography expressed in the form of institutions "that administer knowledge about reality in space and time and organize its growth."[27] The otherworldly future that Christianity projects collapses into this world as the *possibility* of political and institutional utopias.[28] But in Bacon's writings, curiosity also frustrates that topography by locating an enjoyment that serves no obvious use. While doubtless Bacon continually proposes what Blumenberg calls a "politico-morphic" understanding of the world "in which natural laws are interpreted as decreed by divine volition and the role of created things is defined in the plan of creation in terms of service and power," nevertheless he also forms an experience that does not easily move into this new world order.[29] Rather, this experience takes up the problematic of history as the relation to oneself and to others, creating a fragmented, sexed *poiesis* at the epochal threshold.

I propose to read this *poiesis* from two directions: first, as an outcome of Bacon's considerations of legal and scientific judgment; and second, as a backlash formation against his reliance on Protestant hermeneutics. In the first, I shall be concerned with how the political haunts Bacon's thinking about epistemology and the body; in the second, I shall focus more explicitly on sexuality. These two directions meet in a corporeal and an erotic attachment to the inability to move to the very future that Baconian science projects. It is at this syncopic threshold that the sexuality of the Baconian project emerges, precisely as that which does not convert.

## Jurisprudence, Counterjurisprudence, and the Baconian Body Politic

In his writings on common law reform, Bacon asserts what Peter Goodrich, following Deleuze and Guattari, calls a minor-jurisprudence: the expression of another possible form of judgment and the forging of "the means for another consciousness and another sensibility" from within a dominant mode of expression and of thought.[30] In Bacon's estimation, the problem with common law in the early seventeenth century was its form of expression. What concerned Bacon was "not . . . the matter of the laws," whose mixed national origins Bacon finds especially vivifying, but "the manner of their registry, expression, and tradition" (*LL*, 13:63). Bacon's worry was that the presentation of common law worked to secure the centrality of the judge, to the detriment of both legal proceedings and the education of lawyers. In the preface to his *Arguments of Law*, Bacon proposes that presenting common law in the form of pleadings rather than as the decisions of judges "is the more necessary, because the compendious form of reporting resolutions with the substance of the reasons, used lately by Sir Edward Coke, . . . doth not delineate or trace out to the young practisers of law *a method and form of argument for them to imitate*" (*AR*, 7:523, emphasis Bacon's). Bacon extends this proposal beyond the purview of legal reasoning so that it becomes the basis for his version of experimental science. In so doing, I shall argue, Bacon fractures the body, splays it between two dominant expressions, the body under juridical duress, and the body in relation to hygiene and health, both of which combine in his main rhetorical figure for subjectivity at the epochal threshold, the purging of the idols of the mind. Further, I shall argue that in these two expressions of the body, Bacon attempts to corporealize historical change. That is, whereas the insistence on the centrality of judicial reasoning attempts to assert the body of the judge as an allegorical figure that secures continuity, the Baconian body in its splitting attempts to display change as such.

During the sixteenth and seventeenth centuries, the dominant genre of common law literature changed fairly abruptly. The first three decades of the sixteenth century saw the demise of the publication of legal yearbooks. Beginning in 1292 under Edward I as authoritative reports of discussions that took place in courts, the yearbooks extended as a consecutive series no further than 1500, and between 1500 and 1535, only nine volumes were published. Meanwhile, the end of the sixteenth and beginning of the seventeenth century saw the rise of published law reports: Plowden's *Commentaries* (volume 1, 1571; volume 2, 1579); Brooke's *Graunde Abridgement* (1573); Dyer's *Reports* (1585; expanded and republished 1592 and 1601); Keilway's *Reports* (1602); Bendlowes's reports (published as an appendix to Ashe's *Promptuary* (1609); Dalison's *Reports* (1609); and Coke's *Reports* (1600–15; with volumes 12 and 13 published posthumously in 1659). Notebook manuscripts circulated within particular Inns of Court found their way into print, filling the gap left by the demise of the yearbooks, so that by the first quarter of the seventeenth century, and especially with the popularity of Dyer, Plowden, and Coke, the law report became the primary generic expression of English common law both in legal practice and in its popular representations. "There's a parcel of law-books," the law student Fungoso explains in Jonson's *Every Man Out of His Humour.* "There's Plowden, Dyer, Brooke, and Fitzherbert, divers such as I must have ere long."[31]

Whereas the yearbooks had served as guides to techniques of pleading, focusing as much if not more on judicial indecision as on judicial decisiveness, law reports almost always eschewed cases of judicial indecision, in their very form asserting reasoned decisiveness as a judge's primary responsibility.[32] As Plowden writes in the preface to his *Commentaries,* the first published law reports and the only set of law reports besides Coke's published before their author died,

> These reports excel any former book of reports in point of credit and authority, for other reports generally consist of the sudden saying of the judges upon motions by the serjeants and counselors at the bar, whereas all the cases here reported are upon points of law tried and debated upon demurrers or special verdicts, copies whereof were delivered to the judges, who studied and considered them, and for the most part argued in them, and after great and mature deliberation gave judgment thereupon, so that (in my opinion) these reports carry with them the greatest credit and assurance.[33]

The law report explicitly shifts from the yearbooks' assertion of a theater of the trial, where judges give "sudden sayings . . . upon motions by the serjeants and counselors at the bar" to the assertion of a theater of judgment, which displays judges in their reasoning, interpretive, and decision-making capacities. In attempting to explain a fundamental distinction between judicial and private knowledge, Plowden advises that while judges cannot acquit based on private knowledge of a case, they can acquit based on judicial knowledge, which is predicated upon a judge's supposedly superior capability to mobilize statute law. Plowden explains:

> If one is arraigned upon an indictment for an offense which is pardoned by parliament, there you ought not to proceed in it, nor give judgment, if he is found guilty, because it appears to you by

your judicial knowledge that you ought not to arraign him. For the judges ought to take notice of statutes, which appear to them judicial, altho' they are not pleaded, and then the misrecital of that, whereof the judges ought to take notice without recital, is not material.[34]

Judicial knowledge allows, indeed necessitates, that judges apply law not argued in a particular case "which *appear[s] to them* judicial" and that they use this knowledge of law to "correct" the lawyer's "misrecital." In short, judicial knowledge amounts to a privileged relation to the legal text that supersedes its recitation by lawyers. The assertion of a theater of judgment allows Plowden to theorize a version of judicial knowledge that overrules the scene of the trial.

Plowden's version of judicial knowledge is an abstraction of what he presents as the reporter's process of note taking. Explaining his method, Plowden writes,

I have for the most part reported cases in a summary way, collecting together the substance (as it appeared to me) of all that was said on one side, and on the other, and oftentimes of all that was said by the judges themselves, without reciting their arguments *verbatim*. In which case I have purposely omitted much that was said both at the bar and at the bench, for I thought that there were few arguments so pure as not to have some refuse in them, and therefore I thought it best to extract the pure only, and to leave the refuse, then and yet holding that to be the best method of reporting.[35]

In the reporting of case law, what counts is not the "mere" recitation and pleadings of law, but "pure" judicial thought—a purity of thought to be matched by the reporter in his own "excellency of judgment" in relation to the scene of the trial:

He who would reject a great part of what was spoken as vain and superfluous, and relate only that which was pure and material, ought to have not only great understanding and memory, but especially an excellent and distinguishing judgment, for otherwise he may reject as ineffectual that which is very material, and approve as effectual that which is of no weight. . . . This excellency of judgment is to be met with in the greatest perfection in those

who are endued with the greatest degree of reason, for it is said
that *ratio est radius divini luminis*.[36]

The judges' relation to the legal text is literally underwritten by the
court reporters' privileged relation to the legal performance. Rejecting
the "superfluous" and "immaterial" in the name of the pure has the
effect of consolidating the fantasy of a transcendent judgment in
which court reporter and decisive judge meet: *ratio est radius divini
luminus*. Similar to the structure of remarking that Jonathan Goldberg
elaborates in his discussion of Elizabethan secretaries, the law reports
authorize judicial decisiveness and its concurrent systems of reason
through the conscription of the reporter's hand, especially insofar as
the law report pretends to function as what Plowden calls "register
or memorial."[37] The contextualization of the law report's theater of
judgment within the "credit and authority" of memorializing allows
the genre to posit itself as simply mimetic of a judicial thought process, "great and mature deliberation," supposedly necessary for sustaining national justice. Paraphrasing Goldberg: The reporters are the
hands of a power that has inserted itself into other hands, disowned
to serve as the marks that validate judicial knowledge, reasoning, and
decisiveness, granted personal scope and individuality to secure the
hands of those in whose hands they wrote.[38] As a by-product of memorializing, this disowning validates an amanuensis that produces judicial reasoning through institutional amnesia.

In asserting and bolstering the person of the judge in his judicial
decisiveness, the law reports attempted to contextualize and limit
what Ernst Kantorowicz calls the "politico-ecclesiological" theory of
the king's two bodies, which mobilized an explicitly Christian division
of time into *chronos* and *kairos* that subsumed political particularity
within a broad protonational sense of continuity through kingship.[39]
By the time that sixteenth-century jurists were first elaborating this
theory (which, Kantorowicz argues, was practiced in England for
quite some time), the main internal limit to the king's royal prerogative was the crown in Parliament. As an essential component of the
body politic, by the sixteenth century Parliament had legislative authority to override the will of any particular king, even though the
king could through royal prerogative dispense with an individual's obligation to some statute—by granting a monopoly, for example.[40] As

J. G. A. Pocock has demonstrated, common law jurists of the late sixteenth and seventeenth centuries attempted to contextualize and
usurp this sense of national continuity that the king's two bodies permitted by asserting a mythic ancient constitution extending back to
time immemorial and carried forward through custom. The increased
"hardening" and "consolidation" of common law between 1550 and
1600 allowed the seventeenth century to propose a sense of national
historical continuity through the ancient constitution that delimited
monarchical authority by contextualizing it within the history of common law.[41] But also, in positing and authorizing a theater of judgment
that could theorize the king's two bodies, the law reports assert the
position of the judge as another conceptual limit.

In part, this limit was manifest in the theory that judicial decision
and common law, both based on reason, stood as correctives to statute
law. The only case so far as I know in which a judge in fact declares
an act of Parliament null and void is Coke's decision in Bonham's case
(1609)—where Coke asserts that "in many Cases, the Common law
doth controll Acts of Parliament, and sometimes shall adjudge them
to be void: for when an Act of Parliament is against Common Rights
and reason, or repugnant, or impossible to be performed, the Common Law shall controll it, and adjudge such an Act to be void."[42] Nevertheless, once law reports posit judges' interpretive right to measure
statute law by reference to a rational justice to which only judges have
access, they also validate an authority that theoretically can be subsumed neither by the king nor by the crown in Parliament—no matter how nervous or timid judges other than Coke may have been about
exercising that authority in practice.[43]

It would be inadequate, however, to understand the juridical authority posited by the law reports to be simply in opposition to the
doctrine of the king's two bodies. Rather, the goal of this relation,
especially under Coke's direction, was to translate the king's body politic as *corpus mysticum* into the quasi-mystical authority of law instantiated by "reason" as "proper judgment." While judicial reasoning
was produced through the disowning of the reporter's hand, nevertheless, and especially with Coke, judicial reasoning also attempted to
usurp the capacity of the king's body for allegorization, precisely as a
limit to kingship.

Take, as an example, Coke's well-known discussion of Calvin's case

(1608). The "outward" question of this case is "whether a child, born in Scotland since his Majesty's happy coming to the crown of England, be naturalised in England, or no?" as Bacon put it in his arguments for the plaintiff (*CPN*, 7:642). Does the plaintiff, Robert Calvin, born in Scotland after James's accession, have the right to bring legal action in England as a natural born subject? This question centers on the doctrine of the king's two bodies. The defendants argued that the body politic in England isn't the same as the body politic in Scotland; "it is all one as if they were in diverse persons" (*R*, 585). Therefore, when Calvin was born in allegiance to James in Scotland, he was also born out of allegiance to James in England and is, thus, in England an alien. Coke rejects this line of thinking and, siding with the plaintiff, decides instead that "legiance is a quality of mind, and not confined within any place" (*R*, 592). Allegiance is always to the king's natural body and not to the body politic. If things were the other way around, Coke reasons, then allegiance could justify treason: one could legitimately overthrow the king as body natural while ostensibly supporting the king as body politic.

The stakes of this case were extremely high. Its outcome justified England's overstepping its older geographic, political, and juridical boundaries in order to reexpress itself through the monarchy as Great Britain. Since the House of Commons refused to accept the recommendation of the commission, appointed under "An Acte authorizinge certaine Commissioners of the Realme of England to treate withe Commissioners of Scotland, for the weale of bothe kingdomes," 1 Jac., c. 2, to declare that by common law natives of Scotland and England after James's accession were naturalized in both countries, the crown looked to this case as a way to circumvent Parliament's obstinacy. "Though it was one of the shortest and least that ever we argued in this Court," Coke writes, "yet was it the longest and weightiest that ever was argued in any court" (*R*, 586). Bacon concurs: "For whether you do measure it by place, it reacheth not only to the realm of England, but the whole island of Great Britain; or whether you measure it by time, it extendeth not only to the present time, but much more to future generations" (*CPN*, 7:641).

But the stakes are high also because both Coke and Bacon use this case to attempt to redefine the king's two bodies. In his pleadings for the plaintiff, Bacon argues for "the mutual and reciprocal intercourse, . . . or influence or communication of qualities" (*CPN*, 7:668) between the body politic and the body natural: "[A]s [the king's] capacity politic worketh so upon his natural person, as it makes it differ from all other [of] the natural persons of his subjects; so *e converso*, his natural body worketh so upon his politic, as the corporation of the crown utterly differeth from all other corporations within the realm" (*CPN*, 7:667). Bacon gives his main image for this reciprocal relation toward the beginning of his pleadings:

> Law no doubt is the great organ by which the sovereign power doth move, and may be truly compared to the spirits: for if the sinews be without the spirits, they are dead and without motion; if the spirits move in weak sinews, it causeth trembling: so the laws, without the king's power, except the laws be corroborated, will never move constantly, but be full of staggering and trepidation. But towards the king himself the law doth a double office or operation: the first is to entitle the king or design him. . . . The second is,—that whereof we need not fear to speak in good and happy times, such as these are,—to make the ordinary power of the king more definite or regular. (*CPN*, 7:646)

On the one hand, as Bacon imagines it, law is the prosthetic instrument of the king and, as such, needs him in order to function. On the other hand, as prosthesis, the law also serves to limit and to regulate the king in his exercise of power. This image consolidates a Baconian "reason of state" that, as Julie Robin Solomon argues, conceives of good governance as prudent calculation. While Baconian reason of state maintains a strong attachment to kingship, it also instrumentalizes the governing function of the crown so that good governance is defined by submission to good reasoning. Baconian reason of state thereby accommodates James's transcendentalism insofar as it "underscores the hidden, sealed, and nontransferable nature of royal governance," James as spirit-mover; but reason of state also "empties out the political body and purpose of the monarch and prepares the way for constitutional monarchy" insofar as it emphasizes "the transparent, impartial, and exchangeable instrumentality of royal governance."[44]

Even as he decides for the plaintiff, Coke emphasizes the theological limitations of the body politic and compensates for them by bolstering the place of the judge. Allegiance isn't to the body politic, Coke argues, because "the body politic has no soul, for it is framed by the policy of man" (R, 593). With this statement, Coke attempts to sever the sense of instrumental mutuality integral to Bacon's pleadings. The lack of a soul in the body politic demands not the king as spirit-mover but judges and the body of law. Coke's first move is to change the image of law from the organs that the king inhabits to a form of writing that demands specialized knowledge in order to be interpreted:

> A King's Crown is a Hieroglyphick of the Lawes, where Justice &c. is administered. . . . Therefore if you take that which is signified by the Crown, that is, to doe Justice and Judgement, to maintain the Peace of the Land, &c., to separate right from wrong, and the good from the ill; that is to be understood as the capacity of the king, that *in rei veritate* hath capacity, and is adorned and indued with indowments as well of the soul as of the body, and thereby able to doe Justice and Judgement according to right and equity, and to maintain the peace, &c., and to find out and discuss the truth, and not of the invisible and immortal capacity that hath no such indowments; for of itself hath neither body nor soul. (R, 598)

The king, *in rei veritate,* has a soul and therefore has the capacity for justice, but this justice cannot be actualized through the body politic, which is simply man-made policy. In order to actualize this capacity, the king also needs to be able to read a veritable hieroglyphics of law, an ability that elsewhere in his *Reports,* Coke makes it clear the king does not have. In response to James I's attempt to determine the direction of judicial decision, Coke responds that the laws of England "are not to be decided by naturall reason," which James most assuredly had, "but by the artificiall reason and judgment of law, which law is an act which requires long study and experience, before that a man can attain cognizance of it."[45] Here, in Calvin's case, Coke's implication is that justice can only be actualized by the body of the law, which is separate from the king's body natural. Coke's second move is to introduce a different body image of the law. Commenting on the oddness of this case, Coke writes:

> And albeit I concurred with those that adjudged the Plaintif to be no alien, yet do I find a meer stranger in this case, such a one as the eye of the law (our books, and our book cases) never saw, as

the ears of our law (our Reporters) never heard of, nor the mouths of our law (for *Judex est lex loquens*) the Judges our forefathers of the law never tasted; I say, such a one, as the stomach of our law, our exquisite and perfect Records of pleadings, entries, and judgements (that make equal and true distribution of all cases in question) never digested. (*R*, 587)

Over and against Bacon's version of the king as a spirit-mover inhabiting the "great organ" of the law, Coke asserts an allegorical body of law made up of books as eyes, law reporters as ears, judges as mouths, and records of pleadings as stomach. Given the very questions at stake in this case, strikingly absent is the king in any interpretive capacity whatsoever. In effect, Coke upholds the doctrine of the king's two bodies in order to modify it into a nonce-theory of the hieroglyphics of the crown and the interpretive capacity of the judge both as the law's mouthpiece and as the actualization of the crown's soul. Refusing exactly what Kantorowicz argues the body politic as *corpus mysticum* is supposed to accomplish, that is, the political unification of the state through the body of the king, Coke instead reexpresses the politico-ecclesiological urge of this monarchical theory in a mystified version of judicial interpretation and its relation to the crown as supposed font of justice.[46]

In his writings on common law reform, Bacon argues for the reinstatement of court reporters paid for by the crown. This reinstatement does not simply signal Bacon's royalist proclivities, as Julian Martin argues.[47] Rather, this reinstatement mobilizes a royalist position in order to counter the law reports' mystification of judicial reasoning. The job of reporter has been taken over by judges, Bacon explains, "but great Judges are unfit persons to be reporters, for they have either too little leisure or too much authority, as may well appear by those two books, whereof that of my Lord Dier is but a kind of note book, and those of my Lord Cokes too much *de proprio*" (*LL*, 12:86). "Let not the judges meddle with these reports," Bacon writes, "lest from being too fond of their own opinion, and relying on their own authority, they exceed the providence of a reporter" (*DA*, 5:104). In short, Bacon splits the collapse of court reporter and judge precisely in order to limit the judicial authority garnered by the shift from yearbooks to law reports.

In Bacon's analysis, the mystification of judicial reason allows it to "forget" the power relations within which it is situated and from which it emerges. Bacon returns to the problem of independent judicial decisiveness in the opening sentences of his essay "Of Judicature":

> Judges ought to remember that their office is *jus dicere*, and not *jus dare*; to interpret law, and not to make law or give law. Else will it be like the authority of the Church of Rome, which under pretext and exposition of Scripture doth not stick to add and alter; and to pronounce that which they do not find; and by shew of antiquity to introduce novelty. Judges ought to be more learned than witty, more reverend than plausible, and more advised than confident. (*E*, 6:506)

If the problem with law reports is that they allow judges to be more witty than learned, more applauded than reverend, and more confident than advised, then the problem with witty, applauded, confident judges is that, in their claims to authority, they disown the complex set of power relations comprised by the juridical machinery of the court. Rather than authorizing the office of the judge through judicial reasoning, Bacon places judicial decisiveness within the juridical machinery of the court and asserts that "the office of judges may have reference unto the parties that sue, unto the advocates that plead, unto the clerks and ministers of justice underneath them, and to the sovereign or state above them" (*E*, 6:507). What emerges from Bacon's considerations is a form of judicial decisiveness that doesn't abstract from material circumstances but instead maintains considered relations with its constitutive parts: In relation to parties that sue, judges should maintain equity and, in criminal law especially, mercy. In hearing the pleadings of advocates, judges should work "to direct the evidence; to moderate length, repetition, or impertinency of speech; to recapitulate, select and collate the material points of that which hath been said; and to give the rule or sentence" (*E*, 6:508). The clerk, "wary in proceeding, and understanding in the business of the court; is an excellent finger of the court, and doth many times point the way to the judge himself" (*E*, 6:509). And finally, when the welfare of the people or the interests of the nation are at stake, judges ought to "often consult with the king and state" (*E*, 6:509). "Whatsoever is above these," Bacon writes, "is too much; and proceedeth either of glory and willingness to speak, or of impatience to hear, or of shortness of

memory, or of want of a staid and equal attention" (*E*, 6:508). Bacon's
essay implies a critique of the law reports' theater of abstracted reason
by validating in its stead a complex set of mainly institutional negotiations that underwrite and delimit a judicial decisiveness that, without
these limits, threatens to turn judicial interpretation all too readily
into case-law legislation.

But it is in his more philosophical and scientific considerations of
imagination, reason, and judgment that Bacon most fully develops a
jurisprudence counter to that of Coke, the common law judges, and
the law reports. By comparing the office of judges who give law with
the interpretive maneuvers of the Church of Rome, "which under pre-
text and exposition of Scripture doth not stick to add and alter, and
to pronounce that which they do not find," Bacon also implies that
the form of jurisprudence he advocates is linked to the iconoclastic
version of reason elaborated throughout his scientific writings. In the
*Dignity and Advancement of Learning,* Bacon revises a simple opposition between a rhetoric whose "duty and office . . . is not other than
to apply and recommend the dictates of reason to the imagination, in
order to excite the appetite and will," and a logic whose end "is to
teach a form of arguments to serve reason, and to entrap it" (4:455–
56) into a version of reasoned analysis whose function is to break so-
phistical axioms and avoid entrapment. One example of this form of
reasoning is *Of the Colors of Good and Evil,* which Bacon simply inserts
into the *Dignity and Advancement of Learning.* There he cites authoritative axioms—for example, "[W]hat men praise and honour is good;
[what] they dispraise and condemn is evil"—and then goes on to
show how the sophism in question deceives, in the case in hand, by
discounting the reasons of "ignorance, of bad faith, of party spirit and
factions, or the natural disposition of those who praise and blame"
(4:459). Bacon's notes for the *Essays* end up providing another example of this form of judicial reasoning when, following Cicero's use
of legal reasoning, Bacon opposes two sets of commonplaces, "in
which the question is argued and handled on either side, . . . such as
are 'For the Letter of the Law,' and 'For the Intention of the Law.'"
Moreover, Bacon explains, "I extend this kind of oration to other
cases; applying it not only to the judicial kind of oratory, but also to
the deliberative and demonstrative" (4:472). This expanded judicial
form centers on conflict as the equivalent of legal pleading in order

to provoke a judgment that breaks with commonplaces and leads to further reasoning, "from experiments to axioms; which axioms themselves suggest new experiments," as Bacon characterizes it in its scientific manifestation (4:413).

But what, then, of the body? Most obvious, because most insistent, is the body under juridical duress. In order to isolate the causes that will make up his natural history, Bacon argues for the observation of Nature "under constraint and vexed [*constrictae et vexatae*]; that is to say, by the art and the hand of man [*per artem et ministerium humanum*] she is forced out of her natural state, and squeezed and moulded" (*PW*, 4:29/1:141). It isn't at all difficult to see, I suspect, that this isolation of cause relies upon a version of criminal proceedings in which torture produces the "truths" upon which, in turn, legal judgment will rely. In *The Wisdom of the Ancients* as well as in *The Preparation Towards a Natural and Experimental History*, Bacon reads Proteus in his ability to shift forms as an emblem of "the ultimate struggles and efforts of matter" (*PN*, 4:257). Like Nature, Bacon argues, Proteus's secrets and prophesies can only be revealed if he is manacled, which causes him to change shapes until, finally, he resumes his own shape and gives his prophesy. Bacon explains:

> [I]f any skilful Servant of Nature shall bring force to bear on matter, and shall vex it and drive it to extremities as if with the purpose of reducing it to nothing [*et materiam vext atque urgeat, tanquam hoc ipso destinato et proposito, ut illam in nihilum redigat*], then will matter (since annihilation or true destruction is not possible except by the omnipotence of God) finding itself in these straits, turn and transform itself into strange shapes, passing from one change to another till it has gone through the whole circle and finished with the period; when, if the force be continued, it returns at last to itself. And this constraint and binding will be more easily and expeditiously effected, if matter be laid hold on and secured by hands; that is, by its extremities [*Ejus autem constrictionis seu alligationis ratio magis facilis erit et expedita, si materia per manicas comprehendatur, id est per extremitates*]. (*WA*, 6:726/6:652)

Knowing the effects of this vexing will allow for an understanding of cause—an intellectual leap secured specifically by the logic of the trial. Hence, Kenneth Cardwell argues that the Baconian experiment takes the form of an inquisitorial criminal trial, with Nature placed in the position of the suspect and the experimenter taking the position of the examining magistrate.[48] However, Bacon's point in turning to the trial isn't to maintain the status quo of the law but to effect a revision of understanding in relation to the production of knowledge and truth. "The world is not to be narrowed till it will go into the understanding (which has been done hitherto)," Bacon writes, "the understanding is to be expanded and opened [*expandendus . . . et laxandus*] till it can take in the image of the universe, as it is in fact" (*PN*, 4:256/ 1:397). The writers of natural history, Bacon urges, are "to be lowly of mind and search for knowledge in the greater world, and to throw aside all thought of philosophy" until this new natural history is composed (*HN*, 5:131).

To the extent that the experiment also necessitates an iconoclastic breaking of the experimenter's idols of the mind, it's most accurate to understand the experiment-as-trial in relation to hagiography. Hagiography attempts to think broad historical change through the torture of the saint's body by an almost evacuated juridical authority. As Julia Lupton argues, the primary function of the saint's vexed and flayed body is for Christianity to locate as historical cut and, subsequently, to commemorate as iconic relic the shift from a pagan to a Christian world order. The saint's torture proves, through "the perversity of the pagan tyrant . . . the impotence of Roman law in late antiquity," but crucially, to prove it "from the vantage point of the Christian world order." To this extent, "the saints are rebels against one order, but only in the name of another: a theocratic City of God that will finally reinforce rather than dissolve the disciplines of the earthly *polis*."[49] For example, Eusebius will portray the tyrannical Roman rulers as exceptions to a rule of law that retroactively secures the Christianization of Roman authority, the Christian city of God served by earthly, Roman rulers. Both Pilate and Tiberius knew about and accepted as true Christ's resurrection, Eusebius argues, and Tiberius even went so far as to attempt to get the senate to proclaim Christ as a deity; only the senate refused upon some legal technicalities.[50] Some twelve hundred years later, repeating Eusebius's gesture, although this time in order to secure a Protestant national order, John Foxe will level a relentless critique of the papacy, but he will do so in the name of the continuity of the "true church" and from the vantage point of Elizabeth as righteous Protestant ruler. Foxe's Protestant saints rebel against a supposedly bankrupt Catholicism from the vantage point of God's "happy preservation of [Elizabeth's] royal estate" (*AM*, 1:8).

In its insistence on thinking historical change through the vexing and torture of the body, hagiography, Protestant hagiography in particular, instantiates the tactical reversal of authoritative, ecclesiastical judgment, so often the condition for the emergence of a new world order. The effect is a sustained critique of office. For example, Foxe's "Life and Story of Archbishop Cranmer" repeatedly stages scenes of judgment in which Cranmer, under juridical duress, exposes the incompetence and deceitfulness of those who claim the ability to judge him. Early on in the life, as a kind of preparatory anecdote, Foxe tells of a country priest who calls Cranmer a "hosteler" that "hath no more learning than the goslings that go yonder on the green" (8:15–16). The priest is imprisoned, but instead of judging him, Cranmer decides to submit to this priest's accusations. "If I have no learning you may now try it and be out of doubt thereof," Cranmer offers. The priest, of course, refuses, explaining that he is ignorant, knows no Latin, and his "only study hath been to say my service and mass, fair and deliberate" (8:17). Cranmer then questions him on some Bible stories, supposing that at least the priest has read the Bible in English. When the priest cannot answer even these very simple questions, Cranmer charges, "I now well perceive howsoever ye have judged heretofore of my learning, sure I am that you have none at all." He then gives the general moral: "But this is the common practice of all you that be ignorant and superstitious priests, to slander, backbite, and hate all such that are learned and well-affected towards God's word and sincere religion" (8:18). Characterizing Cranmer's strategy quite precisely, the archbishop of Gloucester remarks after Cranmer, on trial, has given him a particularly pointed history lesson, "We come to examine you, and you, methinks, examine us" (8:53). Most famously, at the end of the life, Cranmer recants his previous support of the Act of Supremacy and is forced by Mary to make a public confession of his mistaken support of the Reformation. Instead, however, Cranmer takes the opportunity to renounce the pope "as Christ's enemy, and antichrist, with all his false doctrine." Foxe draws the following lesson:

"I think there was never cruelty more notably or better in time de-
luded and deceived; for it is not to be doubted but they looked for a
glorious victory and a perpetual triumph by this man's recantation;
who, as soon as they heard these things, began to let down their ears,
to rage, fret, and fume; and so much the more, because they could
not revenge their grief—for they could no longer threaten or hurt
him" (8:88). The fulminations of judicial authority at Cranmer's reversal, which result finally in his being burned at the stake, prove the
very impotency of that authority in the face of "righteous" judgment.

Bacon uses the hagiographic trial in order to effect a historical shift
through materiality and epistemic aggression from an authority-based
science to a "new world" governed by the protocols of experimental
science. It may well be, as Bacon proposes at the beginning of book 2
of the *New Organon,* that "of a given body to generate and superin-
duce a new nature or new natures, is the work and aim of Human
Power" and that concurrently "of a given nature to discover the form,
or true specific difference, or nature-engendering nature, or source of
emanation . . . is the work and aim of Human Knowledge" (*NO,*
4:2.1). But these tasks and purposes must also be understood within
the context of the reversal with which Bacon begins the *New Organon's*
first book: "Man, being the servant and interpreter of Nature, can do
and understand so much and only so much [as] he has observed in
fact or in thought of the course of nature, . . . [for] Nature to be commanded must be obeyed" (*NO,* 4:1.1, 3). Before placing the body of
Nature under juridical duress, "man" must submit to a regime of
iconoclasm that effectively rewrites how he knows and how he thinks.

In opposition to Coke's judges, mouthpieces of the law and in-
stantiators of the crown's soul, Bacon insists upon the necessity of
humility in judgment. Since we must "approach with humility and
veneration to unroll the volume of Creation" (*HN,* 5:132), Bacon
presents himself as a "child of time rather than of wit" [*pro partu
temporis quam ingenii*], as a product of chance and not ability (*GI,*
4:11/1:123; *NO,* 4:1.122/1:217). He asserts that he has been successful
"by no other means than the true and legitimate humility of the human spirit" (*GI,* 4:19). He claims that future times will understand
him not as one who has done great things, "but simply made less
account of things that were accounted great" (*NO,* 4:1.97). He ac-

knowledges that he cannot complete the project that he has set out for himself, and he even acknowledges that future generations will find many mistakes in his work (4:1.116, 118). But Bacon demands the same humility from others who participate in his science. One of the main evils, Bacon asserts, that has prevented science from blossoming is the "opinion or conceit; which though of long standing is vain and hurtful; namely, that the dignity of the human mind is impaired by long and close intercourse with particulars, . . . especially since they are laborious to search, ignoble to meditate, harsh to deliver, infinite in number, and minute in subtlety" (*NO*, 4:1.83). Bacon's method debunks this self-importance. "For my way of discovering sciences goes a far way to level men's wits, and leaves little to individual excellence; because it performs everything by the surest rules and demonstrations" (*NO*, 4:1.122). Baconian science demands a humble epistemological pose as the condition for historical change.

The other dominant expression is the body signified within a regime of health. The operations of this expression are perhaps most evident in Bacon's *History of Life and Death*. In this work, experimentation on Nature allows Bacon to assert an axiom, and this axiom then allows him to posit a rule concerning the body's relations to processes within the history of life and death—a rule, it is important to add, that Bacon insists is "imperfect" and "set down . . . provisionally" (*HL*, 5:136). For example, as the result of experimentation, Bacon asserts the axiom that "in nature there is no annihilation; and therefore the thing which is consumed passes into air, or is received into some adjacent body." This axiom allows him subsequently to posit the scientific truth that "there is no consumption, unless that which is lost by one body passes into another" (*HL*, 5:320). The general effect of this rule is to resignify the body within a regime of science.

The study of the "natural forces" of repair and depredation allows Bacon to posit a conscriptive hygienic that becomes the basis for both an ethical relation to one's body and a political relation to authoritative power structures. In the section of his *History of Life and Death* that he considers to be his "systematic inquiry" (*HL*, 5:221), Bacon portrays significant, constitutive body parts—spirit, blood, bowels, juices of the body, the outer parts of the body—in their many relations to the body's environment, including air, food, drugs, and ailments, in order to produce statements concerning the body's repair and depredation that move among the anecdotal, the scientific, and the moral. For example:

> 1.25. The Turks use likewise a kind of herb, called "coffee," which they dry, grind to powder, and drink in warm water. They affirm that it gives them no small vigour both to their courage and their wit. Yet this taken in large quantities will excite and disturb the mind; which shows it to be of a similar nature to opiates. (*HL*, 5:271)
>
> 2.1. Exclusion of the external air tends in two ways to prolong life. First, because most of all things, next to the internal spirit, the external air (although it is as life to the human spirit, and contributes very much to health) preys upon the juices of the body and hastens its desiccation; whence the exclusion of the air conduces to longevity. (*HL*, 5:283)
>
> 4.6. The inhabitants of Orkneys, who live on salt fish, and fish-eaters in general, are long-lived. (*HL*, 5:291)
>
> 6.6. Exercises to distribute the juices over the body should affect all members equally; not (as Socrates says) that the legs should move and the arms rest, nor the contrary; but that all the parts should share in the motion. It is of great use also for longevity that the body should never remain long in the same posture, but should change it every half hour at least, except during sleep. (*HL*, 5:301).

The net effect of these statements is to conscript the body within a quasi-regulatory ethics of health and well-being—what to eat, how to act—that also, de facto, authorizes the truths of nascent experimental science.

But the body submitted to "natural processes" also suspends the authority of office and quite specifically writes that suspension onto the body as its truth. Early in the *History of Life and Death*, Bacon gives the "real truth" of this scientific body:

> In declining age repair takes place very unequally, some parts being repaired successfully enough, others with difficulty and for the worse; so that from this time the human body begins to suffer that torture of Mezentius, *whereby the living die in the embraces of the dead,* and the parts that are easily repaired, by reason of their connection with the parts hardly reparable, begin to decay. For even

after the decline of age the spirit, blood, flesh and fat are still easily repaired, when the drier or more porous parts, as the membranes, tunicles, nerves, arteries, veins, bones, cartilages, most of the bowels, and nearly all the organic parts are repaired with difficulty and loss. Now these parts when they ought to perform their office of repairing the other reparable parts, being impaired in their powers and activities, are no longer equal to their proper functions; and hence it results that very soon the whole tends to dissolution, and those very parts, which in their own natures are most capable of repair, are yet through the failure of the organs of repair no longer able to be similarly repaired, but decay, and in the end totally fail.

[*Vergente aetate, inaequalis admodum fit reparatio; aliae partes reparantur satis foeliciter, aliae aegre et in pejus; ut ab eo tempore corpora humana subire incipiant tormentum illud Mezentii, ut* viva in amplexu mortuorum immoriantur, *atque facile reparabilia, propter aegre reparabilia copulata, deficiant. Nam etiam post declinationem et decursum aetatis, spiritus, sanguis, caro, adeps, facile reparantur; at quae sicciores aut porosiores sunt partes, membranae et tunicae omnes, nervi, arteriae, venae, ossa, cartilagines, etiam viscera pleraque, denique organica fere omnia, difficilius reparantus, et cum jactura. Illae autem ipsae partes, cum ad illas alteras reparabiles partes actu reparandas omnino officium suum praestare debeant, activitate sua ac viribus imminutae, functiones suas amplius exequi non possunt. Ex quo fit, ut paulo post omnia ruere incipiant, et ipsae illae partes quae in natura sua sunt valde reparabiles, tamen deficientibus organis reparationis, nec ipsae similiter amplius commode reparentur, sed minuantur, et tandem deficiant.*] (*HL*, 5:218/2:106, emphasis Bacon's)

The truth of the body is the decay of office: when parts of the body whose office is repair begin to deteriorate, then "very soon the whole tends to dissolution." This truth relies as much on the reversal of the topos by which political harmony is figured as corporeal health as it does on the iconoclastic gesture that Bacon uses to effect a historical shift in the first place. For example, as Sidney repeats the story from Livy's *History of Rome,* the same story with which Shakespeare opens *Coriolanus,* in order to prevent the populace from rebelling against the senate, Menenius Agrippa "telleth them a tale, that there was a time when all the parts of the body made a mutinous conspiracie against the belly, which they thought devoured the fruits of each others labour," thereby in "punishing the belly they plagued themselves."[51] Or, to take a more complex example, in his essay "Of Seditions and Toubles," Bacon considers how "poverty and broken estate" among the nobility, when combined with "want" among the populace, leads to the worst sort of sedition. "For the rebellions of the belly are the worst" (*E*, 6:409). But immediately after posing the body as material cause of political turmoil, Bacon abstracts from it to posit a "politic body" in which "discontentment" is analogous to the humours, "which are apt to gather a preternatural heat and to inflame" (*E*, 6:409). This abstraction allows Bacon to propose a series of metaphorical "antidotes" and "remedies" to cure potential "diseases" in the body politic. The "real truth" of the body that Bacon gives in the *History of Life and Death* literalizes these fables of corporeal health and, in so doing, inscribes onto the hygienic body the body politic's concern for offices. In this way the depredation of the hygienic body as "natural force" is due to a corporealization of a problem in the body politic.

Hence, Bacon's very odd use of Mezentius as an example for natural decay. Mezentius—"scorner of the gods," who along with the other rulers fighting Aeneas "muster[s] forces and strip[s] the wide fields of husbandmen," and whose cruelty arouses "five hundred" to take up arms "against himself"[52]—is doubtless an illustration of what Bacon might call an "unfit head." But his isn't the only office that concerns Bacon here. Mezentius serves as a model of natural decay primarily because the tortured king dies "in the embraces of the dead." After being wounded by Aeneas, Mezentius leaves the battlefield, and his son Lausus takes his place, only to have Aeneas kill him. When Lausus's body is returned to the Etruscans, Mezentius clings to it and confesses his failure to carry out both the office of father and of ruler:

> My son! and did such joy of life possess me, that in my stead I suffered thee to meet the foeman's sword—thee, whom I begat? Am I, thy father, saved by these wounds of thine, and living by thy death? Ah me! now at last is come to me, alas! the bitterness of exile; now is my wound driven deep! Yea, and I, my son, stained thy name with guilt—I, driven in loathing from the throne and scepter of my fathers. Long have I owed my punishment to my country and my people's hate; by any form of death should I have

yielded up my guilty life. Now I live on, and leave not yet daylight
and mankind, but leave I will.

[*tantane me tenuit vivendi, nate voluptas,*
*ut pro me hostili paterer succedere dextrae,*
*wuem genui? tuane haec genitor per volnera servor,*
*morte tua vivens? heu, nunc misero mihi demum*
*exsilium infelix, nuncalte volnus adactum!*
*idem ego, nate, tuum maculavi crimine paternis.*
*debueram patriae paenas odiisque meorum:*
*omnis per mortis animam sontem ispe dedissem.*
*nunc vivo neque adhuc homines lucemque relinquo.*
*sed linquam.*]

(10.846–56)

This abject acceptance of the failure of office stands as the "truth" of
the "natural processes" of death. After describing these processes,
Bacon then gives their cause: the spirit, which "like a gentle flame is
ever preying on the body" [*instar flammae lenis, perpetuo praedato-*
*rius*], along with the air, which "likewise sucks and dries bodies" [*qui*
*etiam corpora sugit et arefacit*], finally "destroy[s] the workshop of the
body with its machines and organs, and make[s] them incapable of
performing the work of repair" [*officinam corporis et machinas et or-*
*gana perdat, et inhabilia reddat ad munus reparationis*] (*HL*, 5:218/
1:106). The anticipation of a historical shift that the body under juridical duress might prompt is frustrated by the body signified within a
regime of health. Rather then encouraging entry into a new age of
science, this spirit refuses an epochal shift, locating the truth of the
scientific and hygienic body with the failed patriarch, the failed ruler,
and most generally the decay of political office.

## The Body that Does Not Convert

Bacon's epochal thinking explicitly attempts to abstract the assertions
of Protestant biblical hermeneutics in order to rearticulate these assertions as both the interpretive preconditions and the historical paradigm for the new philosophy to which experimental science will lead.
Bacon's "purging" of the "the idols of the mind" repeats in a new
context the experience that, for Luther and Calvin, precipitates the
"correct" reading of Scripture, a reading that breaks the "external"

authority of the Catholic Church. The mind, as Calvin writes, is "a perpetual forger of idols" and is for this reason constitutively susceptible to the idolatry that is Catholicism.[53] Therefore, what is needed before the reading of Scripture is a prior experience by which these idols of the mind and, thus, the mind's dependence on Catholic authority are broken. Luther's and Calvin's insistence upon this iconoclastic experience serves as a kind of subjective reiteration of the historiographic schemata that allow Protestantism to situate itself in relation to both church history and Catholic historiography. That is, this experience repeats as subjective the very terms and the very temporality that allow Protestantism to grasp itself as historically different.[54]

In its epoch-making gestures, Baconian science repeats the form of this Protestant historiographic move in order to lay the ground for the subject who comes to science. In *The New Atlantis*—which the Royal Society later took as its model for the institution of experimental, scientific inquiry—Bacon "narrativizes" the formation of the subject of science in an allegory of interpellation. The narrative movement of *The New Atlantis* allegorically reflects the epistemological movement that Bacon gives as steps two and three respectively of his *Great Instauration,* the movement from "Directives for the Interpretation of Nature" to the collection of the "Phenomena of the Universe" as the basis for a "Natural and Experimental History" (*PW,* 4:22). *The New Atlantis* opens with the dynamic of despair and hope over the unknown that is also central to the *New Organon*'s shift from debunked and depleted ancient science to the possibilities of new, experimental science (*NO,* 4:1.92). A group of Spanish seafarers, exploring a distant ocean, give themselves up "for lost men, and [prepare] for death." Yet, sustaining hope, they pray and subsequently see "towards the north, as it were thick clouds, which did put us in hope of land, knowing how that part of the South Sea was utterly unknown, and might have islands or continents that hitherto were not come to light" (*NA,* 3:129). And *The New Atlantis* ends with the description of an institution for experimental science that—with its experiments on the "coagulations, indurations, refrigerations, and conservations of bodies" (*NA,* 3:156); its production of artificial metals used "for curing of some diseases and for prolongation of life in some hermits that choose to live there" (3:157); its experiments on dead things buried in earth, air, or water (3:157); its Waters of Paradise for prolongation of life and baths for restoring and prolonging life (3:158); its "dissections and trials" that explain how to resuscitate life (3:159); and its drinks "insinuated" into the body to extend life and make skin tougher than it would otherwise be (3:160)—would be the ideal place for Bacon to carry out the inquiries into "the Nature of Durable and Non-Durable inanimate bodies" and "touching the desiccation, artefaction, and consumption of bodies inanimate and vegetable," as well as "the inteneration, softening, and renewal of bodies, after they have once commenced to become dry" (*HL*, 5:220), proposed in *History of Life and Death*.

But this movement and, by extension, the allegory of interpellation of the subject of science is interrupted by two surprising moments: first, the Feast of the Family, an obviously political ritual that attempts to align kinship structure, the royalist state, and merchant systems of exchange; and second, this ritual's interpretation by the merchant Joabim, a "circumcised" Jew, the narrator explains, who is left to practice Judaism, since these New World Jews differ from the "Christ-hating" Jews of Europe, who "have a secret inbred rancour against the people among whom they live: these (contrariwise) give unto our Saviour many high attributes, and love the nation of Bensalem extremely" (*NA*, 3:151). These scenes do not simply interrupt the formation of the Baconian subject of science; they substantiate that subject's epistemological and historiographic limits. Baconian science finds its limit in a form of sexuality that recalls and commemorates the purported carnality of the Jews.

The Spanish explorers have landed on the uncharted, New World island of Bensalem. Some inhabitants from Bensalem approach the ship of these explorers and ask, "Are ye Christians?" An affirmative answer to the question is the condition for the explorers to land. The Spanish answer that they are indeed Christians, "fearing the less," the narrator explains, because the Bensalemites themselves appear to be Christian (3:131). Even so, this denial of fear isn't something to be immediately trusted. Once they are alone, quarantined, the Spanish narrator warns his company not to act in any way that is unchristian:

We are come here amongst a Christian people, full of piety and humanity: let us not bring that confusion of face upon ourselves,

as to show our vices or unworthiness before them. Yet there is
more. For they have by commandment (*though in form of cour-*
*tesy*) cloistered us within these walls for three days: *who knoweth*
*whether it be not to take some taste of our manners and conditions?*
... For these men that they have given us for attendance may
withal have an eye upon us. Therefore for God's love, and as we
love the weal of our souls and bodies, let us so behave ourselves
*as we may be at peace with God,* and may find grace in the eyes of
these people. (3:134, emphasis mine)

In his warning, the narrator emphasizes possible apparatuses of sur-
veillance: "[T]hey have by commandment (*though in form of courtesy*)
cloistered us within these walls for three days: *who knoweth whether it*
*be not to take some taste of our manners and conditions?*" And he also
quite cagily refuses sincerity in response to the possibility of being
watched at this particular moment: "[L]et us so behave ourselves *as*
*we may be at peace with God,* and may find grace in the eyes of these
people." While the narrator's admonition does not assume a guilty
conscience concerning Christian identity, this speech—as an example
of what Julie Solomon calls the merchants' "vocational tactic of not
representing the self and its desires"[55]—does assume an anxiety concerning the appropriate, well-mannered enactment of Christianity for
a watchful if courteous audience. At issue here is the outward performance of spiritual peace for an audience who, so think the Spanish,
might be disturbed upon seeing the opposite.

Steven Shapin has argued that seventeenth-century English experimental science and its systems of knowledge are predicated upon
gentlemanliness and the systems of civility in which that social stratum expressed and sustained its notions of sociality. This form of
sociality—based mainly upon a Christian tradition of honor refracted
through both merchant culture and courtliness—prescribed the protocols for truth-telling, Shapin argues, by which scientific knowledge
could be produced and judged as credible.[56] This moment in *The New*
*Atlantis* stands as a narrative precursor to that system of evaluation,
draining sociality of its Christian motive while maintaining its Christian form. A formal courtesy whose content is Christianity is here the
corporeal practice by which identity can traverse national particularity and work itself into a limited transnationalism.[57] To this extent,
the courteous performance of Christian identity formally attempts a

gesture of self-assertion that reiterates a European Christianity purged of its history. In a moment of revelation, the Bensalemites receive "all the canonical books of the Old and New Testament," along with the Apocalypse and "some other books of the New Testament which were not at that time written" (3:138). The immediacy of this scene of revelation translates into an unmediated Christianity that has no institutional or textual history, no history of the Catholic Church, and no history of the Protestant Reformation.

But the history of European Christianity returns nonetheless as Bensalem's and, by extension, experimental science's historiographic unconscious. After all, it is not difficult to notice that Bacon's allegory of interpellation is haunted by the Spanish Inquisition. Though neither present as a narrative event nor obvious as a narrative context, many of *The New Atlantis*'s otherwise disparate images and details concerning the daily life of the Bensalemites cohere around the Spanish Inquisition as a missing referent: the presence of the Spanish explorers, the odd figure of the Jew, the confinement of the explorers in Strangers' House, the rather cagey relation between the state and the members of Salomon's House, and the presence almost everywhere of notaries. The connotative presence of the Spanish Inquisition serves no direct narrative function. Nor does the Spanish Inquisition serve as the "sociopolitical context" of Baconian science. But it is precisely this nonfunctionality that makes these connotations historically significant, specifying what is historically irreducible about Bacon's institution of secular science.

In English accounts, the Spanish Inquisition figures as the antinomic perversion of the law, the point, as Slavoj Zizek puts it, at which "the opposition between the law and its transgressions repeats itself inside . . . the law itself," the scandalous moment when the law, in confrontation with the problem of heresy and disbelief, itself turns heretical and tyrannical.[58] In John Foxe's *Acts and Monuments*, for example, the lives of Nicholas Burton and John Fronton tell how the inquisitors imprison English merchants on trumped-up charges in order to seize their goods and, in the case of Burton, execute them. Such actions demonstrate "the extreme dealing and cruel ravening of those catholic inquisitors of Spain, who, under the pretensed visor of religion, do nothing but seek their own private gain and commodity" (*AM*, 8:513). More pointedly, Montanus's *Discovery and Playne Decla-*

*ration of Sundry Subtill Practices of the Holy Inquisition in Spayne* (1567; English translation 1568), the main source in England for information about the Spanish Inquisition up through the seventeenth century, details the abuses and perversions internal to the Inquisition's legal processes, from familiars whose job it is to entrap unsuspecting Christians to the complicity in the courts between lawyers and the inquisitors. "A bloodier Law used bloodier was never heard or shall," William Warner writes in *Albion's England* (1612). "Tormenting men until they guess by whom they are accus'd, / Which guessed, it against themselves for Evidence is us'd."[59]

The historiographic import of this portrait is that Catholicism becomes the figure for "absolute criminality" against which the Protestant Reformation is asserted and justified as righteous. In "a diligent endeavor to remove the infection that might grow as well of the Jewish and Mahometicall heresies that daily do arise" (a project, by the way, that Montanus endorses), the Spanish Inquisition only concretizes Catholic trust in ritual and law—so Montanus argues—finally turning its aggression against the "true" Reformation itself.[60] In opposition to the Spanish Inquisition, which attempts to teach and convert by "fire and sword," the force of law, the Protestant Reformation, a kind of righteous reiteration of the Inquisition's intentions, teaches and converts by the "sword of God's word."[61]

Because of its dependence on this historiographic model, the Reformation can never entirely supersede the Catholicism against which it pits itself. To compensate, the Reformation tends to translate this historiographic model into a defensive political and psychic formation. English Protestantism historically differentiates itself from Catholicism through iconoclasm, the destruction and desecration of church artifacts. But Protestantism also externalizes the violence of iconoclasm as the pope's evil rage, of which, in its perversion of law, the Inquisition is simply an extension. Whereas Foxe uses Protestant martyrology to demonstrate the impotence of the Roman Church, Montanus uses the Spanish Inquisition to secure that church as a continual threat against which Protestants must defend themselves. As the English translator of the *Discovery* writes, "if the Devil's holines, and his lieuetenaunt generall, the Pope's majestie were a little moved then [at the Council of Trent], they be now (doubt ye not) enraged, and transubstantiat into furour and borne Woodnes, to see their revenues

decay, their monasteries and sinagoges defaced, their villaines defet-
ted, their noble champions slaine."[62] The very assertion of Protestant
England's supremacy goes hand in hand with a paranoid, psychic
after-effect that the Inquisition configures.

The strongest influence that the Spanish Inquisition exerts upon
*The New Atlantis* has little to do with content, but a great deal to do
with form. Perhaps the main generic moment in English anecdotes
concerning the Inquisition, aside from the culmination in martyr-
dom, is the trap by which the unsuspecting victim is set up by a seemingly friendly figure. For example, Foxe tells of San Romanus, who
converts to Protestantism but is subsequently betrayed by Spanish
merchants, "pretending outwardly a fair countenance of much good
will, but secretly practicing his destruction." These merchants send
letters to San Romanus asking to see him, but when he shows up,
"certain friars were set ready to receive him" (*AM*, 4:448). Eventually,
San Romanus is burned at the stake. A similar trick happens to Roche,
an engraver whom an inquisitor urges to break a statue of Mary and,
when Roche does, has him condemned to death for blasphemy
(4:450–51). As Warner explains,

> This Spanish Inquisition is a Trap so slyly set,
> As into it Wise, Godly, Rich, by Blanchers base are set.
> Direct or indirect to answer all is one,
> From th'holy Inquisition escape but very few or none.[63]

*The New Atlantis* actively rejects the Spanish Inquisition as a localized
cultural and historical phenomenon. But in narrativizing the interpellation of the subject of science, *The New Atlantis* repeats this formal
reversal, signaling the dangers that run concurrent with it without
ever actualizing them.

The Spanish narrator's gesture toward civilized transnationalism
is limited through the foregrounding of epistemological invasiveness.
Four days after the Spanish are quarantined, a governor explains that
for the past nineteen hundred years, the "Brethren of Salomon's
House"—the secret scientific community that apparently controls
Bensalem—have been spying on Europe and the rest of the world,
gathering knowledge concerning politics and the sciences (*NA*, 3:146).
Upon hearing this, the Spanish are simply dumbstruck, "astonished
to hear so strange things probably told." While the courtesy of the

earlier moment attempts to forestall anxiety concerning the Other's
desire—when they ask "Are ye Christians," what do they *really expect*
from us?—this second moment exacerbates that anxiety, crystallizing
what the courtesy of the Spanish attempts to preempt into a potentially more provocative, divisive, and epistemologically more aggressive question: What do they *really know* about us?

*The New Atlantis* translates the potential dangers that underlie this
epistemological aggression into posited judgments concerning sex
and the body. A week after the Spanish land on Bensalem, two explorers witness a ceremony in which the father who lives "to see thirty
persons descended of his body alive together" (3:147) blesses his children and chooses one of his sons to live with him as the inheritor of
paternal prestige. Part of the ceremony involves an attempt to translate genealogy and inheritance into mystical props for the ahistorical
continuity of the state. The ceremony begins with a herald entering,
flanked on one side by a young boy carrying a charter "containing gifts
of revenew, and many privileges, exemptions, and points of honour,
granted to the Father of the Family; and it is ever styled and directed,
*To such a one our well-beloved friend and creditor. . . .* For they say the
king is debtor to no man, but for propagation of his subjects" (3:149).
The herald is flanked on the other side by another boy carrying "a
cluster of grapes of gold" (3:149), which the herald delivers to the
father, who subsequently delivers it to the son he chooses as his main
inheritor. This son "beareth it before his father as an ensign of honour
when he goeth in public, ever after; and is thereupon called the Son
of the Vine" (3:150). A fairly conspicuous example of what Bacon calls
in his *Essays* the "pleasing and sensual rites and ceremonies" of superstition (*E,* 6:416), this ritual attempts to assert a set of what Bourdieu
calls irresistible analogies between the royalist state, the patriarchal
family, and a mercantile system of debits and credits. The effect of
these analogies is to evacuate any sense of political motive or historical
change from the royalist state, the patriarchal family, or a mercantilist
system of exchange—a goal reinforced by the history of Bensalem that
the governor tells the Spanish. It is, after all, quite striking that in
Bacon's account of Bensalemite history, there are two main events—
the moment of Christian revelation and the establishment of Salomon's House—and the rest of history is the continuous extension of

these beginnings in the form of Christianity and of experimental science.

For the narrator, the political motives of the Feast of the Family are most interesting. After the description of this feast, the narrative shifts to a conversation between the narrator and the Jewish merchant, Joabim. The narrator asks Joabim if polygamy is admitted in Bensalem, since they place such high value on the generation of offspring. "Because propagation of families proceedeth from the nuptial copulation," the narrator speculates, "I desired to know of him what laws and customs they had concerning marriage; and whether they kept marriage well; and whether they were tied to one wife? For where population is so much affected, and such as with them it seemed to be, there is commonly permission of plurality of wives" (3:151–52). This question causes Joabim to rail against European sexual practices, including the "libertine and impure single life," which too many European men choose; marriage for "alliance, or portion, or reputation," as opposed to "the faithful nuptial union of man and wife"; the "haunting of those dissolute places, or resort to courtesans" and the "meretricious embracements" that happen within them; and "masculine love," which Joabim opposes to "faithful and inviolate friendships" (3:152–53). By the end of this tirade, the narrator has forgotten the inquiry that caused it. He simply responds that this Jew "has come to bring to memory our sins" (3:153).

This general confession—a memory that is also a forgetting—not only specifies what the Bensalemites know about the Europeans, but also gives imaginary substance to the formal infelicity that the second moment in Bacon's allegory of interpellation crystallized and that the first assumed. "Our sinful sex" resolves the previously implied question, "What do they really know about us?" which itself brings into focus the anxieties concerning the desire of the Bensalemites activated by the first question, "Are ye Christians?" The narrator's general confession is not a reference to European sexual practices themselves but instead, given the parameters of subjectivity mapped by this allegory of interpellation, refers to the infelicity upon which interpellation is predicated—refers so forcefully as to be almost, but not quite, equal to it.

This confession attempts to forestall a relation to the flesh, but its proximity to the Jew opens it up. The Jew who knows about "illicit" European sexual practices gives the historically specific underside to the Baconian fantasy of Bensalem. On the one hand, Bacon's Jew positivizes the epistemological threshold of Baconian science as what we might, following Lacan, call a "presentification" of Baconian science's historical real.[64] For, when this science formalizes itself through Protestant iconoclasm, in effect forming a supposedly "antiauthoritarian" group that is both anti-idolatrous and anti-Catholic, it participates in a history of religion and biblical hermeneutics even as it abstracts from its participation in that history. The Jew as epistemological limit is "presentified" neither as the radical outside, nor as the most intimate interior, but as a "commemoratory" image of the rejected inside forced to remain outside, as the extimate Thing around which history circulates. On the other hand, when Bacon's Jew "presentifies" this limit, the limit is also reinscribed as a threshold for the interpellated subject of science. While the historiographic project of Baconian science refuses to recognize and write its relation to a biblical hermeneutics that repeatedly attempts to unwrite the Jews, nevertheless Bacon's Jew emerges to mark that empty place as the place of sexual unruliness around which transnational European identity emerges. The Jew quite specifically as the "prehistoric Other" of Baconian science that is "impossible" for European identity "to forget" affirms sex as what Freud calls *Entfremdet*, something strange to me yet so integral to me that it cannot be forgotten.[65]

# Conclusion:
# Thinking Sexualities and Beyond

Throughout this book, I have argued that a queer historiography must account for particularity as a problem concerning the limit of social thought. Moreover, I have tried to show that queer analyses must attend to the ways in which particular works figure this limit by asserting complex and often ambivalent relations between the past and the future in their various solicitations of readers and spectators, formal solicitations that are erotic as much as anything else. By way of conclusion, I wish to return to the theoretical concerns raised in chapter 1. One of the fundamental contributions of queer theory—what makes it potentially theory and not just another fashionable trend—has been its effort to think about sexuality in order to think beyond sexuality. Moreover, queer theory's commitment to a heterogeneity embodied in the impurity of the flesh sufficiently complicates the positing of this beyond such that it cannot simply be accessible in some idealist, utopian space of political fantasy. Beyond sexuality is *not* sexual practice as political eschatology. But what, then, is it? I shall conclude this book by addressing this question through a brief meditation on Luce Irigaray. Specifically, I shall focus on two proposals that Irigaray makes in the opening pages of *An Ethics of Sexual Difference*, proposals that assert sexuality as an issue of poetics and of time. First, Irigaray writes that "sexual difference is one of the major philosophical issues, if not the issue, of our *age.*" And second, she continues, to think this problem through would involve "the production of a new age of thought, art, poetry, and language: the creation of a new *poetics.*"[1] How can we understand the heterogeneity embodied in the flesh in relation to "a new age of thought"? And even more pointedly, how might the "production" of this age involve a queer poetics in particular?

By and large, readers of Irigaray, at least in Anglo-American circles, have considered her poetics to be a tactics of mimesis that jams the machinery of a totalizing philosophy by developing a "figurative thematics that works against the thematizable." In so doing, Elizabeth Weed argues, Irigaray produces a "sexual difference rich in discursive positivity."[2] In Judith Butler's analysis, Irigaray's is a "radical citational practice," which mimes what is catechretic in philosophical and psychoanalytic discourses in order to "question the exclusionary rules of proprietariness" that govern these discourses.[3] In these accounts, Irigaray's is a poetics of performativity. Through strategic and flamboyant mimicry, Irigaray seemingly pressures totalizing philosophy into displaying its own unadmitted limitations.

However, by considering this poetics solely as a tactics of mimesis, these analyses miss the strong emphasis Iriagaray places on history, culture, and ethics. In her early work, Irigaray famously argues that what she calls hom(m)o-sexual, between-men history—that is, history as we know it—is "based upon the exploitation of one 'class' of producer, namely, women."[4] Moreover, she adds, because this exploitation happens not simply on the level of practice but also on the level of social mediation, in history women "have value only in that they serve as the possibility of, and potential benefit in, relations among men" (*TS*, 172). In *An Ethics of Sexual Difference*, Irigaray returns to this problem of women, representation, and history by thinking of it as a problem of the interval. How can woman find a place that is not simply a gap in a history that values her primarily as a mediator of relations between men? In this history, "woman always tends *toward* without any return to herself as the place where something positive can be elaborated" (*ES*, 9). Because between-men history offers her no place from which to begin, when she tries to get anywhere, woman is faced with the lack of something positive, with a gap. How, then, might we come to understand the relation that Irigaray elaborates between the creation of a new poetics and a seemingly totalized between-men history?

This question speaks directly to contemporary queer theory. How is it, Butler asks, that in the early 1990s queer as a term of degradation has been "turned . . . to signify a new and affirmative set of meanings?" Does this turning signal "a simple reversal of valuations," or "is this a reversal that retains and reiterates the abjected history of the term?"[5] Despite the differences between the two, Irigaray's questions concerning women, representation, and history hold for the queer as well: How can the queer find a place that is not simply an interval in a history that values him or her primarily as an example of what is most detestable, of what should most remain unknown? Doesn't the queer also always tend *toward* without any return to the self as the place where something positive can be elaborated?

While Butler proposes that the turn from degradation to affirmation is primarily a turn of discourse, she also assumes that for queer to be queer, it must be attached to the performing and performative ego. In *Bodies That Matter,* Butler emphasizes both the temporality of gender and how that temporality permits the taking up and taking on of repudiated identities. Butler writes that, on a general level, "the imaginary practice of identification must itself be understood as a double movement: in citing the symbolic, an identification (re)invokes and (re)invests the symbolic law, seeks recourse to it as a constituting authority that precedes its imaginary instancing. The priority and the authority of the symbolic is, however, constituted *through* that recursive turn, such that citation . . . effectively brings into being the very prior authority to which it then defers." This turn, Butler proposes, "takes place through a set of repudiations" that invoke "the heterosexual norm through the exclusion of contestatory possibilities."[6] How, Butler continually asks, might the performance of these "contestatory possibilities" allow for the stylization of a version of freedom that resists conscription by the heterosexual norm? Whereas a normative performative "accumulates the force of authority through the repetition or citation of a prior, authoritative set of practices," Butler argues that through parodic repetition queer performativity appropriates the force of the norm by posing a political position that both recognizes the "constitutive history" of the normative term "queer" and makes claims on that history by "reworking the specific historicity of that term."[7] "Where the uniformity of the subject is expected, where the behavioral conformity of the subject is commanded, there *might be produced* the refusal of the law in the form of the parodic inhabiting of conformity that subtly calls into question the legitimacy of the command, a repetition of the law into hyperbole, a rearticulation of the law against the authority of the one who delivers it."[8]

Butler's is perhaps the most significant attempt to pose sexualities in terms of identitary time, and, to this extent, her analysis is most powerful not in the somewhat banal observation that identity is performative but in the implicit location of queer at a historical threshold. Butler's analysis, at least in my understanding, strongly suggests that the *time* of the queer is never quite equal to the rhythms of the everyday as the support for the repetition of social norms. Rather, this time is oriented toward that repetition's limits. Only, Butler's fascination with relations between performative authority and abject identity tend to prevent her from developing in any strong way the implications of this location. In contrast, Irigaray turns to this disturbing and troubled location in *An Ethics of Sexual Difference* as the basis for a new poetics. Instead of claiming the interval that history offers woman in practices of pleasure and *jouissance,* Irigaray will argue for the ethical importance of decathecting the interval so that between-men history can become something else. Irigaray proposes not the celebration of practices but the translation of the interval into a critical and poetic stance that desubstantiates forms of being that a celebration of practices might otherwise consolidate.

The problem I am here raising with Irigaray is similar to the one that John Champagne raises with Nietzsche's "Uses and Disadvantages of History for Life." Beginning with Nietzsche's contrast between an excess of historical sense deployed by the "toothless and tasteless greybeards" and the unhistorical exuberance of a defiant youth, Champagne asks, What is the value of the historical and the unhistorical for contemporary gay studies? Whereas a monumental history of homosexuality would posit a "transhistorical queerness" that attributes to homosexuality a political heroism, and an antiquarian history of homosexuality would attempt to preserve "all extant accounts of same-sex interaction," finding ancient precursors "to such contemporary figures as the drag queen, the butch dyke, the sweater boy, and the lipstick lesbian . . . in such unlikely places as Renaissance England and the pre-Columbian Americas, among the sandu of India and the Oriental mystics," a critical history of homosexuality, Champagne proposes, would turn to history with an ethical commitment to the unhistorical in order to confront the possibility of being otherwise in the time of our own thought.[9] So conceived, critical history would be, not an attempt to free oneself from the forces of history per se, but an effort to overturn the conservative and stultifying urges of the historicist greybeards both young and old who practice monumental and antiquarian history. Champagne proposes that "a critical history of homosexuality might hold up historical models of gay sexuality and subjectivity only to destroy them. It suggests that rather than adopting current historical models of right homosexual conduct, we must 'work' at becoming gay, forging a new, as yet unanticipated, way of life."[10] Of course, critical history cannot be some naive celebration of the contemporary, as it threatens to be in Champagne's analysis, as if the contemporary were not already a deeply historical delimitation. Rather, the task of a critically queer history would be to introduce an element of the unhistorical into contemporary historical thinking in order to open that thinking to the risk of a future in which the contemporary version of identitary time can become something else.

The unhistorical is by no means the ahistorical. By unhistorical, I mean quite specifically particular forms of thinking that emerge through the aesthetic at the limits of social thought. Moreover, as my analyses of Caravaggio, Marlowe, and Bacon would suggest, what is particularly unhistorical about these forms of thinking is the way in which they develop modes of interpretation that variously frustrate seemingly sound distinctions between past, present, and future in the space between work and reader or spectator. Caravaggio's traversal of typology, Marlowe's development of a literary hermeneutics of sodomy, Bacon's repeated confrontation with the unconvertible as the experience that subtends a desire for epochal history—each case develops a minor, aesthetic mode of thinking that overturns some posited form of identitary time. Throughout my analyses, I have argued that the issue of sexuality lies in the modes of evaluation that the works of Caravaggio, Marlowe, and Bacon solicit. Rather than uniting the material actuality of the given artifact with some coherent meaning, these modes of evaluation call for a queering of the reader/spectator in relation to meaning, history, and a dominant social poetics of the body that serves as the basis for the untimely meditations that the works of Caravaggio, Marlowe, and Bacon—in varying degrees of urgency—demand.

These untimely meditations stand against the dominant form of the civilizing process. As I discussed in chapter 2, the civilizing process involves bringing the force of civic judgment to bear upon oneself before one is judged by some concrete, juridical authority. It is a form of self-assertion that almost immediately refuses the possibilities that it opens up. Irigaray has two terse and specific responses to this anticipatory judgment: first, man affirms his body by establishing domination—no matter how nontyrannical—over the maternal-feminine-natural-material; second, and worse, man forgets what he has done. The mastery of a style of life that civility offers all too quickly turns into a pathetic and life-draining "hibernation" (*ES*, 144) inside "that tentacular technical machine that man has made" (113) and then calls the world. "The world, or worlds, that he constructs," Irigaray writes, "will close over him so tightly that reaching something outside him becomes difficult for him" (99–100). Thus, she will argue that man's forgetting his affirmation through self-assertion results in relations with maternity, paternity, divinity, and his body, all of which symptomatically block all over again the possibility of connection outside. Thus, a "desire to go back towards and into the originary womb" (100) misappropriates the maternal-feminine by making it stand in for the outside; similarly, a "quest for God through the father" and a masturbatory love for one part of the self (61) both exclude the feminine, again placing it as man's limit.

Most significantly, instead of fetishizing the archive and bemoaning the interval, Irigaray develops a hermeneutics that lets history write itself against this dominant form of judgment. "There is," she writes, "the fact that the female does not have the same relation to exteriority as the male" (63). Like Lacan, Irigaray posits at least two relations to the outside that define sexual difference. In Irigaray's account, whereas man attempts to commemorate exteriority in a style of life that amounts to domination of the feminine-maternal-natural-material, or, subsequently, to forget exteriority in neurotic hibernation, woman attempts to accede to exteriority by "bringing herself out" (63). Because man neurotically makes woman, as a mother, serve as the container, "the starting point from which man limits his things," the maternal-feminine "remains the *place separated from 'its' own place*" (10, emphasis Irigaray's). For this reason, woman sustains a privileged relation to the horizons of man's world. She is able to undo "man's work" by creating an interval, something that disturbs man's perspective, at the limits of his world.

Here, at this interval, Irigaray argues, woman finds the possibilities for *jouissance:* "[B]ody-expanse tries to give itself exteriority, to give itself to exteriority, to give itself in an unpunctuated space-time that is also not orgastic in the limited sense of that word" (64). Unfortunately, as with all *jouissance,* if one attempts to claim it, one finds oneself beset with problems. In the case of woman, the first problem, Irigaray points out, is that this version of *jouissance* explicitly equates woman with maternity: "[W]oman is loved/loves herself through the children she *gives birth to*" (63). The second problem is that, when it comes to group formation, claiming this *jouissance* produces mediocrity as the group's dominant rule. Once acceding to exteriority is established as acceding to maternity, then the *jouissance* of giving oneself exteriority turns into a striving "to achieve the post of *the unique one: the mother of mothers*" (102, emphasis Irigaray's). The symptom of this striving is the repetition within the group of phrases such as "like you" and "me too" that prevent any woman from achieving the post of the unique one and instead make every woman as mediocre as every other woman. In these phrases "like you" and "me too," Irigaray writes, "we have no proof of love, but a judgmental statement that prevents the woman from standing out from an undifferentiated grouping, from a sort of primitive community of women, unconscious utopias or atopias that some women exploit at times to prevent one of their number from affirming her identity" (103).

Instead of claiming this *jouissance* of the interval, Irigaray argues for the interval's decathexis. For, she argues, it is by emptying the interval of the *jouissance* it offers that history can open up onto something else. Irigaray argues for a hermeneutics that attempts to reverse the direction of history *from the inside* in order to open up history to the possibilities exteriority offers. Irigaray's analysis implies the necessity of emptying practices of *jouissance* so that woman can sublimate her *jouissance* into an ethics of sexual difference by which she can find herself "through the images of herself already deposited in history and the conditions of production of the work of man, and not on the basis of his work" (10).

Irigaray insists on the problematicization of specifically secular history, first by translating woman's *jouissance* of the interval, a *jouissance* expressed as space, into a temporal modality. To this extent, Irigaray shares with Caravaggio, Marlowe, and Bacon the attempt to develop a *poiesis* that extends the flesh at the limits of the civilizing process. Irigaray figures this temporal modality by reference to angels: "mediators of that which has not yet happened, of what is still going to happen, of what is on the horizon." Angels figure the endless "reopening [of] the enclosures of the universe, of universes, identities, the unfolding of actions, of history. . . . The angel is that which unceasingly *passes through the envelope(s)* or *container(s)*" (15, emphasis Irigaray's). Irreducible to the interval to which woman is referred, angels sublimate the *jouissance* of the interval that blocks woman's relation to exteriority into "passage" as a temporal modality.

If she were to stop here, Irigaray would simply be repeating as a feminist project Christian typology. Potentially, by mobilizing an allegory of the new birth against a version of genealogy that is expressly patrilineal, Christian typology has something to offer antipatriarchal historiography. Only, in its insistence on a spirit opposed to the flesh, Christian typology establishes itself in dialectical tension with racial particularity and carnality and relies on abstraction from maternal birth into an allegorical birth that needs no women at all. Thus, in her second move, Irigaray refers the time of angels to mucous. Why mucous? Since it is known by both man and woman "in the prenatal and loving night," mucous locates the sameness of the Other—the possibility of a meeting between sameness and the Other. Only, she argues, since mucous is more important for women in "setting up the intimacy of bodily perception and its threshold" (109), it locates this sameness as one that makes no pretense to the cunning of gender neutrality. In its specificity, and alongside the general temporal modality of angels, mucous introduces the remainder, the forgotten, into between-men history in order to open that history up to something else. That is, in her insistence on angels and mucous, Irigaray allows for the development of a postsecular, radically psychoanalytic hermeneutics that would reverse the direction of history as genealogy of the fathers sublated into a sense of the spirit in which woman still has no place. In this reversal, Irigaray offers woman the ability to constitute "memory in the space where man at times closes himself off inside a *pathos* of memory, inside a nostalgia that forgets the threshold, the flesh" (141).

To constitute as memory a thinking of the flesh where the civilizing process, in an affirmation of the aestheticized body, has posited an anticipatory judgment: this will not simply lead to practices of *jouissance,* critical and otherwise, that block exteriority and thus reauthenticate between-men history. Rather, to constitute this memory is to open up history to something else. Might not the attempt to evacuate the *jouissance* of the interval offer the grounds for—forgive the paradoxical formulation of the phrase—an authentically queer poetics?

## Chapter One

1. Gilles Deleuze and Félix Guattari, *Kafka: Toward a Minor Literature*, trans. Dana Polan (Minneapolis: University of Minnesota Press, 1986), 16–27.

2. Eve Kosofsky Sedgwick, *Tendencies* (Durham: Duke University Press, 1993), 110.

3. David M. Halperin, *One Hundred Years of Homosexuality* (New York: Routledge, 1990), 29.

4. I am not claiming that sexuality is particularized because it is the singular experience of an individual. Rather, I am claiming that it is particularized as the limit of a certain form of thought. For a critique of authoritative grounds of experience, see Joan W. Scott, "The Evidence of Experience," *Critical Inquiry* 17 (1991): 773–97. See also Michel de Certeau, *The Writing of History*, trans. Tom Conley (New York: Columbia University Press, 1988), 83–86.

5. From the introduction to *Premodern Sexualities*, ed. Louise Fradenburg and Carla Freccero, with the assistance of Kathy Lavezzo (New York: Routledge, 1996), xiv.

6. Historicality is Heidegger's term. He uses it to designate "the state of Being that is constitutive for Dasein's 'historicizing' as such," and he argues that it is the possibility for historical thinking that historicism, in its positing a secure history of being, refuses to acknowledge or account for. See Martin Heidegger, *Being and Time*, trans. John Macquarrie and Edward Robinson (New York: Harper and Row, 1962), intro., 2.6.19–20.

7. Valerie Traub, "The (In)Significance of Lesbian Desire," in *Queering the Renaissance*, ed. Jonathan Goldberg (Durham: Duke University Press, 1994), 72, 62.

8. Jonathan Goldberg, *Sodometries: Renaissance Texts/Modern Sexualities* (Stanford: Stanford University Press, 1992), 22. For an essay that develops this practice by mobilizing erotic/poetic equivocation against a retrospective heterosexual history, see Goldberg's "The History That Will Be," in Fradenburg and Freccero, *Premodern Sexualities*, 3–21.

9. Pierre Bourdieu, *The Logic of Practice*, trans. Richard Nice (Stanford: Stanford University Press, 1990), 71.

10. Cornelius Castoriadis, *The Imaginary Institution of Society*, trans. Kathleen Blamey (Cambridge: Massachusetts Institute of Technology Press, 1987), 202–11.

11. See Sigmund Freud, "On Narcissism: An Introduction," in *General Psychological Theory*, ed. Philip Rieff (New York: Collier, 1963), 74. The term "prestigious imitation" comes from Marcel Mauss. Mauss writes:

> The notion of education could be superimposed upon that of imitation. For there are particular children with very strong imitative faculties, others with very weak ones, but all of them go through the same education, such that we can understand the continuity of the concatenations. What takes place is a prestigious imitation. The child, the adult, imitates actions that have succeeded, which he has seen successfully performed by people in whom he has confidence and who have authority over him. The action is imposed from without, from above, even if it is an exclusively biological action, involving his body. The individual borrows the series of movements of which he is composed from the action executed in front of him, or with him, by others.
>
> It is precisely this notion of the prestige of the person who performs the ordered, authorized, tested action vis-à-vis the imitating individuals, that contains all the social element. The imitative action that follows contains the psychological element and the biological element. (Marcel Mauss, "Techniques of the Body," in *Incorporations,* ed. Jonathan Crary and Sanford Kwinter [New York: Zone Books, 1992], 459)

12. Sigmund Freud, *Civilization and Its Discontents,* trans. James Strachey (New York: Norton, 1961), 37–39, 70–78.

13. Judith Butler, *The Psychic Life of Power: Theories in Subjection* (Stanford: Stanford University Press, 1997), 66.

14. Keith Thomas, introduction to *A Cultural History of Gesture,* ed. Jan Bremmer and Herman Roodenburg (Ithaca: Cornell University Press, 1992), 5–6.

15. I think that this relation to the limit of social thought is what Mario DiGangi is after when he proposes an orderly and a disorderly homoeroticism in his study of Renaissance English drama. See *The Homoerotics of Early Modern Drama* (Cambridge: Cambridge University Press, 1997).

16. Sigmund Freud, *The Ego and the Id,* trans. Joan Riviere, ed. James Strachey (New York: Norton, 1962), 16.

17. Freud, "On Narcissism," 58.

18. Jacques Lacan, *Ecrits* (Paris: Editions du Seuil, 1966), 113; *Ecrits: A Selection,* trans. Alan Sheridan (New York: Norton, 1977), 18–19. Hereafter citations to this work give the page reference to the French edition first and to Alan Sheridan's translation second.

19. Ibid., 113/19.

20. Sigmund Freud, "Splitting of the Ego in the Defensive Process," in *Sexuality and the Psychology of Love,* trans. Philip Rieff (New York: Collier, 1963), 220–23. Kristeva's analyses tend to focus on the flexibility of this double inscription in the production of new symptomologies. See, for example, Julia Kristeva, *Powers of Horror: An Essay on Abjection,* trans. Leon S. Roudiez (New York: Columbia University Press, 1982), 8–12, 34–41; *Tales of Love,* trans. Leon S. Roudiez (New York: Columbia University Press, 1987), 21–56; and *Nations without Nationalism,* trans. Leon S. Roudiez (New York: Columbia University Press, 1993), 49–64. Judith Butler tries to rework this double inscription of the body through the recursive temporality of the

performative in *Bodies That Matter: On the Discursive Limits of "Sex"* (New York: Routledge, 1993), 93–119. Butler's reworking strongly implies that this double positing of epistemological space developed by Freud and his followers has the status of event but not necessarily the status of history.

21. In his translator's notes to Lacan's *Seminar Eleven: The Four Fundamental Concepts of Psychoanalysis,* ed. Jacques-Alain Miller (New York: Norton, 1978), Alan Sheridan gives the following definition of *jouissance:* "There is no adequate translation in English of this word. 'Enjoyment' conveys the sense, contained in jouissance, of enjoyment of rights, of property, etc. Unfortunately, in modern English, the word has lost the sexual connotations it still retains in French. ('Jouir' is slang for 'to come.') 'Pleasure,' on the other hand, is pre-empted by 'plaisir,'—and Lacan uses the two terms quite differently. 'Pleasure' obeys the law of homeostasis that Freud evokes in *Beyond the Pleasure Principle,* whereby, through discharge, the psyche seeks the lowest possible level of tension. 'Jouissance' transgresses this law and, in that respect, it is *beyond* the pleasure principle" (Lacan, *Seminar Eleven,* 281). Lacan distinguishes this understanding of thinking and sexuality from Jung's reliance on archetypes (ibid., 152–53). Cf. Lacan's discussion of *jouissance* in *Seminar Seven: The Ethics of Psychoanalysis,* trans. Dennis Porter (New York: Norton, 1992), 167–204.

22. Sigmund Freud, *The Interpretation of Dreams,* trans. James Strachey (New York: Avon Books, 1965), 605.

23. Ibid., 641, emphasis Freud's.

24. Ibid., 639.

25. Sigmund Freud, *Project for a Scientific Psychology,* in *The Standard Edition of the Complete Psychological Works of Sigmund Freud,* ed. and trans. James Strachey (New York: Norton, 1950), 1:326; Lacan, *Seminar Seven,* 43–84.

26. Monique David-Ménard, *Hysteria from Freud to Lacan: Body and Language in Psychoanalysis,* trans. Catherine Porter (Ithaca: Cornell University Press, 1989), 149–50.

27. Norbert Elias, *The Civilizing Process,* trans. Edmund Jephcott (Oxford: Basil Blackwell, 1994), 443–524. While there have been over the past ten or so years a number of excellent studies on the Renaissance construction of interiority, the general problem with these studies has been that, by considering the problems of civility as spatial, they can't recognize in exteriority its full disrupting force. See, for example, Francis Barker, *The Tremulous Private Body* (New York: Methuen, 1984); Philippe Ariès and Georges Duby, eds., *A History of Private Life,* trans. Arthur Goldhammer (Cambridge: Harvard University Press, 1987–91), vols. 2 and 3; Anna Bryson, "Gesture, Demeanour, and the Image of the Gentleman," in *Renaissance Bodies: The Human Figure in English Culture, 1540–1660,* ed. Lucy Gent and Nigel Llewellyn (London: Reaktion Books, 1990), 136–53; Patricia Fumerton, *Cultural Aesthetics: Renaissance Literature and the Practice of Social Ornamentation* (Chicago: University of Chicago Press, 1991); and, to a large extent writing against the tenor of these, Joel Fineman, *Shakespeare's Perjured Eye: The Invention of Poetic Subjectivity in the Sonnets* (Berkeley and Los Angeles: University of California Press, 1986); and Katharine Eisaman Maus, *Inwardness and the Theater in the English Renaissance* (Chicago: University of Chicago Press, 1995). Two studies that attend to issues of power and force quite innovatively are Barbara Correll, *The End of Conduct: Grobianus and the Renaissance Text of the Subject* (Ithaca: Cornell University Press, 1996); and Jonathan Goldberg, *Writing Matter: From the Hands of the English Renaissance* (Stanford:

Stanford University Press, 1990). Correll focuses on the abject and the corrosion of conduct, while Goldberg mobilizes an Elias-based model to reinterpret Derrida's "violence of the letter" through readings of Renaissance writing techniques.

To my mind, one of the most innovative uses of Elias has been in the field of science and literature, where Gail Kern Paster argues for relations between the corporealization of shame and its representation in Renaissance London drama. See *The Body Embarrassed: Drama and the Disciplines of Shame in Early Modern England* (Ithaca: Cornell University Press, 1993); also Katherine Rowe, "'God's Handy Worke': Divine Complicity and the Anatomist's Touch," in *The Body in Parts: Fantasies of Corporeality in Early Modern Europe*, ed. David Hillman and Carla Mazzio (New York: Routledge, 1997), 285–309.

28. Elias, *The Civilizing Process*, 43, 57.

29. Ibid., 59.

30. Biblical citations are from the New Jerusalem Bible, unless otherwise noted.

31. See the groundbreaking essay by Daniel and Jonathan Boyarin, "Diaspora: Generation and the Ground of Jewish Identity," *Critical Inquiry* 19 (summer 1993): 693–725; and Daniel Boyarin's *A Radical Jew: Paul and the Politics of Identity* (Berkeley and Los Angeles: University of California Press, 1994). See also Thomas H. Luxon, *Literal Figures: Puritan Allegory and the Reformation Crisis in Representation* (Chicago: University of Chicago Press, 1995), especially his reading of allegory and typology, 34–62, and his reading of Pauline stories of identity, 102–9, 114–29. For a comparison between Renaissance humanist historiography and Pauline reformation historical thinking, see Anthony Kemp, *The Estrangement of the Past: A Study in the Origins of Modern Historical Consciousness* (New York: Oxford University Press, 1991), 96–104. And for an analysis of typology, nineteenth- and early-twentieth-century historiography, and Renaissance literature, see Julia Reinhard Lupton, *Afterlives of the Saints: Hagiography, Typology, and Renaissance Literature* (Stanford: Stanford University Press, 1996).

32. Hans Blumenberg, *The Legitimacy of the Modern Age*, trans. Robert M. Wallace (Cambridge: Massachusetts Institute of Technology Press, 1983), 137.

33. Fredric Jameson's *The Political Unconscious: Narrative as a Socially Symbolic Act* (Ithaca: Cornell University Press, 1981), 17–102, is both an example of this recuperation and an extraordinary attempt to open it up to a new dialectical reversal.

34. Nicholas of Cusa, *Of Learned Ignorance*, trans. Fr. Germain Heron (New Haven: Yale University Press, 1954), 2.7.

35. Giordano Bruno, *Cause, Principle, and Unity: Five Dialogues*, trans. Jack Lindsay (New York: International Publishers, 1962), 111–12; Benedict de Spinoza, *The Ethics*, trans. R. H. M. Elwes (New York: Dover, 1955), part 2, first definition, and part 4, proof of the fourth proposition.

36. Jacques Lacan, *Television*, trans. Denis Hollier, Rosalind Kraus, and Annette Michelson, ed. Joan Copjec (New York: Norton, 1990), 185, 204–5, 214–15.

37. Jacques Lacan, *Seminar Twenty: Encore*, trans. Bruce Fink (New York: Norton, 1998), 15.

38. Ibid., 111–12.

39. Michel Foucault, *The History of Sexuality*, vol. 1, *An Introduction*, trans. Robert Hurley (New York: Random House, 1980), 43.

40. David M. Halperin, "Forgetting Foucault: Acts, Identities, and the History of Sexuality," *Representations* 63 (summer 1998): 99, emphasis Halperin's; see also Eve

Sedgwick's critical discussion of "paradigm shifts" in *Epistemology of the Closet* (Berkeley and Los Angeles: University of California Press, 1990), 44–48.

Halperin's argument is against the "ritual invocation" of Foucault's works—always minus *The Order of Things* and *The Archaeology of Knowledge*, I would add—which "has had the effect of reducing the operative range of this thought to a small set of received ideas, slogans, and bits of jargon that have now become so commonplace and familiar as to make a more direct engagement with Foucault's texts entirely dispensable" ("Forgetting Foucault," 93–94), a diagnosis with which I agree. If Foucault were writing social history, as many of his readers seem to believe, then his characterization of sodomy as simply a set of practices with few consequences for identification would be easy to dismiss.

For a subtle analysis of the invention of sodomy, see Mark D. Jordan, *The Invention of Sodomy in Christian Theology* (Chicago: University of Chicago Press, 1997).

41. See Goldberg, *Sodometries*, 18–22; Valerie Traub, *Desire and Anxiety: Circulations of Sexuality in Shakespearean Drama* (New York: Routledge, 1992), 12.

42. See Friedrich Nietzsche, "The Uses and Disadvantages of History for Life," in *Untimely Meditations*, trans. R. J. Hollingdate (Cambridge: Cambridge University Press, 1983), 60–65.

43. Michel Foucault, *The Use of Pleasure*, vol. 2 of *The History of Sexuality*, trans. Robert Hurley (New York: Vintage, 1990), 80–81, 92.

44. Michel Foucault, *The Archaeology of Knowledge*, trans. A. M. Sheridan Smith (New York: Pantheon, 1972), 28, 91, 121.

45. Ibid., 55.

46. Gilles Deleuze, *Foucault*, trans. Seán Hand (Minneapolis: University of Minnesota Press, 1986), 107.

47. Lacan, *Seminar Seven*, 20. Where the English translation writes "actualized," the French has "se présentifie." Cf. Jacques Lacan, *Le séminaire livre VII: L'ethique de la psychanalyse* (Paris: Editions du Seuil, 1986), 28.

48. See, for example, Jacques Lacan, "Kant with Sade," trans. James B. Swenson, Jr., *October* 51 (winter 1989): 67; *Seminar Eleven*, 184–86, 243; and *Seminar Twenty*, 21–25, 93–95. See also Parveen Adams's excellent discussion in *The Emptiness of the Image: Psychoanalysis and Sexual Differences* (London: Routledge, 1996), 92–93, 151–52.

49. Foucault, *The Use of Pleasure*, 11, 13, emphasis Foucault's. In doing this, Foucault repeats Heidegger's consistent return to the Greeks in order to rethink the history of being insofar as being has been debased by Western metaphysics. As Deleuze remarks in something of an aside, the implicit philosophical project of late Foucault is to introduce into that Heideggerian history the necessity of thinking sexuality (see Deleuze, *Foucault*, 107–8). Since this might seem like an outlandish claim to many of Foucault's English-speaking readers, it is worthwhile to recall Foucault's statement in one of his late interviews: "Heidegger has always been for me the essential philosopher. . . . I probably wouldn't have read Nietzsche if I hadn't read Heidegger. I tried to read Nietzsche in the fifties, but Nietzsche by himself said nothing to me. Whereas Nietzsche and Heidegger—what a shock!" (from "The Return of Morality," interview conducted by Gilles Barbadette and Andre Serla, *Les Nouvelles*, June 28–July 5, 1984; reprinted in Michel Foucault, *Foucault Live: Interviews, 1966–84*, ed. Sylvère Lotringer, trans. John Johnston [New York: Semiotext[e], 1989], 326).

50. Foucault, *The Use of Pleasure*, 9.

51. Ibid., 26–27. For a discussion of the implications of Foucault's approach for contemporary historical methodologies, see Robert Castel, "'Problematicization' as a Mode of Reading History," trans. Paula Wissing, in *Foucault and the Writing of History*, ed. Jan Goldstein (Oxford: Basil Blackwell, 1994), 237–52.

52. Maurice Merleau-Ponty, *The Visible and the Invisible*, ed. Claude Lefort, trans. Alphonso Lingis (Evanston: Northwestern University Press, 1973), 141.

53. Lacan, *Seminar Twenty*, 121.

54. Ibid., 105.

55. For Lacan's remarks on history and the subject of the statement, see ibid., 45–46.

56. Ibid., 44–45; cf. *Le séminaire livre XX: Encore* (Paris: Editions du Seuil, 1975), 44.

57. This phrase occurs at the end of the first chapter of *Discipline and Punish*. Foucault writes, "I would like to write the history of this prison, with all the political investments of the body that it gathers together in its closed architecture. Why? Simply because I am interested in the past? No, if one means by that writing a history of the past in terms of the present. Yes, if one means writing the history of the present" (*Discipline and Punish: The Birth of the Prison*, trans. Alan Sheridan [New York: Vintage Books, 1979], 31).

58. In other words, this is a being that is, in Heidegger's magisterial terms, "authentic":

> Only an entity which, in its Being, is essentially futural so that it is free for its death and can let itself be thrown back upon its factical "there" by shattering itself against death—that is to say, only an entity which, as futural, is equiprimordially in the process of having been, can, by handing down to itself the possibility it has inherited, take over its own thrownness and can be in the moment of vision for "its time." Only authentic temporality which is at the same time finite, makes possible something like fate—that is to say, authentic historicality. (Heidegger, *Being and Time*, 2.5.74.385)

59. Michel Foucault, "Friendship as a Way of Life," *Le Gai Pied*, April 6, 1980; reprinted in *Foucault Live*, 204–5.

60. Ibid., 205, 206. It is to this extent that homosexual thought maintains what David Lloyd, in a very different context, calls the "subalternity effect." Reworking Joel Fineman's concept of "subjectivity effect," Lloyd writes, "the social space of the 'subaltern' designates not some sociological datum of an objective and generalizable kind, but is an effect emerging in and between historiographic discourses." The project of writing a history of the "subaltern," Lloyd argues, must combine

> with a performative engagement which could be seen . . . to desire the derivation of emergent from residual practices. This is not, however, to seek legitimate contemporaneous acts or practices by appealing to past forms, opposing thereby an alternative but no less spurious mode of historical continuity to that of dominant narratives. . . . The object is . . . to reapprehend social processes in terms of the uncloseable struggle between the "self-evident" and continuity of dominant repre-

sentations and those other cultural forms whose apparent "irrationality" and sporadic temporality is as much the effect as the cause of their marginalization. ("David Lloyd, "Discussion outside History: Irish New Histories and the 'Subalternity Effect,'" *Subaltern Studies* 9 [1996]: 263–64).

I would like to thank Katherine O'Brien O'Keeffe for passing Lloyd's essay along to me.

61. Foucault, "Friendship," 209.

62. Michel Foucault, "The Concern for Truth," interview conducted by François Ewald, *Le Magazine Littéraire,* May 1984; reprinted in *Foucault Live,* 303; and "Friendship," 204.

63. Leo Bersani, *Homos* (Cambridge: Harvard University Press, 1995), 81.

64. Ibid., 95, 99.

## Chapter Two

1. Norbert Elias, *The Civilizing Process,* trans. Edmund Jephcott (Oxford: Basil Blackwell, 1994), 453, emphasis Elias's. See also 156–68, and, for a more general analysis, 443–29.

2. Lacan develops this concept of extimacy in relation to art in *Seminar Seven: The Ethics of Psychoanalysis,* trans. Dennis Porter (New York: Norton, 1992), 139–54; see also Jacques-Alain Miller, "Extimacy," *Prose Studies* 11 (1988): 121–30.

3. See Maria Serena Mazzi, "Cronache de periferia della stato florentino: Reati contro la morale ne primo quattrocento." *Studi Storici* 27 (1986): 609–35.

4. Richard Trexler, "La prostitution florentine au XVe siècle: Patronage et clientèles, *Annales: Economies, Socìetes, Civilisations* 36 (1981): 983–1015; Maria Serena Mazzi, *Prostitute e lenoni nella Firenze del quattrocento* (Milan: Saggiatore, 1991), 200–31; and Michael Rocke, *Forbidden Friendships: Homosexuality and Male Culture in Renaissance Florence* (Oxford: Oxford University Press, 1996), 30–32. The 1403 law is from the *Provvisioni Registri* 92, 9$^r$ (April 24, 1403), cited in Rocke, *Forbidden Friendships,* 30; and the 1404 proposal is from the *Libri Fabarum* 47, 187$^v$ (March 12, 1404), cited in ibid., 31–32.

5. Rocke, *Forbidden Friendships,* 34–35.

6. Ibid., 45–59.

7. Bernardino of Siena, *La Prediche Volgari,* ed. Ciro Cannarozzi (Pistoia: Tip. Cav. Alberto Pacinotto, 1934), 2:48; the English translation is from Michael Rocke's important essay, "Sodomites in Fifteenth-Century Tuscany: The Views of Bernardino of Siena," in *The Pursuit of Sodomy: Male Homosexuality in Renaissance and Enlightenment Europe,* ed. Kent Gerard and Gert Hekma (New York: Harrington Park Press, 1989), 7.

8. Peter Stallybrass and Allon White, *The Politics and Poetics of Transgression* (Ithaca: Cornell University Press, 1986), 193.

9. Bernardino of Siena, *La Prediche,* 2:87.

10. Gene Brucker, *The Civic World of Early Renaissance Florence* (Princeton: Princeton University Press, 1977), 474–500; and Dale Kent, *The Rise of the Medici: Faction in Florence, 1426–1434* (Oxford: Oxford University Press, 1978), 11–26, 239–52.

11. Gino Capponi, "Ricordi de Gino di Neri Capponi," in *Miscellanea di studi offerta a A. Balduini e B. Bianchi,* ed. Gianfranco Folena (Padua: Presso Il Seminario de Filologia Moderna dell'Università, 1962), 34.

12. See Richard Trexler, *Public Life in Renaissance Florence* (Ithaca: Cornell University Press, 1980), 28–30.

13. Andrea Zorzi, "The Florentines and Their Public Offices in the Early Fifteenth Century: Competition, Abuses of Power, and Unlawful Acts," in *History from Crime,* ed. Edward Muir and Guido Ruggiero, trans. Corrada Biazzo Curry, Margaret A. Gallucci, and Mary M. Gallucci (Baltimore: Johns Hopkins University Press, 1994), 110.

14. Lauro Martines, *Lawyers and Statecraft in Renaissance Florence* (Princeton: Princeton University Press, 1968), 143–45.

15. For a discussion of the Otto di Guardia in relation to the development of Florentine government as a centralized oligarchy, see Andrea Zorzi, *L'amministrazione della giustizia penale nella repubblica fiorentina: Aspetti e problemi* (Florence: Leo S. Olschki Editore, 1988), 32–46; and for an extended discussion of the Conservatori delle Leggi, see Zorzi, "Florentines and Their Public Offices," 110–129.

16. S. K. Cohen, Jr., "Criminality and the State in Renaissance Florence, 1344–1466," *Journal of Social History* 14 (1981): 211–33; see also Marvin Becker, "Changing Patterns of Violence and Justice in Fourteenth- and Fifteenth-Century Florence," *Comparative Studies in Society and History* 18 (1976): 281–96.

17. Leon Battista Alberti, *I Libri Della Famiglia,* in *Opere Volgari,* ed. Cecil Grayson (Bari: G. Laterza, 1960), 1:204; translated as *The Family in Renaissance Florence* by Renée New Watkins (Columbia: University of South Carolina Press, 1969), 196, translation slightly altered. Subsequent citations of this work are to these editions and appear parenthetically in the text, with the Italian page number following the English.

18. See Angelo Cicchetti and Raul Mordenti, *I libri di famiglia in Italia* (Rome: Edizioni di Storia e Lettura, 1985), 116; Zorzi, "Florentines and Their Public Offices," 121; Stephanie H. Jed, *Chaste Thinking: The Rape of Lucrece and the Birth of Humanism* (Bloomington: Indiana University Press, 1989), 89–97.

19. Leon Battista Alberti, *On Painting,* trans. Cecil Grayson (London: Phaidon, 1972; reprint, New York: Penguin, 1991), 54. References to the Italian are from *Opere Volgari,* vol. 3. Subsequent citations of this work are to these editions and are given parenthetically in the text as *DP;* the Italian page number follows the English.

20. Antonia di Tucci Manetti, *La Vita di Filippo Brunelleschi,* 55–56; translated by Catherine Enggass as *The Life of Brunelleschi,* with an introduction and notes by Howard Saalman (University Park: Pennsylvania State University Press, 1970), 42.

21. *The Notebooks of Leonardo da Vinci,* ed. Jean Paul Richter (New York: Dover, 1970), 1:30; Hubert Damisch, *The Origin of Perspective,* trans. John Goodman (Cambridge: Massachusetts Institute of Technology Press, 1994), 48; Joan Kelly [Gadol], *Leon Battista Alberti: Universal Man of the Early Renaissance* (Chicago: University of Chicago Press, 1969), 70–81.

22. Damisch, *Origin of Perspective,* 49. This is the reason that Lacan turns to painting and perspective in order to discuss the gaze as *objet a.* Perspective is the form that allows us to consider consciousness: seeing oneself seeing oneself. See *Seminar Eleven: The Four Fundamental Concepts of Psychoanalysis,* ed. Jacques-Alain Miller, trans. Alan Sheridan (New York: Norton, 1978), 82. For a useful analysis of

perspective as a discourse, see James Elkins, *The Poetics of Perspective* (Ithaca: Cornell University Press, 1994).

23. Erwin Panofsky, *Perspective as Symbolic Form*, trans. Charles S. Wood (New York: Zone Books, 1991), 66. It is important to note that the movement toward mathematical unity is occasioned by technological forces that enter from outside the history that Panofsky gives. For example, Martin Kemp argues that Brunelleschi's demonstrations and Alberti's, Leonardo's, and Dürer's subsequent formalizations of perspective all relied on a knowledge of medieval surveying techniques. See Kemp, *The Science of Art: Optical Themes in Western Art from Brunelleschi to Seurat* (New Haven: Yale University Press, 1990), 167–73.

24. Elias, *Civilizing Process*, 63; see also Arnold Hauser, *Mannerism: The Crisis of the Renaissance and the Origin of Modern Art* (Cambridge: Harvard University Press, 1965), 94–130.

25. From the thirteenth-century *Book of Nurture and School of Good Manners*, quoted in Elias, *Civilizing Process*, 69.

26. Michael Baxandall, *Painting and Experience in Fifteenth-Century Italy* (Oxford: Oxford University Press, 1972), 34.

27. Ibid., 36.

28. See Paul Hill, *The Light of Early Italian Painting* (New Haven: Yale University Press, 1987), chap. 1.

29. *Leonardo on Painting*, ed. Martin Kemp, selected and trans. Martin Kemp and Margaret Walker (New Haven: Yale University Press, 1987) 59, 65.

30. Louis Hjelmslev, *Prolegomena to a Theory of Language*, trans. Francis J. Whitfield (Madison: University of Wisconsin Press, 1961), 47–60.

31. Gilles Deleuze and Félix Guattari, *A Thousand Plateaus: Capitalism and Schizophrenia*, trans. Brian Massumi (Minneapolis: University of Minnesota Press, 1987), 44.

32. *Metaphysics*, 6.2, from *The Basic Works of Aristotle*, ed. Richard McKeon (New York: Random House, 1941). All references to Aristotle are from this edition; Deleuze and Guattari, *Thousand Plateaus*, 43.

33. In *Opera di Baldassare Castiglione, Giovanni Della Casa, Benvenuto Cellini*, ed. Carlo Cordié (Milan: Riccardo Ricciardi, n.d.), 32; translated by George Bull as *The Book of the Courtier* (New York: Penguin, 1967), 54. Subsequent citations from *The Book of the Courtier* are to these editions and appear parenthetically in the text as *BC*, with page references to the Italian edition following those from the English translation, which I have in some instances altered slightly.

34. Giovanni Della Casa, *Galateo*, trans. Konrad Eisenbichler and Kenneth Bartlett (Toronto: Centre for Reformation and Renaissance Studies, 1994), 38. Subsequent citations from this work are to this edition and appear parenthetically in the text as *G*. Italian citations are from Carlo Cordié's *Opere do Castiglione, Della Casa, Cellini*, and the Italian page number follows the English.

35. For detailed discussions of the political negotiations during the *calamità*, see Eric Cochrane, *L'Italia del cinquecento, 1530–1630* (Bari: Gius. Laterza e Fili, 1989), 3–55; J. R. Hale and M. E. Mallett, *The Military Organization of a Renaissance State: Venice c. 1400–1617* (Cambridge: Harvard University Press, 1984), 221–27, which focuses on the treaty of Cambrai and wars that resulted from it; and Lauro Martines, *Power and Imagination: City-States in Renaissance Italy* (New York: Knopf, 1979), 277–96.

36. Martines, *Power and Imagination,* 288.

37. Ibid.

38. Ibid., Deleuze and Guattari, *Thousand Plateaus,* 357.

39. Francesco Guicciardini, *Storia d'Italia,* in *Opere di Francesco Guicciardini,* ed. Emanuella Lugnani Scarano (Turin: Unione Tipografico, 1981), 2:162. See also Simon Pepper and Nicholas Adams, *Firearms and Fortifications: Military Architecture and Siege Warfare in Sixteenth-Century Siena* (Chicago: University of Chicago Press, 1986), 8–10; and Christopher Duffy, *Siege Warfare: The Fortress in the Early Modern World, 1494–1660* (London: Routledge, 1979), 8–10.

40. Hale and Mallett, *Military Organization,* 382; Bert S. Hall, *Weapons and Warfare in Renaissance Europe: Gunpowder, Technology, and Tactics* (Baltimore: Johns Hopkins University Press, 1997), 166–68.

41. J. R. Hale, "The Early Development of the Bastion: An Italian Chronology, c. 1450– c. 1535," in *Europe in the Late Middle Ages,* ed. J. R. Hale, J. R. L. Highfield, and B. Smalley (Evanston: Northwestern University Press, 1965), 491; reprinted in *Renaissance War Studies,* ed. J. R. Hale (London: Hambledon Press, 1983), 1–30.

42. See Horst De la Croix, "Military Architecture and the Radical City Plan in Sixteenth-Century Italy," *Art Bulletin* 42 (1960): 263–90; and Hale, "Development of the Bastion," 466–94.

43. Leon Battista Alberti, *On the Art of Building in Ten Books,* trans. Joseph Rykwert, with Neil Leach and Robert Tavernor (Cambridge: Massachusetts Institute of Technology Press, 1988), 4.

44. Niccolò Machiavelli, *The Discourses,* ed. Bernard Crick, trans. Leslie J. Walker (New York: Penguin, 1970; reprint, 1983), 322. Subsequent citations of this work are to this edition and are given in the text as *D.* Italian citations are from Niccolò Machiavelli, *Tutte le Opere* (Florence: Sansoni, 1989). The Italian page number follows the English.

45. Luigi Guicciardini, *The Sack of Rome,* trans. James H. McGregor (New York: Italica Press, 1993), 61. So far as I can tell, most Italian editions of *Il Sacco di Roma* attribute the work to Lodovico Guicciardini. McGregor does not discuss the reasons for his attribution in his translation.

46. F. Guiciardini, *Storia d'Italia,* 3:1758.

## Chapter Three

1. Max Weber, *From Max Weber: Essays in Sociology,* ed. and trans. H. H. Gerth and C. Wright Mills (New York: Oxford University Press, 1946; reprint, 1958), 267–301.

2. Julia Reinhard Lupton, *Afterlives of the Saints: Hagiography, Typology, and Renaissance Literature* (Stanford: Stanford University Press, 1996), 107.

3. Daniel and Jonathan Boyarin, "Diaspora: Generation and the Ground of Jewish Identity," *Critical Inquiry* 19 (summer 1993): 708, 697; see Augustine's *Adversus Judaeos,* in *Treatises on Marriage and Other Subjects,* ed. Roy J. Deferrari, trans. Charles T. Wilcox et al. (New York: Fathers of the Church, 1955), chap. 7. See also Daniel Boyarin's subtle reading of how Paul was not an anti-Semite but did firmly place "the Jewish question" at the heart of post-Pauline Christianity in *A Radical Jew: Paul and the Politics of Identity* (Berkeley and Los Angeles: University of California Press, 1994), 136–57.

4. Augustine, *On Free Choice of the Will,* trans. Anna S. Benjamin and L. H. Hackstaff (New York: Bobbs-Merrill, 1964), 8, 87.

5. See, for example, *On the Origin of the World* or the Valentinian *Tripartite Tractate* in *The Nag Hammadi Library,* ed. James Robinson et al. (1978; San Francisco: Harper and Row, 1988).

6. Hans Blumenberg, *The Legitimacy of the Modern Age,* trans. Robert M. Wallace (Cambridge: Massachusetts Institute of Technology Press, 1983), 131.

7. Donald Posner, "Caravaggio's Homo-Erotic Early Works," *Art Quarterly* 34 (1971): 304–5. See also James M. Saslow, *Ganymede in the Renaissance* (New Haven: Yale University Press, 1986), 200.

8. Giovanni Baglione, *Le Vite di pittori, scultori, et architetti* (Rome, 1642), cited in Hibbard, *Caravaggio,* 352; translations altered slightly.

9. Creighton Gilbert, *Caravaggio and His Two Cardinals* (University Park: Pennsylvania State University Press, 1995), 208–9.

10. David Carrier, "The Transfiguration of the Commonplace: Caravaggio and His Interpreters," *Word and Image* 3 (January–March 1987): 41–73. While Carrier's interpretation of homosexuality relies on Foucault's discussion in which "the homosexual" becomes a personage through nineteenth-century medico-juridical discourses, for Carrier, sexuality appears to have no relation whatsoever to equivocation, discourse, or exteriority, which is in no way the case with Foucault.

11. Jacques Lacan, *Seminar Eleven: The Four Fundamental Concepts of Psychoanalysis,* ed. Jacques-Alain Miller, trans. Alan Sheridan (New York: Norton, 1978), 136–48.

12. Eve Kosofsky Sedgwick, *Tendencies* (Durham: Duke University Press, 1993), 8–9, emphasis Sedgwick's.

13. Leo Bersani and Ulysse Dutoit, *Caravaggio's Secrets* (Cambridge: Massachusetts Institute of Technology Press, 1998), 79.

14. Guilio Mancini, *Considerazioni sulla pittura* (manuscript of 1617–21); reprinted in Hibbard, *Caravaggio,* 350.

15. Giovanni Bellori, *Le vite de pittori, scultori e archetetti moderni* (Rome, 1672), reprinted in Hibbard, *Caravaggio,* 371.

16. Arnold Hauser, *The Social History of Art,* trans. Stanley Godman (New York: Vintage, 1957; reissued 1985), 2:184.

17. Giorgio Vasari, *On Technique,* trans. Louisa S. Macelhouse (New York: Dover, 1960), 205.

18. Giorgio Vasari, *Lives of the Artists,* trans. George Bull (New York: Penguin, 1965; reprint, 1987), 1:250, 253.

19. Jacques Lacan, *Seminar Three: The Psychoses,* ed. Jacques-Alain Miller, trans. Russell Grigg (New York: Norton, 1993), 305.

20. René Descartes, *The Passions of the Soul,* art. 53, in *The Philosophical Works of Descartes,* trans. Elizabeth S. Haldane and G. R. T. Ross (Cambridge: Cambridge University Press, 1911; reprint, 1979), 1:358.

21. Ibid., art. 70, 362.

22. Leon Battista Alberti, *On Painting,* trans. Cecil Grayson (London: Phaidon, 1972; reprint, New York: Penguin, 1991), 73, 76.

23. In his famous reading of this painting, Walter Friedlander quotes Acts 9:7: "The men which journeyed with [Saul] stood speechless, hearing a voice, but seeing

no man." This is important to note because, while Friedlander's analysis is quite accurate in its detailed explanations of how the space of this painting is organized around the "dialectically contrasted elements" of the horse's bulk and the rapid foreshortening of Paul's body, nevertheless, he does not attach this dialectic to "the powerful voice penetrating" Paul's "mind and body." See Walter Friedlander, *Caravaggio Studies* (Princeton: Princeton University Press, 1955; reprint, New York: Schocken, 1969), 3, 18–19, 24.

24. The spread legs of this pose appear to be particular to Caravaggio's Paul. Compare Caravaggio's Paul with Raphael's, Michelangelo's, and Zuccari's. Friedlander argues that in Caravaggio's *Conversion of St. Paul,* Paul's spread-legged, supine pose cites Tintoretto's *St. Mark Rescuing a Slave* and Signorelli's *Signs of Destruction.* See Friedlander, *Caravaggio Studies,* 3–7, 18–20. In the Tintoretto, the slave is supine and expressly closed-legged, whereas in the Signorelli, the supine figure—posed much like Caravaggio's Paul—has a man standing on his groin.

25. See Sigmund Freud, "Negation," in *General Psychological Theory,* ed. Philip Rieff (New York: Collier, 1963), 213–17.

26. See Lacan, *Seminar Eleven,* 179. See also Slavoj Zizek, *Looking Awry: An Introduction to Jacques Lacan through Popular Culture* (Cambridge: Massachusetts Institute of Technology Press, 1991), 5.

27. Lacan, *Seminar Eleven,* 243.

28. See Joan Copjec, *Read My Desire: Lacan against the Historicists* (Cambridge: Massachusetts Institute of Technology Press, 1994), 188. For analysis of voice as *objet a,* see Slavoj Zizek, *Enjoy Your Symptom! Jacques Lacan in Hollywood and Out* (New York: Routledge, 1992), 116–20; Mladen Dolar, "The Object Voice," in *Gaze and Voice as Love Objects,* ed. Renata Salecl and Slavoj Zizek (Durham: Duke University Press, 1996), 7–31; Parveen Adams, *The Emptiness of the Image: Psychoanalysis and Sexual Differences* (London: Routledge, 1996), 67–69.

29. Jacques Lacan, *Seminar Twenty: Encore,* trans. Bruce Fink (New York: Norton, 1998), 21.

30. Luce Irigaray, *An Ethics of Sexual Difference,* trans. Carolyn Burke and Gillian C. Gill (Ithaca: Cornell University Press, 1993), 15.

31. Freud, *The Ego and the Id,* ed. James Strachey, trans. Joan Riviere (New York: Norton, 1962); "Instincts and Their Vicissitudes," in *General Psychological Theory,* ed. Philip Rieff (New York: Collier, 1963), 99.

32. Freud, *The Ego and the Id,* 44–45.

33. Ibid.

34. Jacques Lacan, *Seminar Seven: The Ethics of Psychoanalysis,* trans. Dennis Porter (New York: Norton, 1992), 109. To this extent, Lacan argues, sublimation is very close to the clinical structure of perversion.

35. Guy Hocquenghem, *Homosexual Desire,* trans. Daniella Dangoor (Durham: Duke University Press, 1993), 95; Sigmund Freud, "Psychoanalytic Notes on an Autobiographical Account of a Case of Paranoia," in *Three Case Histories,* ed. Philip Rieff (New York: Collier, 1963), 164.

36. Hocquenghem, *Homosexual Desire,* 150.

37. Ibid., 97.

38. Ibid., 103.

39. Ibid., 50.

40. Leo Bersani, *Homos* (Cambridge: Harvard University Press, 1995), 101, 164.

41. Freud, "Negation," 215.

42. Ibid., 215–16, emphasis Freud's.

43. Lacan, *Seminar Seven*, 112.

44. Sigmund Freud, *Civilization and Its Discontents*, trans. James Strachey (New York: Norton, 1961), 26.

45. Lacan, *Seminar Eleven*, 113.

46. Cited in Hibbard, *Caravaggio*, 307.

47. Ibid., 353.

48. See Tim Dean, "Sex and Syncope," *Raritan* 15 (winter 1996): 77; see also Catherine Clément, *Syncope: The Philosophy of Rapture*, trans. Sally O'Driscoll and Deirdre M. Mahoney (Minneapolis: University of Minnesota Press, 1994). Dean's main point in using this term is to elaborate the politico-aesthetic implications of Leo Bersani's *Homos*. Dean is interested in nuancing Bersani's concept of "homoness" with the notion of syncope precisely because of the ways in which syncope allows the self-shattering of sexuality to operate "prophylactically" (81) in aesthetic practices—as a kind of safe sex way to deal with the deadly dangers of *jouissance* in the age of AIDS.

49. See Michael Fried's comments on Caravaggio and temporality in his "Thoughts on Caravaggio," *Critical Inquiry* 24 (autumn 1997): 13–57.

50. I am here indebted to Parveen Adams's discussion of Francis Bacon's paintings in "The Violence of Paint," in *Emptiness of the Image*, 108–21. Adams argues specifically that painting offers a way to think about a violence of psychical deflation that is outside the phallic vocabulary of castration so central to psychoanalysis. While Adams argues for the political and therapeutic importance of the concept of castration, her work is also dedicated to finding other models that can embody and extend this concept.

51. Sigmund Freud, "Analysis Terminable and Interminable," in *Therapy and Technique*, ed. Philip Rieff (New York: Collier, 1963), 271.

52. Lacan, *Seminar Eleven*, 273. For a discussion of identification with the "fall of the object" especially in relation to Lacan's crucial notion of the pass, see Anne Dunand, "The End of the Treatment," *Newsletter of the Freudian Field* 4 (1990): 120–33. See also Charles Shepherdson, "Vital Signs: The *Place* of Memory in Psychoanalysis," *Research in Phenomenology* 23 (1994): 61–66.

53. Alfred Moir, *Caravaggio* (New York: Harry Abrams, 1982; reprint, 1989), 116.

## Chapter Four

1. Here is Eliot's remarkable sentence: "But Marlowe, the most thoughtful, the most blasphemous (and, therefore, probably the most Christian) of his contemporaries, is always an exception." See T. S. Eliot, "Shakespeare and the Stoicism of Seneca," in *Selected Essays* (London: Faber and Faber, 1972), 133; also C. L. Barber, "The forme of Faustus fortunes good or bad," in *Creating Elizabethan Tragedy: The Theater of Marlowe and Kyd*, ed. Richard P. Wheeler (Chicago: University of Chicago Press, 1988), 102.

2. Stephen Greenblatt, *Renaissance Self-Fashioning: From More to Shakespeare* (Chicago: University of Chicago Press, 1980), 221; Jonathan Goldberg, *Sodometries: Renaissance Texts/Modern Sexualities* (Stanford: Stanford University Press, 1992), 123.

3. Philip Sidney, *An Apologie for Poetrie*, in *Elizabethan Critical Essays*, ed. G. Gregory Smith (London: Oxford University Press, 1904), 1:184–86, 156. For a useful

analysis of Sidney's *Defense* as a performance, see Margaret W. Ferguson's *Trials of Desire: Renaissance Defenses of Poetry* (New Haven: Yale University Press, 1983), 137–62. In using the word "performative," I follow J. L. Austin's analysis in *How to Do Things with Words,* ed. J. O. Urmson and Marina Sbisa (Cambridge: Harvard University Press, 1975). As is well known, Austin begins by distinguishing between the "constative," or statements judged by their truth or falsity, and "performative," or statements judged by their felicity or infelicity—how well they perform in relation to a set of conventions. In the process of his analysis, however, Austin demonstrates that constatives are performatives that ignore their performativity. And this leads Austin to develop a theory of the utterance based on force. See also Shoshana Felman, *The Literary Speech Act: Don Juan with J. L. Austin, or Seduction in Two Languages,* trans. Catherine Porter (Ithaca: Cornell University Press, 1983).

4. See Joel Fineman, *Shakespeare's Perjured Eye: The Invention of Poetic Subjectivity in the Sonnets* (Berkeley and Los Angeles: University of California Press, 1986), 1–48.

5. Doctor Faustus, line 799, B-text, in *The Works of Christopher Marlowe,* ed. C. F. Tucker Brooke (Oxford: Clarendon Press, 1910). Subsequent quotations from the plays and poetry of Marlowe are to this edition and are cited by parenthetically in the text by line number. My argument is developed from both the A-text and the B-text, though I quote from the A-text unless otherwise noted.

6. *The Acts and Monuments of John Foxe,* ed. Rev. George Townsend (New York: AMS Press, 1965), 1:vii. Subsequent quotations from Foxe's *Acts and Monuments* are to this edition and are cited parenthetically in the text as *AM* by volume and page number.

7. Anthony Kemp, *The Estrangement of the Past: A Study in the Origins of Modern Historical Consciousness* (New York: Oxford University Press, 1991), 84–85.

8. John Calvin, *Institutes of the Christian Religion,* ed. John T. MacNeill, trans. Ford Lewis Battles (Philadelphia: Westminster Press, 1960), 1.9.8.

9. I quote here from the Geneva Bible.

10. Bruce R. Smith, *Homosexual Desire in Shakespeare's England: A Cultural Poetics* (Chicago: University of Chicago Press, 1991; reprint, 1994), 44.

11. *Statutes of the Realm,* 5 Eliz. c. 17.

12. Goldberg, *Sodometries,* 1–26.

13. Harry Berger, Jr., "Bodies and Texts," *Representations* 17 (winter 1987): 149.

14. Elaine Scarry, *The Body in Pain: The Making and Unmaking of the World* (New York and Oxford: Oxford University Press, 1985), 184–85.

15. Bruster develops the thesis of Jean-Christophe Agnew that the Elizabethan theater was a laboratory or proxy for market economy. Bruster argues that the theaters were not just laboratories; they were markets. See Douglas Bruster, *Drama and the Market in the Age of Shakespeare* (Cambridge: Cambridge University Press, 1992), 8–9. For Bruster's analysis of commodification, see 63–96. See also Jean-Christophe Agnew, *Worlds Apart: The Market and the Theater in Anglo-American Thought, 1550–1750* (Cambridge: Cambridge University Press, 1986), ix–xiv.

16. "Mate" cannot here mean checkmate (i.e., defeat) because the Carthaginians, under Hannibal, *won* the battle of Trasymenus.

17. The announcement of a form whose performance differs from the form itself is a device that runs throughout the play. Think, for example, of the way that Mephostophilis performs the damnation of Faustus dressed like a friar, or, in the comic

scenes, the way that Wagner performs illogical arguments in the form of logic. My favorite example is Faustus's first incantation:

> Now that the gloomy shadow of the night,
> Longing to view Orions drisling looke,
> Leapes from th'antartike world vnto the skie
> And dimmes the welkin with her pitchy breath . . .
> (B-text, 235–38)

The referent of this speech is impossible to discern if we assume a one-to-one correspondence between words and things. How can the night, itself a lack of light, have a shadow whose pitchy breath dims what is already dark? While this speech announces the performance of the act of darkening, the referent of this speech is the aurora borealis, which "leaps from th'antartike world" to "dim" (that is, lighten) that the sky with "her pitchy [that is, bright] breath."

18. As Emily Bartels points out, the issue is not exactly the "good" or "bad," but the "form" of Faustus's fortunes itself—"a form that uncovers the dependence of authority on subversion." See "Authorizing Subversion: Strategies of Power in Marlowe's *Doctor Faustus*," *Renaissance Papers*, 1989, 67. Bartels expands this argument in *Spectacles of Strangeness: Imperialism, Alienation, and Marlowe* (Philadelphia: University of Pennsylvania Press, 1993), 111–42. Cf. Jonathan Dollimore, *Radical Tragedy: Religion, Ideology, and Power in the Drama of Shakespeare and His Contemporaries* (Chicago: University of Chicago Press, 1986), 109–19.

19. This account is the same one that Lacan gives for the subject of psychoanalysis when he says that a signifier is that which represents the subject for another signifier. By this statement, Lacan means that subjectivity is an effect of the recursivity of signification that, as Judith Butler has argued, constitutes both the "imaginary instancing" of identity and the "authority of the symbolic"—not necessarily in the form of the law but, I would add, in its precise historical form. See Judith Butler, *Bodies That Matter: On the Discursive Limits of "Sex"* (New York: Routledge, 1993), 108–9. There is no signified that guarantees either the authority of the symbolic or the stability of the subject that is an effect of this recursivity. "There is no Other of the Other," as Lacan puts it; there is only a "signifier of a lack in the Other." See *Ecrits: A Selection*, trans. Alan Sheridan (New York: Norton, 1977), 316–17.

20. *Summa Theologica*, book 1, quest. 76, art. 2, in *The Basic Works of Saint Thomas Aquinas*, ed. Anton C. Pegis (New York: Random House, 1945). Subsequent citations of Aquinas are from this edition.

21. Sigmund Freud, *Jokes and Their Relation to the Unconscious*, ed. and trans. James Strachey (New York: Norton, 1960; reprint, 1989), 138.

22. William Empson, "Two Proper Crimes," *Nation* 163 (October 19, 1946): 444–45; emphasis Empson's.

23. Michael Goldman, "Marlowe and the Histrionics of Ravishment," in *Two Renaissance Mythmakers: Christopher Marlowe and Ben Jonson*, ed. Alvin Kernan (Baltimore: Johns Hopkins University Press, 1977), 23.

24. Marjorie Garber, "Closure and Enclosure in Marlowe," in Kernan, *Two Renaissance Mythmakers*, 17. This backwards and forwards movement of words is the source of Faustus's escape from the theological: "Bell, Booke, and Candle. Candle, Booke, and Bell," Faustus says, mocking the friars' attempt to exorcise him. "Forward and backward, to curse Faustus to hell!" (B-text, 1095–96).

25. Ovid, *Metamorphoses*, trans. Frank Justus Miller (Cambridge: Harvard University Press, 1921), 3.176; subsequent citations of this work are given parenthetically in the text.

26. George Sandys, *Ovid's Metamorphoses Englished, Mythologized, and Represented in Figures*, ed. Karl K. Hulley and Stanley T. Vandersall (Lincoln: University of Nebraska Press, 1970), 151; emphasis Sandys's.

27. Francis Bacon, *Wisdom of the Ancients*, in *The Works of Francis Bacon*, ed. James Spedding, Robert Leslie Ellis, and Douglas Denon Heath (London: Longman, 1857–74; reprint, Stuttgart-Bad Cannstatt: F. Frommann, G. Holzboog, 1962–63), 6:719.

28. Sandys, *Ovid's Metamorphoses Englished*, 150. As Helkiah Crooke writes, "sometimes [the clitoris] groweth to such a length that it hangeth without the cleft like a mans member, especially when it is fretted with the touch of the cloaths, and so strutteth and groweth to a rigiditie as doth the yarde [or penis] of a man. And this part it is which those wicked women do abuse called Tribades (often mentioned by many authors, and in some states worthy to be punished) to their natural and unnatural lusts." Quoted in Valerie Traub, "The (In)Significance of Lesbian Desire," in *Queering the Renaissance*, ed. Jonathan Goldberg (Durham: Duke University Press, 1994), 66.

29. For instance, W. W. Greg argues that the B-text is the original, while Constance Brown Kuriyama opts for the A-text. See Greg's editorial comments in *Marlowe's* Doctor Faustus, *1604–1616: Parallel Texts* (Oxford: Clarendon Press, 1950); and Kuriyama's "Dr. Greg and *Doctor Faustus*: The Supposed Originality of the 1616 Text," *English Literary Renaissance* 5 (1975): 171–97. See also Leah Marcus, "Textual Indeterminacy and Ideological Difference: The Case of *Doctor Faustus*," *Renaissance Drama* 20 (1989): 5, and William Empson's posthumous study, *Faustus and the Censor: The English Faust-Book and Marlowe's* Doctor Faustus, recovered and edited by John Henry Jones (New York: Basil Blackwell, 1987).

30. Greenblatt, *Renaissance Self-Fashioning*, 200, emphasis Greenblatt's.

31. For a brilliant reading of how ends work in *Doctor Faustus*, see Edward A. Snow, "Marlowe's *Doctor Faustus* and the Ends of Desire," in Kernan, *Two Renaissance Mythmakers*, 70–110.

32. Berger, "Bodies and Texts," 157.

33. Sandys, *Ovid's Metamorphoses Englished*, 152.

34. Plutarch, *Moralia*, trans. Howard North Fowler (Cambridge: Harvard University Press, 1949), 10:9.

35. See Ed Cohen, "Legislating the Norm: From Sodomy to Gross Indecencies," *South Atlantic Quarterly* (winter 1989): 187.

36. Alan Bray, "Homosexuality and the Signs of Male Friendship in Elizabethan England," in Goldberg, *Queering the Renaissance*, 50–51.

37. Goldberg, *Sodometries*, 19. Bruce Smith argues that there were two main shifts in sixteenth- and seventeenth-century England concerning sodomy, a shift in ideology, "a progression from religious to political to personal ways of thinking about sodomy," and "an increasing exactitude about just what homosexual acts are" (Smith, *Homosexual Desire*, 41–53).

38. Sigmund Freud, "Negation," in *General Psychological Theory*, ed. Philip Rieff (New York: Collier, 1963), 213–17. Freud explains that "the subject-matter of a re-

pressed image or thought can make its way into consciousness on condition that it is *denied*. Negation is a way of taking account of what is repressed; indeed, it is actually a removal of the repression, though not, of course, an acceptance of what is repressed" (213–14).

39. Ibid., 215–16, emphasis Freud's.

40. Judith Butler, *Gender Trouble: Feminism and the Subversion of Identity* (New York: Routledge, 1990), 141.

41. Lacan, *Ecrits: A Selection*, 213.

42. Following the work of Eve Sedgwick and Judith Butler, I would further propose that the performative assertion of the heterosexual masculine, *Je m'affirme être un homme . . .* , is rendered felicitous or infelicitous by its relation to the reiterated conventions of homosociality and that the possible infelicity that all performative assertions assume is rendered an epistemological anxiety around which subjectivity is constituted. While this infelicity and anxiety are structurally part and parcel of any sense of subjectivity constituted by and within an economy of exchange (Lacan's insight), historically at least after the middle of the nineteenth century this infelicity gets named "homosexuality" and this temporally situated anxiety gets spatialized as "the closet." See Butler, *Bodies That Matter*, esp. chaps. 3 and 4; Sedgwick, *Between Men: English Literature and Male Homosocial Desire* (New York: Columbia University Press, 1985); and *Epistemology of the Closet* (Berkeley and Los Angeles: University of California Press, 1990), 67–90.

43. See "Commentaire de Jean Hyppolite sur la 'Verneinung,'" in Jacques Lacan, *Ecrits* (Paris: Editions du Seuil, 1966), 886. A translation of this commentary appears in the appendix of Lacan's, *Seminar One: Freud's Papers on Technique*, ed. Jacques-Alain Miller, trans. John Forrester (New York: Norton, 1988), 289–97.

44. Rainolds, *Th'Overthrow of Stage Plays* (1599), quoted in Bray, "Homosexuality and Male Friendship," 41.

45. Reginald Scot, *The Discoverie of Witchcraft* (New York: De Capo Press, 1971), 3.19.71–72; *Malleus Maleficarum*, trans. Rev. Montague Summers (New York: Dover, 1971), 25, 30.

46. See Gordon Teskey's suggestive remarks on irony, allegory, and the market in *Allegory and Violence* (Ithaca: Cornell University Press, 1996), 68–69.

47. Barber, "The forme of Faustus fortunes," 109–20.

48. Aristotle, *De Anima*, 1.4.408b.13, 3.8.4321.1, in *The Basic Works of Aristotle*, ed. Richard McKeon (New York: Random House, 1941); Acquinas, *Summa Theologica*, book 1, quest. 76, art. 3.

49. Pietro Pomponazzi, "On the Immortality of the Soul," in *The Renaissance Philosophy of Man*, ed. Ernst Cassirer, Paul Oskar Kristeller, and John Herman Randall, Jr. (Chicago: University of Chicago Press, 1948), 298.

50. Karl Marx, *Capital*, ed. Frederick Engels, trans. Samuel Moore and Edward Aveling (New York: International Publishers, 1967), 1:176, translation slightly modified. For a detailed explanation of this process, see chapters 6 and 7.

51. For an analysis of the mechanization of human labor and the humanization of the machine in the early modern period, see Lewis Mumford, *Technics and Civilization* (New York: Harcourt, Brace, Jovanovich, 1963), 107–50, where Mumford discusses the way that the "manu-facture" of goods resulted in specialization and technologization of the body's motions.

52. *Everyman*, lines 76–79, in *Medieval Drama*, ed. David Bevington (Boston:

Houghton Mifflin, 1975). All citations are to this edition and are hereafter cited parenthetically in the text by line number.

53. James Peele, *The Manner and Fourme How to Keepe a Perfect Reconynge* (London, 1553), STC 19547, Aiii^r.

54. John Mellis, *A Briefe Instruction How to Keepe Bookes of Accompts* (London, 1588), STC 18794, A7^r. Mellis's book is a reprint of Hugh Oldcastle's 1543 *Brief Instruction*, which is no longer extant.

55. James Peele, *The Pathe Waye to Perfectnes, in th' Accomptes of Debitour, and Creditour* (London, 1569), STC 19548, *ii^v.

56. Mellis, *A Briefe Instruction*, A6^v–A7^v.

57. In his *Lectures on Genesis*, Luther attributes the invention of what I am calling a literary mode of representation to the serpent when he describes the way that Satan corrupts the Word with his question "Did God really command you not to eat from every tree of Paradise?" As Luther argues, Satan's distortion uses the Word against itself in order to introduce doubt, or "unbelief." See *Lectures on Genesis*, trans. George V. Shick and Paul D. Pahl, in *Luther's Works*, ed. Jaroslav Pelikan and Helmut Lehman, 55 vols. (Saint Louis and Philadelphia: Concordia and Fortress Presses, 1958–86), 1:146–54.

58. For perhaps the most famous version of this argument, see Harry Levine, *The Overreacher: A Study of Christopher Marlowe* (Cambridge: Harvard University Press, 1952), 111ff.

## Chapter Five

1. See John Aubrey, *Brief Lives* (Oxford: Clarendon Press, 1898), 1:71; Simonds D'Ewes, *The Autobiography and Correspondence of Sir Simonds D'Ewes, Bart., During the Reigns of James I and Charles I*, ed. James O. Halliwell (London: R. Bently, 1845), 1:192; and, for Mrs. Bacon's letter, Alan Bray, *Homosexuality in Renaissance England* (London: Gay Men's Press, 1982), 49. See also Bray's discussion on same-sex relations between masters and servingmen in ibid., 45–51; as well as Bray, "Homosexuality and the Signs of Male Friendship in Elizabethan England," in *Queering the Renaissance*, ed. Jonathan Goldberg (Durham: Duke University Press, 1994), 53–56.

2. David M. Halperin, *One Hundred Years of Homosexuality* (New York: Routledge, 1990), 25, emphasis Halperin's.

3. Ibid., 33.

4. Jacques Lacan, *Seminar Eleven: The Four Fundamental Concepts of Psychoanalysis*, ed. Jacques-Alain Miller, trans. Alan Sheridan (New York: Norton, 1978), 214, emphasis Lacan's.

5. See ibid., 149–60; and also "The Meaning of the Phallus," in *Feminine Sexuality: Jacques Lacan and the Ecole Freudienne*, ed. Juliet Mitchell and Jacqueline Rose, trans. Jacqueline Rose (New York: Norton, 1982), 80–81.

6. Lacan, *Seminar Eleven*, 206.

7. Michel Foucault, "The Concern for Truth," interview conducted by François Ewald, *Le Magazine Littéraire*, May 1984; reprinted in Michel Foucault, *Foucault Live: Interviews, 1966–84*, ed. Sylvère Lotringer, trans. John Johnston (New York: Semiotext[e], 1989), 296. For a discussion of Foucault and problematicization, see Robert Castel, "'Problematicization' as a Mode of Reading History," trans. Paula Wissing, in *Foucault and the Writing of History*, ed. Jan Goldstein (Oxford: Basil Blackwell, 1994), 237–52.

8. Francis Bacon, *The Masculine Birth of Time,* from Benjamin Farrington's translation in *The Philosophy of Francis Bacon* (Liverpool: Liverpool University Press, 1964), 62, 70. All quotations from *The Masculine Birth of Time* are from this translation and are hereafter cited parenthetically in the text as *MB.* Citations in the Latin original are from *The Works of Francis Bacon,* ed. James Spedding, Robert Leslie Ellis, and Douglas Denon Heath, 14 vols. (London: Longman, 1857–74; reprint, Stuttgart–Bad Cannstatt: F. Frommann, G. Holzboog, 1962–63), 3:529, 537. Page references to the Latin follow those to the English translation.

9. Evelyn Fox Keller, *Reflections on Gender and Science* (New Haven: Yale University Press, 1985), 37.

10. Unless otherwise noted, all citations of Francis Bacon are from *The Works of Francis Bacon* and are identified parenthetically in the text by volume and page number, except for quotations from the *New Organon,* which are identified by volume, book number, and aphorism number. I use the following abbreviations for specific works: *AL* for *Of the Proficiency and Advancement of Learning; AR* for *The Arguments of Law; CPN* for *In the Case of the Post-Nati of Scotland; DA* for *Of the Dignity and Advancement of Learning; E* for *The Essays; GI* for *The Great Instauration; HL* for the *History of Life and Death; HN* for *Historia Naturalis and Experimentalis; NA* for *The New Atlantis; NO* for *New Organon; PN* for *Preparative Towards a Natural and Experimental History; PW* for *Plan of the Work;* and *WA* for *Wisdom of the Ancients.* Critics sometimes refer to volumes 8 through 14 of *The Works* as *The Letters and the Life of Francis Bacon* and number them 1 through 7. I keep the volume numbers from *The Works* and refer to the occasional writings as *LL.* Throughout, page references to the Latin follow those from the English translation.

11. Keller, *Reflections on Gender and Science,* 34.

12. Ibid., 42.

13. Mark Breitenberg, *Anxious Masculinity in Early Modern England* (Cambridge: Cambridge University Press, 1996), 72, 82.

14. Breitenberg critiques an earlier attempt of mine to think relations between sexuality, writing, and epistemology in Baconian science. Breitenberg concedes the importance of introducing "Bacon's own sexual practices into an analysis of his epistemology," but argues that in so doing I too strongly oppose homosexuality and heterosexuality. Perhaps. However, Breitenberg also opposes homosexuality with heterosexuality, only he does so in order to dismiss homosexuality in the name of Bacon's supposedly conservative class politics: "Bacon's homoerotic practices do not prevent him from figuring his new science in a heterosexual economy—that rhetoric was widely available and it has as much to do with status and class purity as it does with gender" (ibid., 72). See my essay "The Epistemology of Expurgation: Bacon and *The Masculine Birth of Time.*" in Goldberg, *Queering the Renaissance,* 236–52. My introduction to this chapter expands the argument that I gave there.

At stake in Breitenberg's dismissal, as well as in the difference between my analysis and his, is how to read. Breitenberg's analysis is part of a critical trend that reads a narrative of political conservatism in Bacon's metaphors of conquest, imperialism, and sexual difference, in his royalist politics, and in his general project binding knowledge and power. Usually practitioners of this critical trend imply that their own politics are by comparison more liberal, but since this implicit comparison posits politics as little more than sanctimonious moralism, I find myself extremely wary of its claims as well as its analyses. Ronald Levao characterizes this critical trend quite succinctly: "Even as the scheme would locate the complex phenomenon of Baconian science within a broader cultural field, its dedication to a teleological, highly moralized, narrative constrains the resourcefulness of both the texts and the culture it reads, telling them through a singular story whose own authority is protected rather than challenged by an acknowledgment of occulted, contradictory, residual, and emergent strains of discourse." I can only agree with Levao that Bacon "is just the sort of writer to encourage and destabilize such narratives," and I would add that to read Bacon otherwise seriously underestimates and misapprehends the complexity of his thinking, his politics, and his science. See Ronald Levao, "Francis Bacon and the Mobility of Science," *Representations* 40 (fall 1992): 2–3.

15. Abraham Cowley, "To the Royal Society," lines 95–96, in Cowley, *Poems,* ed. A. R. Waller (Cambridge: Cambridge University Press, 1905).

16. Stanley Fish, *Self-Consuming Artifacts: The Experience of Seventeenth-Century Literature* (Berkeley and Los Angeles: University of California Press, 1972), 78–155; Charles Whitney, *Francis Bacon and Modernity* (New Haven: Yale University Press, 1986), 105–25, 173–204.

17. Hans Blumenberg, *The Legitimacy of the Modern Age,* trans. Robert M. Wallace (Cambridge: Massachusetts Institute of Technology Press, 1983), 42–43.

18. Anthony Kemp, *The Estrangement of the Past: A Study in the Origins of Modern Historical Consciousness* (New York: Oxford University Press, 1991), 6.

19. Blumenberg, *Legitimacy of the Modern Age,* 131.

20. Ibid., 138.

21. Ibid., 137, 142.

22. Gérald Sfez, "Deciding on Evil," in *Radical Evil,* ed. Joan Copjec (London: Verso, 1996), 126–27; see also Maurice Merleau-Ponty, *Signs,* trans. Richard C. McCleary (Evanston: Northwestern University Press, 1964), 215.

23. See Eric Cochrane's discussion of Bruni and Florentine humanist historiography in *Historians and Historiography in the Italian Renaissance* (Chicago: University of Chicago Press, 1981), 3–33; Nancy Struever, *The Language of History in the Renaissance* (Princeton: Princeton University Press, 1970), 101–43; Donald J. Wilcox, *The Development of Florentine Humanist Historiography in the Fifteenth Century* (Cambridge: Harvard University Press, 1969), 32–129; and Louis Ferdinand Green, *Chronicle into History* (Cambridge: Cambridge University Press, 1972).

24. Machiavelli, *The Prince,* trans. George Bull (New York: Penguin, 1961), 133; *Tutte le Opere* (Florence: Sansoni, 1989), 296.

25. Augustine, *Confessions,* trans. William Watts (Cambridge: Harvard University Press, 1988), 2:10.35, translation slightly altered.

26. See, for example, Augustine, *On Christian Doctrine,* trans. D. W. Robertson, Jr. (New York: Macmillan, 1958), 1.1–22; see Blumenberg, *Legitimacy of the Modern Age,* 309–23.

27. Blumenberg, *Legitimacy of the Modern Age,* 278.

28. Thus Denise Albanese argues for a homologous relation between new science epistemology and new world exploration. In the case of Bacon, a "nascent imperialism," she argues, is "constellated with an equally nascent empiricism" in which monarchical authority is anxiously overdetermined. See Albanese, *New Science, New World* (Durham: Duke University Press, 1996), 99. As Julie Robin Solomon argues, since commerce and voyages of discovery, not royal authority, "make and sustain empire," Bacon's appropriation of mercantilist vocational tactics threatened to dis-

place apparatuses of royal sovereignty. But, she goes on to argue, royal authority reemerges "as the sovereignty of the material world and of those who have access to it." While Bacon translates merchant ethics into an epistemological position that grounds science, he also reasserts royal prerogative in the discursive networks that cluster around his characterizations of material particularity. See Solomon, *Objectivity in the Making: Francis Bacon and the Politics of Inquiry* (Baltimore: Johns Hopkins University Press, 1998), 162.

29. Blumenberg, *Legitimacy of the Modern Age*, 390.

30. Gilles Deleuze and Félix Guattari, *Kafka: Toward a Minor Literature*, trans. Dana Polan (Minneapolis: University of Minnesota Press, 1986), 17; see also Peter Goodrich, *Law in the Courts of Love* (London: Routledge, 1996), 2–3.

31. Ben Jonson, *Works*, ed. C. H. Herford and Percy Simpson, 11 vols. (Oxford: Oxford University Press, 1925–52), 3:2.3.146–50.

32. See L. W. Abbott, *Law Reporting in England, 1485–1585* (London: Athlone Press, 1973), 10, 210; Joseph Henry Beale, *A Bibliography of Early English Law Books* (Cambridge: Harvard University Press, 1920), 98–104; J. H. Baker, *The Legal Profession and the Common Law* (London: Hambledon Press, 1986), 472. I should make it clear that I am here reversing the relation between document and history that these scholars all assert. Whereas each of the above thinks of the document as reflecting change in the judicial system, I am arguing that the form of law reporting enabled historical change. To a certain extent, then, I follow Richard Helgerson's analysis of Coke's reprinting of Littleton's *Tenures* in *The First Part of the Institutes of the Laws of England*. See Helgerson, *Forms of Nationhood: The Elizabethan Writing of England* (Chicago: University of Chicago Press, 1992), 88–101.

33. Edmund Plowden, *The Commentaries or Reports* (Dublin: H. Watts, 1792), 1:xi.

34. Ibid., 1:83–84.

35. Ibid., 1:vii.

36. Ibid., 1:viii.

37. Ibid., 1:xv.

38. See Jonathan Goldberg's extraordinary discussion in *Writing Matter: From the Hands of the English Renaissance* (Stanford: Stanford University Press, 1990), 263ff.

39. Ernst H. Kantorowicz, *The King's Two Bodies: A Study in Mediaeval Political Theology* (Princeton: Princeton University Press, 1957; reprint, 1997), 15, 171–73.

40. G. R Elton, ed., *The Tudor Constitution*, 2d ed. (Cambridge: Cambridge University Press, 1982), 20–23.

41. J. G. A. Pocock, *The Ancient Constitution and the Feudal Law: A Study of English Historical Thought in the Seventeenth Century* (Cambridge: Cambridge University Press, 1957).

42. Edward Coke, *The Reports of Edward Coke* (London, 1658), Wing C4944, 358. Subsequent citations of this work appear parenthetically in the text as *R*.

43. Elton, *Tudor Constitution*, 238–40.

44. Solomon, *Objectivity in the Making*, 188–89. For a reading of Bacon's animist materialism and its relation to the body of the civilizing process, see Gail Kern Paster, "Nervous Tension: Networks of Blood and Spirit in the Early Modern Body," in *The Body in Parts: Fantasies of Corporeality in Early Modern Europe*, ed. David Hillman and Carla Mazzio (New York: Routledge, 1997), 107–12.

45. Edward Coke, *The Twelfth Part of the Reports* (London, 1658), Wing C4969, 65.

46. See Goodrich, *Courts of Love,* 20–21.

47. Julian Martin, *Francis Bacon, the State, and the Reform of Natural Philosophy* (Cambridge: Cambridge University Press, 1992), 106–29 and passim.

48. Kenneth Cardwell, "Francis Bacon, Inquisitor," in *Francis Bacon's Legacy of Texts: "The Art of Discovery Grows with Discovery,"* ed. William Sessions (New York: AMS Press, 1990), 269–89; see also Martin, *Francis Bacon,* 164–75.

49. Julia Reinhard Lupton, *Afterlives of the Saints: Hagiography, Typology, and Renaissance Literature* (Stanford: Stanford University Press, 1996), 51–52.

50. Eusebius, *The Ecclesiastical History,* trans. Kirsopp Lake (Cambridge: Harvard University Press, 1973), 1.2.5; see also, Kemp, *Estrangement of the Past,* 16 and passim.

51. Philip Sidney, *An Apologie for Poetrie,* in *Elizabethan Critical Essays,* ed. G. Gregory Smith (London: Oxford University Press, 1904), 1:174.

52. Virgil, *Aeneid,.* trans. H. Rushton Fairclough (Cambridge: Harvard University Press, 1986), 2:10.204–5, 8.7–8. Subsequent citations are to this edition and appear parenthetically in the text.

53. John Calvin, *Institutes of the Christian Religion,* ed. John T. MacNeill, trans. Ford Lewis Battles (Philadelphia: Westminster Press, 1960), 1.11.8.

54. For a discussion of Protestantism and historiography, see Kemp, *Estrangement of the Past,* 66–104. For a discussion of Protestant hermeneutics, authority, and experience, see Gerald L. Bruns, *Hermeneutics Ancient and Modern* (New Haven: Yale University Press, 1992), 145–50.

55. Solomon, *Objectivity in the Making,* 108.

56. Steven Shapin, *A Social History of Truth: Civility and Science in Seventeenth-Century England* (Chicago: University of Chicago Press, 1994), 65–124.

57. See Charles Whitney, "Merchants of Light: Science as Colonization in the *New Atlantis,*" in Sessions, *Francis Bacon's Legacy of Texts,* 261–62.

58. Slavoj Zizek, *Tarrying with the Negative: Kant, Hegel, and the Critique of Ideology* (Durham: Duke University Press, 1993), 30.

59. William Warner, *Albion's England* (1612; New York: Georg Olms Verlag Hildesheim, 1971), 230.

60. Reginaldus Gonsalvius Montanus, *A Discovery of Sundry Subtill Practices of the Holy Inquisition of Spayn* (London, 1568), STC 11996, Bi$^v$.

61. Ibid., Bvi$^r$.

62. Ibid., Aiii$^r$.

63. Warner, *Albion's England,* 230.

64. Jacques Lacan, *Seminar Seven: The Ethics of Psychoanalysis,* trans. Dennis Porter (New York: Norton, 1992), 20.

65. Ibid., 71.

## Chapter Six

1. Luce Irigaray, *An Ethics of Sexual Difference,* trans. Carolyn Burke and Gillian C. Gill (Ithaca: Cornell University Press, 1993), 9, emphasis mine in the first quote, Irigaray's in the second. Subsequent citations of this work are given parenthetically in the text as *ES.*

2. Elizabeth Weed, "A Question of Style," in *Engaging with Irigaray: Feminist*

*Philosophy and Modern European Thought,* ed. Carolyn Burke, Naomi Schor, and Margaret Whitford (New York: Columbia University Press, 1994), 102.

3. Judith Butler, *Bodies That Matter: On the Discursive Limits of "Sex"* (New York: Routledge, 1993), 37–38.

4. Luce Irigaray, *This Sex Which Is Not One,* trans. Catherine Porter (Ithaca: Cornell University Press, 1985), 173. Subsequent citations of this work appear parenthetically in the text as *TS.*

5. Butler, *Bodies That Matter,* 223.

6. Ibid., 108–9.

7. Ibid., 227, 230. This argument extends Butler's earlier discussion in *Gender Trouble: Feminism and the Subversion of Identity* (New York: Routledge, 1990), 142–49.

8. Ibid., 122, emphasis mine.

9. John Champagne, *The Ethics of Marginality: A New Approach to Gay Studies* (Minneapolis: University of Minnesota Press, 1995), 136, 138; Friedrich Nietzsche, "The Uses and Disadvantages of History for Life," in *Untimely Meditations,* trans. R. J. Hollingdate Cambridge: (Cambridge University Press, 1983), 115.

10. Champagne, *Ethics,* 142.

# BIBLIOGRAPHY

Abbott, L. W. *Law Reporting in England, 1485–1585*. London: Athlone Press, 1973.

Adams, Parveen. *The Emptiness of the Image: Psychoanalysis and Sexual Differences*. London: Routledge, 1996.

Agnew, Jean-Christophe. *Worlds Apart: The Market and the Theater in Anglo-American Thought, 1550–1750*. Cambridge: Cambridge University Press, 1986.

Albanese, Denise. *New Science, New World*. Durham: Duke University Press, 1996.

Alberti, Leon Battista. *On Painting*. Trans. Cecil Grayson. London: Phaidon, 1972. Reprint, New York: Penguin, 1991.

———. *On the Art of Building in Ten Books*. Trans. Joseph Rykwert, with Neil Leach and Robert Tavernor. Cambridge: Massachusetts Institute of Technology Press, 1988.

———. *Opere Volgari*. Ed. Cecil Grayson. 3 vols. Bari: G. Laterza, 1960.

———. *The Family in Renaissance Florence*. Trans. Renée New Watkins. Columbia, S.C.: University of South Carolina Press, 1969.

Ariès, Philippe, and Georges Duby, eds. *A History of Private Life*. Trans. Arthur Goldhammer. 5 vols. Cambridge: Harvard University Press, 1987–91.

Aristotle. *The Basic Works of Aristotle*. Ed. Richard McKeon. New York: Random House, 1941.

Aubrey, John. *Brief Lives*. 2 vols. Oxford: Clarendon Press, 1898.

Augustine. *Adversus Judaeos*. In *Treatises on Marriage and Other Subjects*, ed. Roy J. Deferrari, trans. Charles T. Wilcox et al., 387–414. New York: Fathers of the Church, 1955.

———. *Confessions*. Trans. William Watts. 2 vols. Cambridge: Harvard University Press, 1988.

———. *On Christian Doctrine*. Trans. D. W. Robertson, Jr. New York: Macmillan, 1958.

———. *On Free Choice of the Will*. Trans. Anna S. Benjamin and L. H. Hackstaff. New York: Bobbs-Merrill, 1964.

Austin, J. L. *How to Do Things with Words*. Ed. J. O. Urmson and Marina Sbisa. Cambridge: Harvard University Press, 1975.

Bacon, Francis. *The Masculine Birth of Time*. Trans. Benjamin Farrington. In *The Philosophy of Francis Bacon*, by Benjamin Farrington, 61–72. Liverpool: Liverpool University Press, 1964.

————. *The Works of Francis Bacon.* Ed. James Spedding, Robert Leslie Ellis, and Douglas Denon Heath. 14 vols. London: Longman, 1857–74. Reprint, Stuttgart–Bad Cannstatt: F. Frommann, G. Holzboog, 1962–63.

Baglione, Giovanni. *Le vite de' pittori, scultori, et architetti.* Rome, 1672. Reprinted in *Caravaggio,* by Howard Hibbard (New York: Harper and Row, 1983), 351–56.

Baker, J. H. *The Legal Profession and the Common Law.* London: Hambledon Press, 1986.

Barber, C. L. "The forme of Faustus fortunes good or bad." *Tulane Drama Review* 8 (1964): 92–119. Reprinted in *Creating Elizabethan Tragedy: The Theater of Marlowe and Kyd,* ed. Richard P. Wheeler (Chicago: University of Chicago Press, 1988), 87–130.

Barker, Francis. *The Tremulous Private Body.* New York: Methuen, 1984.

Bartels, Emily C. "Authorizing Subversion: Strategies of Power in Marlowe's *Doctor Faustus.*" *Renaissance Papers,* 1989, 65–74.

————. *Spectacles of Strangeness: Imperialism, Alienation, and Marlowe.* Philadelphia: University of Pennsylvania Press, 1993.

Baxandall, Michael. *Painting and Experience in Fifteenth-Century Italy.* Oxford: Oxford University Press, 1972.

Beale, Joseph Henry. *A Bibliography of Early English Law Books.* Cambridge: Harvard University Press, 1920.

Becker, Marvin. "Changing Patterns of Violence and Justice in Fourteenth- and Fifteenth-Century Florence." *Comparative Studies in Society and History* 18 (1976): 281–96.

Bellori, Giovanni Pietro. *Le vite de pittori, scultori e archetetti moderni.* Rome, 1672. Reprinted in *Caravaggio,* by Howard Hibbard (New York: Harper and Row, 1983), 360–74.

Benjamin, Walter. *Theses on the Philosophy of History.* In *Illuminations,* ed. Hannah Arendt, trans. Harry Zohn, 253–64. New York: Schocken, 1968.

Berger, Harry, Jr. "Bodies and Texts." *Representations* 17 (winter 1987): 144–66.

Bernardino of Siena. *La Prediche Volgari.* Vol. 2. Ed. Ciro Cannarozzi. Pistoia: Tip. Cav. Alberto Pacinotto, 1934.

Bersani, Leo. *Homos.* Cambridge: Harvard University Press, 1995.

Bersani, Leo, and Ulysse Dutoit. *Caravaggio's Secrets.* Cambridge: Massachusetts Institute of Technology Press, 1998.

Blumenberg, Hans. *The Legitimacy of the Modern Age.* Trans. Robert M. Wallace. Cambridge: Massachusetts Institute of Technology Press, 1983.

Bourdieu, Pierre. *The Logic of Practice.* Trans. Richard Nice. Stanford: Stanford University Press, 1990.

Boyarin, Daniel. *A Radical Jew: Paul and the Politics of Identity.* Berkeley and Los Angeles: University of California Press, 1994.

Boyarin, Daniel, and Jonathan Boyarin. "Diaspora: Generation and the Ground of Jewish Identity." *Critical Inquiry* 19 (summer 1993): 693–725.

Bray, Alan. "Homosexuality and the Signs of Male Friendship in Elizabethan England." In *Queering the Renaissance,* ed. Jonathan Goldberg, 40–61. Durham: Duke University Press, 1994.

————. *Homosexuality in Renaissance England.* London: Gay Men's Press, 1982.

Breitenberg, Mark. *Anxious Masculinity in Early Modern England.* Cambridge: Cambridge University Press, 1996.

Brucker, Gene. *The Civic World of Early Renaissance Florence*. Princeton: Princeton University Press, 1977.

Bruno, Giordano. *Cause, Principle, and Unity: Five Dialogues*. Trans. Jack Lindsay. New York: International Publishers, 1962.

Bruns, Gerald L. *Hermeneutics Ancient and Modern*. New Haven: Yale University Press, 1992.

Bruster, Douglas. *Drama and the Market in the Age of Shakespeare*. Cambridge: Cambridge University Press, 1992.

Bryson, Anna. "Gesture, Demeanour, and the Image of the Gentleman." In *Renaissance Bodies: The Human Figure in English Culture, 1540–1660*, ed. Lucy Gent and Nigel Llewellyn, 136–53. London: Reaktion Books, 1990.

Butler, Judith. *Bodies That Matter: On the Discursive Limits of "Sex."* New York: Routledge, 1993.

———. *Gender Trouble: Feminism and the Subversion of Identity*. New York: Routledge, 1990.

———. *The Psychic Life of Power: Theories in Subjection*. Stanford: Stanford University Press, 1997.

Calvin, John. *Institutes of the Christian Religion*. Ed. John T. MacNeill, trans. Ford Lewis Battles. 2 vols. Philadelphia: Westminster Press, 1960.

Capponi, Gino. "Ricordi de Gino di Neri Capponi." In *Miscellanea di studi offerta a A. Balduini e B. Bianchi*, ed. Gianfranco Folena, 29–39. Padua: Presso Il Seminario de Filologia Moderna dell'Università, 1962.

Cardwell, Kenneth, F.S.C. "Francis Bacon, Inquisitor." In *Francis Bacon's Legacy of Texts: "The Art of Discovery Grows with Discovery,"* ed. William Sessions, 269–89. New York: AMS Press, 1990.

Carrier, David. "The Transfiguration of the Commonplace: Caravaggio and His Interpreters." *Word and Image* 3 (January–March 1987): 41–73.

Castel, Robert. "'Problematicization' as a Mode of Reading History." Trans. Paula Wissing. In *Foucault and the Writing of History*, ed. Jan Goldstein, 237–52. Oxford: Basil Blackwell, 1994.

Castiglione, Baldassare. *The Book of the Courtier*. Trans. George Bull. New York: Penguin, 1967.

———. *Opera di Baldassare Castiglione, Giovanni Della Casa, Benvenuto Cellini*. Ed. Carlo Cordié. Milan: Riccardo Ricciardi, n.d.

Castoriadis, Cornelius. *The Imaginary Institution of Society*. Trans. Kathleen Blamey. Cambridge: Massachusetts Institute of Technology Press, 1987.

Certeau, Michel de. *The Writing of History*. Trans. Tom Conley. New York: Columbia University Press, 1988.

Champagne, John. *The Ethics of Marginality: A New Approach to Gay Studies*. Minneapolis: University of Minnesota Press, 1995.

Cicchetti, Angelo, and Raul Mordenti. *I libri di famiglia in Italia*. Rome: Edizioni di Storia e Lettura, 1985.

Clément, Catherine. *Syncope: The Philosophy of Rapture*. Trans. Sally O'Driscoll and Deirdre M. Mahoney. Minneapolis: University of Minnesota Press, 1994.

Cochrane, Eric. *Historians and Historiography in the Italian Renaissance*. Chicago: University of Chicago Press, 1981.

———. *L'Italia del cinquecento, 1530–1630*. Bari: Gius. Laterza e Fili, 1989.

Cohen, Ed. "Legislating the Norm: From Sodomy to Gross Indecencies." *South Atlantic Quarterly* (winter 1989): 181–217.

Cohen, S. K., Jr. "Criminality and the State in Renaissance Florence, 1344–1466." *Journal of Social History* 14 (1981): 211–33.

Coke, Edward. *The Reports of Edward Coke.* London, 1658. Wing C4944.

———. *The Twelfth Part of the Reports.* London, 1658. Wing C4969.

Copjec, Joan. *Read My Desire: Lacan against the Historicists.* Cambridge: Massachusetts Institute of Technology Press, 1994.

Correll, Barbara. *The End of Conduct: Grobianus and the Renaissance Text of the Subject.* Ithaca: Cornell University Press, 1996.

Cowley, Abraham. *Poems.* Ed. A. R. Waller. Cambridge: Cambridge University Press, 1905.

Damisch, Hubert. *The Origin of Perspective.* Trans. John Goodman. Cambridge: Massachusetts Institute of Technology Press, 1994.

David-Ménard, Monique. *Hysteria from Freud to Lacan: Body and Language in Psychoanalysis.* Trans. Catherine Porter. Ithaca: Cornell University Press, 1989.

Dean, Tim. "Sex and Syncope." *Raritan* 15 (winter 1996): 64–86.

De la Croix, Horst. "Military Architecture and the Radical City Plan in Sixteenth-Century Italy." *Art Bulletin* 42 (1960): 263–90.

Deleuze, Gilles. *Foucault.* Trans. Seán Hand. Minneapolis: University of Minnesota Press, 1986.

Deleuze, Gilles, and Félix Guattari. *Kafka: Toward a Minor Literature.* Trans. Dana Polan. Minneapolis: University of Minnesota Press, 1986.

———. *A Thousand Plateaus: Capitalism and Schizophrenia.* Trans. Brian Massumi. Minneapolis: University of Minnesota Press, 1987.

Della Casa, Giovanni. *Galateo.* Trans. Konrad Eisenbichler and Kenneth Bartlett. Toronto: Centre for Reformation and Renaissance Studies, 1994.

———. *Opera di Baldassare Castiglione, Giovanni Della Casa, Benvenuto Cellini.* Ed. Carlo Cordié. Milan: Riccardo Ricciardi, n.d.

Descartes, René. *The Passions of the Soul.* In *The Philosophical Works of Descartes,* trans. Elizabeth S. Haldane and G. R. T. Ross, 1:329–427. Cambridge: Cambridge University Press, 1911. Reprint, 1979.

D'Ewes, Simonds. *The Autobiography and Correspondence of Sir Simonds D'Ewes, Bart., During the Reigns of James I and Charles I.* Ed. James O. Halliwell. 2 vols. London: R. Bently, 1845.

DiGangi, Mario. *The Homoerotics of Early Modern Drama.* Cambridge: Cambridge University Press, 1997.

Dolar, Mladen. "The Object Voice." In *Gaze and Voice as Love Objects,* ed. Renata Salecl and Slavoj Zizek, 7–31. Durham: Duke University Press, 1996.

Dollimore, Jonathan. *Radical Tragedy: Religion, Ideology, and Power in the Drama of Shakespeare and His Contemporaries.* Chicago: University of Chicago Press, 1986.

Duffy, Christopher. *Siege Warfare: The Fortress in the Early Modern World, 1494–1660.* London: Routledge, 1979.

Dunand, Anne. "The End of the Treatment." *Newsletter of the Freudian Field* 4 (1990): 120–33.

Elias, Norbert. *The Civilizing Process.* Trans. Edmund Jephcott. Oxford: Basil Blackwell, 1994.

Eliot, T. S. "Shakespeare and the Stoicism of Seneca." In *Selected Essays,* 126–40. London: Faber and Faber, 1972.

Elkins, James. *The Poetics of Perspective.* Ithaca: Cornell University Press, 1994.

Elton, G. R, ed. *The Tudor Constitution.* Cambridge: Cambridge University Press, 1960. 2d ed., 1982.

Empson, William. *Faustus and the Censor: The English Faust-Book and Marlowe's Doctor Faustus.* Recovered and ed. John Henry Jones. New York: Basil Blackwell, 1987.

———. "Two Proper Crimes." *The Nation* 163 (October 19, 1946): 444–45.

Eusebius. *The Ecclesiastical History.* Trans. Kirsopp Lake. 2 vols. Cambridge: Harvard University Press, 1973.

*Everyman.* In *Medieval Drama,* ed. David Bevington, 939–63. Boston: Houghton Mifflin, 1975.

Felman, Shoshana. *The Literary Speech Act: Don Juan with J. L. Austin, or Seduction in Two Languages.* Trans. Catherine Porter. Ithaca: Cornell University Press, 1983.

Ferguson, Margaret W. *Trials of Desire: Renaissance Defenses of Poetry.* New Haven: Yale University Press, 1983.

Fineman, Joel. *Shakespeare's Perjured Eye: The Invention of Poetic Subjectivity in the Sonnets.* Berkeley and Los Angeles: University of California Press, 1986.

Fish, Stanley. *Self-Consuming Artifacts: The Experience of Seventeenth-Century Literature.* Berkeley and Los Angeles: University of California Press, 1972.

Foucault, Michel. *The Archaeology of Knowledge.* Trans. A. M. Sheridan Smith. New York: Pantheon, 1972.

———. "The Concern for Truth." Interview by François Ewald in *Le Magazine littéraire,* May 1984. Reprinted in *Foucault Live: Interviews, 1966–84,* ed. Sylvère Lotringer, trans. John Johnston (New York: Semiotext[e]: 1989), 293–308.

———. *Discipline and Punish: The Birth of the Prison.* Trans. Alan Sheridan. New York: Vintage Books, 1979.

———. "Friendship as a Way of Life." *Le Gai Pied,* April 6, 1980. Reprinted in *Foucault Live: Interviews, 1966–84,* ed. Sylvère Lotringer, trans. John Johnston (New York: Semiotext[e]: 1989), 203–9.

———. *The History of Sexuality.* Volume 1, *An Introduction.* Trans. Robert Hurley. New York: Random House, 1980.

———. *The History of Sexuality.* Volume 2, *The Use of Pleasure.* Trans. Robert Hurley. New York: Vintage, 1990.

———. "The Return of Morality." Interview by Gilles Barbadette and Andre Serla in *Les Nouvelles,* June 28–July 5, 1984. Reprinted in *Foucault Live: Interviews, 1966–84,* ed. Sylvère Lotringer and trans. John Johnston (New York: Semiotext[e]: 1989), 317–31.

Foxe, John. *The Acts and Monuments of John Foxe.* Ed. Rev. George Townsend. 8 vols. New York: AMS Press, 1965.

Freud, Sigmund. "Analysis Terminable and Interminable." In *Therapy and Technique,* ed. Philip Rieff, 233–71. New York: Collier, 1963.

———. *Civilization and Its Discontents.* Trans. James Strachey. New York: Norton, 1961.

———. *The Ego and the Id.* Ed. James Strachey, trans. Joan Riviere. New York: Norton, 1962.

———. "Instincts and Their Vicissitudes." In *General Psychological Theory,* ed. Philip Rieff, 83–103. New York: Collier, 1963.

————. *The Interpretation of Dreams.* Trans. James Strachey. New York: Avon Books, 1965.

————. *Jokes and Their Relation to the Unconscious.* Trans. and ed. James Strachey. New York: Norton, 1960. Reprint, 1989.

————. "Negation." In *General Psychological Theory,* ed. Philip Rieff, 213–17. New York: Collier, 1963.

————. "On Narcissism: An Introduction." In *General Psychological Theory,* ed. Philip Rieff, 56–82. New York: Collier, 1963.

————. *Project for a Scientific Psychology.* In *The Standard Edition of the Complete Psychological Works of Sigmund Freud,* ed. and trans. James Strachey, 1:295–397. New York: Norton, 1950.

————. "Psychoanalytic Notes on an Autobiographical Account of a Case of Paranoia." In *Three Case Histories,* ed. Philip Rieff, 103–86. New York: Collier, 1963.

————. "Splitting of the Ego in the Defensive Process." In *Sexuality and the Psychology of Love,* trans. Philip Rieff, 220–23. New York: Collier, 1963.

Fried, Michael. "Thoughts on Caravaggio." *Critical Inquiry* 24 (autumn 1997): 13–57.

Friedlander, Walter. *Caravaggio Studies.* Princeton: Princeton University Press, 1955. Reprint, New York: Schocken, 1969.

Fumerton, Patricia. *Cultural Aesthetics: Renaissance Literature and the Practice of Social Ornamentation.* Chicago: University of Chicago Press, 1991.

Garber, Marjorie. "Closure and Enclosure in Marlowe." In *Two Renaissance Mythmakers: Christopher Marlowe and Ben Jonson.* Baltimore: Johns Hopkins University Press, 1977. 3–21

*The Geneva Bible: A Facsimile of the 1560 Edition.* Madison: University of Wisconsin Press, 1969.

Gilbert, Creighton. *Caravaggio and His Two Cardinals.* University Park: Pennsylvania State University Press, 1995.

Goldberg, Jonathan. "The History That Will Be." In *Premodern Sexualities,* ed. Louise Fradenburg and Carla Freccero, with the assistance of Kathy Lavezzo. New York: Routledge, 1996.

————. *Sodometries: Renaissance Texts/Modern Sexualities.* Stanford: Stanford University Press, 1992.

————. *Writing Matter: From the Hands of the English Renaissance.* Stanford: Stanford University Press, 1990.

Goldman, Michael. "Marlowe and the Histrionics of Ravishment." In *Two Renaissance Mythmakers: Christopher Marlowe and Ben Jonson,* 22–40. Baltimore: Johns Hopkins University Press, 1977.

Goodrich, Peter. *Law in the Courts of Love.* London: Routledge, 1996.

Green, Louis Ferdinand. *Chronicle into History.* Cambridge: Cambridge University Press, 1972.

Greenblatt, Stephen. *Renaissance Self-Fashioning: From More to Shakespeare.* Chicago: University of Chicago Press, 1980.

Greg, W. W., ed. *Marlowe's Doctor Faustus, 1604–1616: Parallel Texts.* Oxford: Clarendon Press, 1950.

Guicciardini, Francesco. *Storia d'Italia.* In *Opere di Francesco Guicciardini,* ed. Emanuella Lugnani Scarano. 3 vols. Turin: Unione Tipografico, 1981.

Guicciardini, Luigi. *The Sack of Rome.* Trans. James H. McGregor. New York: Italica Press, 1993.

Hale, J. R. "The Early Development of the Bastion: An Italian Chronology, c. 1450–c. 1535." In *Europe in the Late Middle Ages,* ed. J. R. Hale, J. R. L. Highfield, and B. Smalley, 466–94. Evanston: Northwestern University Press, 1965. Reprinted in *Renaissance War Studies,* ed. J. R. Hale (London: Hambledon Press, 1983), 1–30.

Hale, J. R., and M. E. Mallett. *The Military Organization of a Renaissance State: Venice c. 1400–1617.* Cambridge: Harvard University Press, 1984.

Hall, Bert S. *Weapons and Warfare in Renaissance Europe: Gunpowder, Technology, and Tactics.* Baltimore: Johns Hopkins University Press, 1997.

Halperin, David M. "Forgetting Foucault: Acts, Identities, and the History of Sexuality." *Representations* 63 (summer 1998): 92–120.

———. *One Hundred Years of Homosexuality.* New York: Routledge, 1990.

Hammill, Graham. "The Epistemology of Expurgation: Bacon and *The Masculine Birth of Time.*" In *Queering the Renaissance,* ed. Jonathan Goldberg, 236–52. Durham: Duke University Press, 1994.

Hauser, Arnold. *Mannerism: The Crisis of the Renaissance and the Origin of Modern Art.* Cambridge: Harvard University Press, 1965.

———. *The Social History of Art.* 4 vols. Trans. Stanley Godman. New York: Vintage, 1957. Reissued 1985.

Heidegger, Martin. *Being and Time.* Trans. John Macquarrie and Edward Robinson. New York: Harper and Row, 1962.

Helgerson, Richard. *Forms of Nationhood: The Elizabethan Writing of England.* Chicago: University of Chicago Press, 1992.

Hibbard, Howard. *Caravaggio.* New York: Harper and Row, 1983.

Hill, Paul. *The Light of Early Italian Painting.* New Haven: Yale University Press, 1987.

Hjelmslev, Louis. *Prolegomena to a Theory of Language.* Trans. Francis J. Whitfield. Madison: University of Wisconsin Press, 1961.

Hocquenghem, Guy. *Homosexual Desire.* Trans. Daniella Dangoor. Durham: Duke University Press, 1993.

Irigaray, Luce. *An Ethics of Sexual Difference.* Trans. Carolyn Burke and Gillian C. Gill. Ithaca: Cornell University Press, 1993.

———. *This Sex Which Is Not One.* Trans. Catherine Porter. Ithaca: Cornell University Press, 1985.

Jameson, Fredric. *The Political Unconscious: Narrative as a Socially Symbolic Act.* Ithaca: Cornell University Press, 1981.

Jed, Stephanie H. *Chaste Thinking: The Rape of Lucrece and the Birth of Humanism.* Bloomington: Indiana University Press, 1989.

Jonson, Ben. *Works.* Ed. C. H. Herford and Percy Simpson. 11 vols. Oxford: Oxford University Press, 1925–52.

Jordan, Mark D. *The Invention of Sodomy in Christian Theology.* Chicago: University of Chicago Press, 1997.

Kantorowicz, Ernst H. *The King's Two Bodies: A Study in Mediaeval Political Theology.* Princeton: Princeton University Press, 1957. Reprint, 1997.

Keller, Evelyn Fox. *Reflections on Gender and Science.* New Haven: Yale University Press, 1985.

Kelly [Gadol], Joan. *Leon Battista Alberti: Universal Man of the Early Renaissance.* Chicago: University of Chicago Press, 1969.

Kemp, Anthony. *The Estrangement of the Past: A Study in the Origins of Modern Historical Consciousness.* New York: Oxford University Press, 1991.

Kemp, Martin. *The Science of Art: Optical Themes in Western Art from Brunelleschi to Seurat.* New Haven: Yale University Press, 1990.

Kent, Dale. *The Rise of the Medici: Faction in Florence, 1426–1434.* Oxford: Oxford University Press, 1978.

Kristeva, Julia. *Nations without Nationalism.* Trans. Leon S. Roudiez. New York: Columbia University Press, 1993.

———. *Powers of Horror: An Essay on Abjection.* Trans. Leon S. Roudiez. New York: Columbia University Press, 1982.

———. *Tales of Love.* Trans. Leon S. Roudiez. New York: Columbia University Press, 1987.

Kuriyama, Constance Brown. "Dr. Greg and *Doctor Faustus:* The Supposed Originality of the 1616 Text." *English Literary Renaissance* 5 (1975): 171–97.

Lacan, Jacques. *Ecrits.* Paris: Editions du Seuil, 1966.

———. *Ecrits: A Selection.* Trans. Alan Sheridan. New York: Norton, 1977.

———. "Kant with Sade." Trans. James B. Swenson, Jr. *October* 51 (winter 1989): 55–75

———. *Le séminaire livre VII: L'ethique de la psychanalyse.* Paris: Editions du Seuil, 1986.

———. *Le séminaire livre XX: Encore.* Paris: Editions du Seuil, 1975.

———. *Seminar Eleven: The Four Fundamental Concepts of Psychoanalysis.* Ed. Jacques-Alain Miller, trans. Alan Sheridan. New York: Norton, 1978.

———. *Seminar One: Freud's Papers on Technique.* Ed. Jacques-Alain Miller, trans. John Forrester. New York: Norton, 1988.

———. *Seminar Seven: The Ethics of Psychoanalysis.* Trans. Dennis Porter. New York: Norton, 1992.

———. *Seminar Three: The Psychoses.* Ed. Jacques-Alain Miller, trans. Russell Grigg. New York: Norton, 1993.

———. *Seminar Twenty: Encore.* Trans. Bruce Fink. New York: Norton, 1998.

———. "The Meaning of the Phallus." In *Feminine Sexuality: Jacques Lacan and the Ecole Freudienne,* ed. Juliet Mitchell and Jacqueline Rose, trans. Jacqueline Rose, 74–85. New York: Norton, 1982.

———. *Television.* Ed. Joan Copjec, trans. Denis Hollier, Rosalind Kraus, and Annette Michelson. New York: Norton, 1990.

Leonardo da Vinci. *Leonardo on Painting.* Ed. Martin Kemp, trans. Martin Kemp and Margaret Walker. New Haven: Yale University Press, 1987.

———. *The Notebooks of Leonardo da Vinci.* Ed. Jean Paul Richter. New York: Dover, 1970.

Levao, Ronald. "Francis Bacon and the Mobility of Science." *Representations* 40 (fall 1992): 1–32.

Levine, Harry. *The Overreacher: A Study of Christopher Marlowe.* Cambridge: Harvard University Press, 1952.

Lloyd, David. "Discussion outside History: Irish New Histories and the 'Subalternity Effect.'" *Subaltern Studies* 9 (1996): 261–80.

Lupton, Julia Reinhard. *Afterlives of the Saints: Hagiography, Typology, and Renaissance Literature.* Stanford: Stanford University Press, 1996.

Luther, Martin. *Lectures on Genesis.* Trans. George V. Shick and Paul D. Pahl. Vols. 1–8 of *Luther's Works,* ed. Jaroslav Pelikan and Helmut Lehman. 55 vols. Saint Louis and Philadelphia: Concordia and Fortress Presses, 1958–86.

Luxon, Thomas H. *Literal Figures: Puritan Allegory and the Reformation Crisis in Representation.* Chicago: University of Chicago Press, 1995.

Machiavelli, Niccolò. *The Discourses.* Ed. Bernard Crick, trans. Leslie J. Walker. New York: Penguin, 1970. Reprint, 1983.

———. *The Prince.* Trans. George Bull. New York: Penguin, 1961.

———. *Tutte le Opere.* Florence: Sansoni, 1989.

*Malleus Maleficarum.* Trans. Rev. Montague Summers. New York: Dover, 1971.

Mancini, Giulio. *Considerazioni sulla pittura.* Manuscript of 1617–21. Reprinted in *Caravaggio,* by Howard Hibbard, 346–51. New York: Harper and Row, 1983.

Manetti, Antonio di Tucci. *La Vita di Filippo Brunelleschi.* Translated by Catherine Enggass as *The Life of Brunelleschi.* Introduction and notes by Howard Saalman. University Park: Pennsylvania State University Press, 1970.

Marcus, Leah. "Textual Indeterminacy and Ideological Difference: The Case of *Doctor Faustus.*" *Renaissance Drama* 20 (1989): 1–29.

Marlowe, Christopher. *The Works of Christopher Marlowe.* Ed. C. F. Tucker Brooke. Oxford: Clarendon Press, 1910.

Martin, Julian. *Francis Bacon, the State, and the Reform of Natural Philosophy.* Cambridge: Cambridge University Press, 1992.

Martines, Lauro. *Lawyers and Statecraft in Renaissance Florence.* Princeton: Princeton University Press, 1968.

———. *Power and Imagination: City-States in Renaissance Italy.* New York: Knopf, 1979.

Marx, Karl. *Capital.* Vol. 1. Ed. Frederick Engels, trans. Samuel Moore and Edward Aveling. New York: International Publishers, 1967.

Maus, Katharine Eisaman. *Inwardness and the Theater in the English Renaissance.* Chicago: University of Chicago Press, 1995.

Mauss, Marcel. "Techniques of the Body." In *Incorporations,* ed. Jonathan Crary and Sanford Kwinter, 455–77. New York: Zone Books, 1992.

Mazzi, Maria Serena. "Cronache de periferia della stato Florentino: Reati contro la morale ne primo quattrocento." *Studi Storici* 27 (1986): 609–35.

———. *Prostitute e lenoni nella Firenze del quattrocento.* Milan: Saggiatore, 1991.

Mellis, John. *Briefe Instruction How to Keepe Bookes of Accompts.* London, 1588. STC 18794.

Merleau-Ponty, Maurice. *Signs.* Trans. Richard C. McCleary. Evanston: Northwestern University Press, 1964.

———. *The Visible and the Invisible.* Ed. Claude Lefort, trans. Alphonso Lingis. Evanston: Northwestern University Press, 1973.

Miller, Jacques-Alain. "Extimacy." *Prose Studies* 11 (1988): 121–30.

Moir, Alfred. *Caravaggio.* New York: Harry Abrams, 1982. Reprint, 1989.

Montanus, Reginaldus Gonsalvius. *A Discovery of Sundry Subtill Practices of the Holy Inquisition of Spayne.* London, 1568. STC 11996.

Mumford, Lewis. *Technics and Civilization.* New York: Harcourt, Brace, Jovanovich, 1963.

*The Nag Hammadi Library.* 1978. Ed. James Robinson et al. San Francisco: Harper and Row, 1988.

Nietzsche, Friedrich. "The Uses and Disadvantages of History for Life." In *Untimely Meditations,* trans. R. J. Hollingdate, 59–123. Cambridge: Cambridge University Press, 1983.

*The New Jerusalem Bible.* New York: Doubleday, 1985.

Nicholas of Cusa. *Of Learned Ignorance.* Trans. Fr. Germain Heron. New Haven: Yale University Press, 1954.

Ovid. *Metamorphoses.* Trans. Frank Justus Miller. Cambridge: Harvard University Press, 1921.

Panofsky, Erwin. *Perspective as Symbolic Form.* Trans. Charles S. Wood. New York: Zone Books, 1991.

Paster, Gail Kern. *The Body Embarrassed: Drama and the Disciplines of Shame in Early Modern England.* Ithaca: Cornell University Press, 1993.

———. "Nervous Tension: Networks of Blood and Spirit in the Early Modern Body." In *The Body in Parts: Fantasies of Corporeality in Early Modern Europe,* ed. David Hillman and Carla Mazzio, 107–25. New York: Routledge, 1997.

Peele, James. *The Manner and Fourme How to Keepe a Perfect Reconynge.* London, 1553. STC 19547.

———. *The Pathe Waye to Perfectnes, in th' Accomptes of Debitour, and Creditour.* London, 1569. STC 19548.

Pepper, Simon, and Nicholas Adams. *Firearms and Fortifications: Military Architecture and Siege Warfare in Sixteenth-Century Siena.* Chicago: University of Chicago Press, 1986.

Plowden, Edmund. *The Commentaries or Reports.* 2 vols. Dublin: H. Watts, 1792.

Plutarch. *Moralia.* Trans. Howard North Fowler. Cambridge: Harvard University Press, 1949.

Pocock, J. G. A. *The Ancient Constitution and the Feudal Law: A Study of English Historical Thought in the Seventeenth Century.* Cambridge: Cambridge University Press, 1957.

Pomponazzi, Pietro. *On the Immortality of the Soul.* In *The Renaissance Philosophy of Man,* ed. Ernst Cassirer, Paul Oskar Kristeller, and John Herman Randall, Jr., 280–381. Chicago: University of Chicago Press, 1948.

Posner, Donald. "Caravaggio's Homo-Erotic Early Works." *Art Quarterly* 34 (1971): 301–24.

Rocke, Michael. *Forbidden Friendships: Homosexuality and Male Culture in Renaissance Florence.* Oxford: Oxford University Press, 1996.

———. "Sodomites in Fifteenth-Century Tuscany: The Views of Bernardino of Siena. In *The Pursuit of Sodomy: Male Homosexuality in Renaissance and Enlightenment Europe,* ed. Kent Gerard and Gert Hekma, 7–31. New York: Harrington Park Press, 1989.

Rowe, Katherine. "'God's Handy Worke': Divine Complicity and the Anatomist's Touch." In *The Body in Parts: Fantasies of Corporeality in Early Modern Europe,* ed. David Hillman and Carla Mazzio, 285–309. New York: Routledge, 1997.

Sandys, George. *Ovid's Metamorphoses Englished, Mythologized, and Represented in Figures.* Ed. Karl K. Hulley and Stanley T. Vandersall. Lincoln: University of Nebraska Press, 1970.

Saslow, James M. *Ganymede in the Renaissance.* New Haven: Yale University Press, 1986.

Scarry, Elaine. *The Body in Pain: The Making and Unmaking of the World.* New York: Oxford University Press, 1985.

Scot, Reginald. *The Discoverie of Witchcraft.* New York: De Capo Press, 1971.

Scott, Joan W. "The Evidence of Experience." *Critical Inquiry* 17 (1991): 773–97.

Sedgwick, Eve Kosofsky. *Between Men: English Literature and Male Homosocial Desire*. New York: Columbia University Press, 1985.

———. *Epistemology of the Closet*. Berkeley and Los Angeles: University of California Press, 1990.

———. *Tendencies*. Durham: Duke University Press, 1993.

Sfez, Gérald. "Deciding on Evil." In *Radical Evil*, ed. Joan Copjec, 126–49. London: Verso, 1996.

Shapin, Steven. *A Social History of Truth: Civility and Science in Seventeenth-Century England*. Chicago: University of Chicago Press, 1994.

Shepherdson, Charles. "Vital Signs: The *Place* of Memory in Psychoanalysis." *Research in Phenomenology* 23 (1994): 22–72.

Sidney, Philip. *An Apologie for Poetrie*. In *Elizabethan Critical Essays*, ed. G. Gregory Smith, 1:148–207. London: Oxford University Press, 1904.

Smith, Bruce R. *Homosexual Desire in Shakespeare's England: A Cultural Poetics*. Chicago: University of Chicago Press, 1991. Reprint, 1994.

Snow, Edward A. "Marlowe's *Doctor Faustus* and the Ends of Desire." In *Two Renaissance Mythmakers: Christopher Marlowe and Ben Jonson*, ed. Alvin Kernan, 70–110. Baltimore: Johns Hopkins University Press, 1977.

Solomon, Julie Robin. *Objectivity in the Making: Francis Bacon and the Politics of Inquiry*. Baltimore: Johns Hopkins University Press, 1998.

Spinoza, Benedict de. *The Ethics*. Trans. R. H. M. Elwes. New York: Dover, 1955.

Stallybrass, Peter, and Allon White. *The Politics and Poetics of Transgression*. Ithaca: Cornell University Press, 1986.

*The Statutes of the Realm*. 11 vols. London: G. Eyre and A. Strahan, 1810–28. Reprint, London: Dawson of Pall Mall, 1963.

Struever, Nancy. *The Language of History in the Renaissance*. Princeton: Princeton University Press, 1970.

Teskey, Gordon. *Allegory and Violence*. Ithaca: Cornell University Press, 1996.

Thomas Aquinas. *The Basic Works of Saint Thomas Aquinas*. Ed. Anton C. Pegis. New York: Random House, 1945.

Thomas, Keith. Introduction to *A Cultural History of Gesture*, ed. Jan Bremmer and Herman Roodenburg, 1–14. Ithaca: Cornell University Press, 1992.

Traub, Valerie. *Desire and Anxiety: Circulations of Sexuality in Shakespearean Drama*. New York: Routledge, 1992.

———. "The (In)Significance of Lesbian Desire." In *Queering the Renaissance*, ed. Jonathan Goldberg, 62–83. Durham: Duke University Press, 1994.

Trexler, Richard. "La prostitution florentine au XVe siècle: Patronage et clientèles. *Annales: Economies, Sociètes, Civilisations* 36 (1981): 983–1015.

———. *Public Life in Renaissance Florence*. Ithaca: Cornell University Press, 1980.

Vasari, Giorgio. *Lives of the Artists*. Trans. George Bull. 2 vols. New York: Penguin, 1965. Reprint, 1987.

———. *Vasari on Technique*. Trans. Louisa S. Macelhouse. New York: Dover, 1960.

Virgil. *Aeneid*. Trans. H. Rushton Fairclough. 2 vols. Cambridge: Harvard University Press, 1986.

Warner, William. *Albion's England*. 1612. New York: Georg Olms Verlag Hildesheim, 1971.

Weber, Max. *From Max Weber: Essays in Sociology*. Ed. and trans. H. H. Gerth and C. Wright Mills. New York: Oxford University Press, 1946. Reprint, 1958.

Weed, Elizabeth. "A Question of Style." In *Engaging with Irigaray: Feminist Philosophy and Modern European Thought,* ed. Carolyn Burke, Naomi Schor, and Margaret Whitford, 79–109. New York: Columbia University Press, 1994.

Whitney, Charles. *Francis Bacon and Modernity.* New Haven: Yale University Press, 1986.

———. "Merchants of Light: Science as Colonization in the *New Atlantis.*" In *Francis Bacon's Legacy of Texts: "The Art of Discovery Grows with Discovery,"* ed. William Sessions, 255–68. New York: AMS Press, 1990.

Wilcox, Donald J. *The Development of Florentine Humanist Historiography in the Fifteenth Century.* Cambridge: Harvard University Press, 1969.

Zizek, Slavoj. *Enjoy Your Symptom! Jacques Lacan in Hollywood and Out.* New York: Routledge, 1992.

———. *Looking Awry: An Introduction to Jacques Lacan through Popular Culture.* Cambridge: Massachusetts Institute of Technology Press, 1991.

———. *Tarrying with the Negative: Kant, Hegel, and the Critique of Ideology.* Durham: Duke University Press, 1993.

Zorzi, Andrea. *L'amministrazione della giustizia penale nella repubblica florentina: Aspetti e problemi.* Florence: Leo S. Olschki Editore, 1988.

———. "The Florentines and Their Public Offices in the Early Fifteenth Century: Competition, Abuses of Power, and Unlawful Acts." In *History from Crime,* ed. Edward Muir and Guido Ruggiero, trans. Corrada Biazzo Curry, Margaret A. Gallucci, and Mary M. Gallucci, 110–34. Baltimore: Johns Hopkins University Press, 1994.

# INDEX